GREEN BIZ

GREEN BIZ

50 GREEN, PROFITABLE COMPANIES
REVEAL THEIR STRATEGIES AND SUCCESSES

Introduction by Mindy Lubber, president, Ceres

AMERICAN
BENCHMARK
PRESS

Grateful acknowledgment to the following companies for the use of their photos in "Green Strategies": Aspen Skiing Company, Aveda, Bank of America, Baxter, The Body Shop, Bristol-Myers Squibb, Coca-Cola, FPL Group, Green Mountain Coffee Roasters, Herman Miller, Inc., Hewlett-Packard, HSBC, Interface, McDonald's, Mohawk Fine Papers, Nike, Nova Nordisk, PG&E, Sun Microsystems, and Tesla Motors.

To learn more about Random House Custom Media's branded content products, write to custommedia@randomhouse.com.

This book may be purchased for business or promotional use for special sales. For information, write to: Special Markets Department, Random House, Inc., 1745 Broadway, New York, NY, 10019 or specialmarkets@randomhouse.com.

Library of Congress Cataloging-in-Publication Data

Green Biz: 50 green, profitable companies reveal their strategies and successes / introduction by Mindy Lubber.—1st ed.
    p. cm.
  Includes index.
  1. Green marketing—Case studies.   2. Sustainable development—Case studies.   I. Random House Custom Media.
  HF5413.G725 2008
  658.4'083—dc22   2008014937

ISBN 978-0-307-38349-5

Printed in China

Profiles written by Bill Baue, Deirdre Cossman, Jennifer Freeman, Blythe Hamer, Nicholas P. Sullivan, and Amy S. Wilensky

Design by Filip Zawodnik

10 9 8 7 6 5 4 3 2 1

First Edition

Contents

Introduction   vii

Green Strategies   1

Alcoa   14
AMD   18
Aspen Skiing Company   22
Aveda   26
Bank of America   30
Baxter International   34
Ben & Jerry's   38
The Body Shop   42
BP   46
Bristol-Myers Squibb   50
BT   54
Citi   58
Clif Bar & Company   62
Coca-Cola   66
FPL Group   70
General Electric   74
Goldman Sachs   78
Google   82
Green Mountain Coffee Roasters   86
Herman Miller, Inc.   90
Hewlett-Packard   94
Honda   98
HSBC   102
IBM   106

IKEA   110

Intel   114

Interface   118

Levi Strauss & Co.   122

McDonald's   126

Mohawk Fine Papers   130

National Grid   134

Nike   138

Novo Nordisk   142

Patagonia   146

PG&E   150

Rio Tinto   154

SC Johnson & Son   158

Seventh Generation   162

Staples   166

Starbucks   170

StatoilHydro   174

Stonyfield Farm   178

SunEdison   182

Sun Microsystems   186

Tesla Motors   190

Timberland   194

Toshiba   198

Toyota   202

Vodafone   206

Xanterra Parks & Resorts   210

A Green Book Made by a Green House   214

Company Contacts   216

Green Partners   218

Green Terms and Abbreviations   222

Index   229

Introduction
Mindy S. Lubber

Companies that help the environment, the economy, and people aren't just good social citizens. They are smart businesses.

Investors and consumers are rewarding companies for being sustainable—creating blueprints for integrating environmental and social challenges while building profits and long-term prosperity. Already, members of the Investor Network on Climate Risk, a coalition of institutional investors managing $5 trillion in assets, are changing their investment strategies based on how companies are managing the risks and opportunities from climate change. Wall Street firms are creating new index funds that leverage energy efficiency, clean energy, and social responsibility.

The 50 companies highlighted in this book are leading the business community in sustainable best practices. They are using creative strategies to minimize their adverse impacts on society and the environment while simultaneously achieving short-term cost savings and improving their long-term financial health.

Tackling the immense environmental and social challenges of the 21st century will require bold action by governments, individuals, and businesses. On climate change, we need unprecedented international collaboration and new regulatory frameworks that will reduce greenhouse gas emissions. We need changes in behavior and consumption patterns from billions of people. And from businesses, we need inspired innovation—especially in renewable energy, investment, corporate responsibility, and insightful leadership—that takes a long view of global prosperity and the social and environmental conditions that can sustain it.

There is much evidence in this book that large and small corporations are beginning to embrace their role as leaders of change. "Sustainability," a term rarely heard in corporate boardrooms and executive suites a decade ago, is now a mantra recited by CEOs. Companies are stepping forward in a variety of ways. Pacific Gas and Electric Company is exploiting energy efficiency to save Californians billions of dollars on their energy bills. General Electric is inventing a range of clean energy technologies. Green Mountain Coffee Roasters is sourcing organically grown, fair-trade coffee. McDonald's and IKEA are requiring suppliers to meet social and environmental standards, and Toyota and Honda are manufacturing low-emission hybrid vehicles. Nike is instilling green design and manufacturing processes, and Sun Microsystems is saving millions of dollars on office-space costs by encouraging employees to work from home.

What is especially striking about these and other examples is how many different ways sustainability can be integrated into corporate strategies. These companies are recognizing their most significant negative impacts, as well as identifying opportunities for positive change, and as a result are creating innovative solutions to address climate change, water scarcity, toxic waste, and sustainable development. For example, health and beauty product maker Aveda is reducing the carbon footprint of its product lines by sourcing organic ingredients from indigenous farmers and packing products in 100% postconsumer recycled materials.

Baxter, the multibillion-dollar health care company, has invested millions in energy conservation programs for its facilities and has set ambitious reduction targets for water use and waste generation, all while reaping huge cost savings far in excess of its investments. FPL Group, which serves half of Florida, is the nation's largest provider of renewable energy, much of it originating from a 2,000-acre solar farm in California's Mojave Desert. Herman Miller, the office design firm and manufacturer of office furnishings, has a Design for the Environment team that ensures that every product the company designs is environmentally sensitive, from the materials and energy used in its creation to recycling at the end of the product's useful life. And Bank of America, one of the world's largest financial institutions, is leveraging its $20 billion environmental initiative toward new sustainability projects, including mortgages that reward homeowners for installing energy-efficient features, real estate financing earmarked for building projects that meet stringent environmental standards, and corporate financing targeted at the development of new green products and technology.

These efforts need to be celebrated, but it is only a start. Even the companies profiled here aren't yet where they need to be. Toyota, widely perceived as one of the greenest of the automakers for its broad investment in hybrid technology, continues to produce gas-guzzling luxury cars, SUVs, and trucks and has lobbied in the United States against higher fuel efficiency standards. Coca-Cola, which has made impressive strides reducing water consumption in its operations and manufacturing processes, continues to market bottled water products that are little different from tap water and require huge amounts of energy and materials to bottle and distribute.

Every company profiled here needs to be bolder and do more, especially in regard to climate change, arguably the biggest sustainability challenge of our time. Installing solar panels and buying carbon offsets is not enough. These actions alone will not reduce greenhouse gas emissions to the levels that are needed to avoid potentially catastrophic consequences for our planet. Entrenching climate-friendly practices more deeply into companies—across all operations, global supply chains, product lines, and employees (including the board of directors and CEO)—is needed immediately and universally.

But be inspired. These 50 companies are trailblazers to a more sustainable world.

Mindy S. Lubber

Ceres is the largest coalition of investor groups, environmental organizations, and investment funds in North America. Ceres engages directly with companies on environmental and social issues to help them achieve long-term business value and to improve management quality through stakeholder engagement, public disclosure, and performance improvements.

Green Strategies

As companies invest more time, money, and energy into becoming sustainable, their strategies invariably become more consolidated and clearly defined. Though each company has a different set of variables to work with, certain categories of effort begin to emerge. Listed below are the common strategies successfully employed by the companies profiled in this book. If a company had an obvious strength in using any given strategy, its logo is listed under the definition and may be used as a guide for readers interested in learning in more detail how that particular method has been implemented. The lists are not meant to be exclusive but are intended to act as indicators of what strategies work for which kinds of businesses.

Alternative Energy

As the climate crisis and peak oil converge, companies see alternative fuels less as an exotic option and more as an imperative transition. Some companies are taking steps to directly provide their energy needs from renewable sources, such as wind, solar, and biofuels. However, the emerging nature of the alternative energy sector can make direct purchase of alternative energy cost-prohibitive, and in most regions clean electricity cannot be purchased directly. For these reasons, many companies are purchasing renewable energy credits (RECs), which support clean energy projects.

The rapid growth of RECs has led to criticism, which has enhanced the need for widely respected certification protocols such as Green-e, which validates that the credits sold actually support renewable energy projects that would not have happened without this financial boost—a concept known as "additionality" in the field.

IMPLEMENTED BY:

   Google HSBC ◆ IBM

RESOURCES:
American Council on Renewable Energy (ACORE), www.acore.org
Green-e, www.green-e.org

Alternative Transportation

The current petroleum-based, single-passenger transportation system for getting employees to work is coming into question, and alternative transportation is taking its place. Hybrids, flex-fuel vehicles, and biodiesel are all gaining popularity, as are carpooling, car sharing, cooperative car ownership, and public mass transit. Companies are supporting these trends to various degrees and in various ways, from producing the vehicles filling these needs to offering incentives for employees to take advantage of these opportunities.

IMPLEMENTED BY:

Bank of America   **HONDA**   RIO TINTO   SCJohnson A Family Company   TESLA MOTORS   **TOYOTA**

RESOURCES:
California Energy Commission Alternative Fuel Vehicles and High-Efficiency Vehicles, www.energy.ca.gov/afvs

Biodiversity and Land Conservation

For some companies, supporting biodiversity and land conservation represents a philanthropic effort, but for others, it shows enlightened self-interest. For example, pharmaceutical companies rely on ingredients from rain forests and other lands that are becoming endangered. Promoting biodiversity represents another avenue for these companies to protect their vital business interests, as well as integrating the indigenous community.

IMPLEMENTED BY:

ALCOA   bp   Bristol-Myers Squibb   Goldman Sachs   PG&E Pacific Gas and Electric Company

RESOURCES:
International Union for Conservation of Nature (IUCN), www.biodiversity.org

Certification: Organic, Sustainable Forestry, Sustainable Fishing, Fair Trade

Separating the wheat from the chaff when it comes to the environmental and social sustainability of products harvested from the earth requires certification to distinguish the integrity of bona fide suppliers from freeloaders. A number of certification schemes have arisen, with a shakedown leaving the most reliable certifiers still standing. In the U.S. organic field, the USDA now oversees certification.

In forestry, Forest Stewardship Council (FSC) certification is the gold standard, as is Marine Stewardship Council (MSC) certification for fish. These certification schemes seek to balance the need for business growth with the need to sustain and preserve dwindling natural resources. Seeking to ensure a livable income for farmers, fair trade focuses more on social concerns than on environmental sustainability, though its guidelines also address environmental issues. As well, progressive practices tend to create a clustering effect, as Fair Trade certification often begets organic certification and vice versa.

IMPLEMENTED BY:

RESOURCES:
USDA Organic Certification, www.usda.gov
Forest Stewardship Council, www.fsc.org/en
Marine Stewardship Council, www.msc.org
Fairtrade Labelling Organizations International, www.fairtrade.net

Climate Change

In a remarkably short period of time, climate change has transformed from a peripheral issue that many CEOs denied or ignored into a core business issue requiring top-level engagement. While most climate strategies focus on avoiding the business risks that will accompany the disruptive nature of global warming, companies increasingly see business opportunities to profit from climate mitigation and adaptation solutions. While this may sound distressingly opportunistic to some, others recognize that the profit motive may advance environmental solutions more efficiently than anything else.

IMPLEMENTED BY:

  Bank of America Google HSBC

 RIO TINTO

RESOURCES:
U.S. Climate Action Partnership (USCAP), www.us-cap.org
Investor Network on Climate Risk (INCR), www.incr.com

Consumer Messaging, Labeling

The rise of green business responds in large part to consumer demand for environmentally beneficial products and services, so communicating environmental initiatives to the public becomes ever more crucial. Marketing and advertising highlight environmental and green attributes as key selling points. Timberland was among the pioneers of using labels, akin to nutrition labels on food, to communicate the environmental impact and emissions associated with the manufacture of its products.

However, the rise in green marketing is accompanied by a rise in "greenwashing," or communicating false and misleading environmental claims. A recent study by TerraChoice, "The Six Sins of Greenwashing," identified a half dozen ways that green claims are misrepresented, and found only a single instance of verifiable environmental claims in over a thousand product claims studied. This trend has prompted the Federal Trade Commission to seek public comment on the need to revise its "green guides" governing environmental claims for the first time in over a decade.

The flip side of greenwashing is "greenmuting," a term coined by Bob Langert of McDonald's and referring to companies remaining silent on their positive environmental initiatives for fear of being accused of greenwashing. Yet another is "brownwashing," or the diminishment of environmental claims for competitive or political purposes—for example, a 2007 CNW Marketing Research study that found the Hummer H2 to be more environmentally sound than a Toyota Prius has come under great scrutiny and raised questions about the bias of the source.

IMPLEMENTED BY:

RESOURCES:
Federal Trade Commission Green Guides, www.ftc.gov/bcp/conline/pubs/buspubs/greenguides.shtm
TerraChoice, "The Six Sins of Greenwashing," www.terrachoice.com/files/6_sins.pdf
Bob Langert, "The Six Sins of Greenmuting," http://csr.blogs.mcdonalds.com/default.asp?item=292036

Emissions Measurement, Reduction, and Trading

Global scientific consensus suggests an urgent need to reduce greenhouse gas emissions at least 80% by 2050 (if not earlier) to avoid catastrophic climate change. Companies realize emissions reductions will soon be mandatory throughout the world and are moving rapidly to measure and reduce emissions where they can, and trade what they can't. Shareholder pressure in the form of the Carbon Disclosure Project (CDP), a group of 385 institutional investors with over $57 trillion under management that annually asks the biggest companies in the world to report their emissions, is another powerful driver of corporate emissions measurement.

A number of yardsticks exist for measuring GHG emissions, the most widely used being the Greenhouse Gas Protocol created by the World Business Council on Sustainable Development (WBCSD) and the World Resources Institute (WRI). Carbon trading is the market-based mechanism for promoting emissions reductions endorsed by the Kyoto Protocol and the European Union with its Emission Trading Scheme, so companies are adopting this practice. However, activists express skepticism, questioning whether carbon trading is merely a way to make money while delaying substantive emissions reductions.

IMPLEMENTED BY:

RESOURCES:
Greenhouse Gas Protocol, www.ghgprotocol.org
European Union Emission Trading Scheme (EU ETS), http://ec.europa.eu
Carbon Disclosure Project (CDP), www.cdproject.net
Climate Counts, www.climatecounts.org

Employee Engagement

As the term "human resources" suggests, employees represent a vital resource, so companies do well to treat them sustainably, and also benefit from worker wisdom on how to advance corporate sustainability. The issue of sustainability crosses the boundary between the personal and the professional, so companies that acknowledge this overlap and seek to connect with employees over sustainability issues can thrive. For example, a recent study by Towers Perrin shows that companies with the highest percentage of engaged workers make more money. Examples of companies engaging with employees on sustainability include supporting telecommuting (incentive programs to buy clean cars, which can save carbon emissions) or use of public mass transit to commute.

IMPLEMENTED BY:

RESOURCES:
Towers Perrin Global Workforce Study, www.towersperrin.com

Energy Efficiency

Energy efficiency is perhaps the most attractive environmental initiative for companies, as saving energy usually simultaneously saves money. As such, it represents low-hanging fruit for companies beginning their green journey. The broad range of areas where companies use energy can lead them further down the green path, providing opportunities for energy and financial savings. Companies can focus on energy efficiency in their own operations as well as efficiency of their products, a key selling point in a world of diminishing resources. Energy efficiency is particularly important for energy-intensive sectors, such as information technology, where computer servers consume extraordinary amounts of power.

IMPLEMENTED BY:

RESOURCES:
American Council for an Energy Efficient Economy, www.aceee.org
EPA Report on Server and Data Center Energy Efficiency, www.energystar.gov
McKinsey Global Institute, "The Case for Investing in Energy Productivity," www.mckinsey.com

Green Building

The establishment of Leadership in Energy and Environmental Design (LEED) certification by the U.S. Green Building Council in 2000 has helped fuel the green building movement, which applies environmental considerations to the architecture and construction of buildings large and small. LEED standards call for the use of environmentally responsible building materials to create safer, healthier work and living spaces, as well as reducing energy consumption and emissions—important factors given that commercial buildings account for about 60% of U.S. electricity use and 30% of greenhouse gas emissions. LEED-certified green building practices apply not only to new construction but also to existing buildings, as well as to commercial interiors and retail space, which have unique considerations.

IMPLEMENTED BY:

RESOURCES:
U.S. Green Building Council, www.usgbc.org
Leadership in Energy and Environmental Design (LEED), www.usgbc.org
Environmental Building News, https://www.buildinggreen.com

Green Manufacturing

The manufacturing phase creates the biggest environmental impact in many products' life cycles, upping the importance of green manufacturing, which reduces environmental impacts through energy efficiency, emissions and pollution reductions, and nontoxic raw materials, among other factors.

IMPLEMENTED BY:

RESOURCES:
Consortium on Green Design and Manufacturing, http://cgdm.berkeley.edu

Green Product Design

Green product design integrates environmental considerations into products from the moment they are scribbled on a cocktail napkin or drawing board. For example, green chemistry seeks to replace toxic chemicals in products and production processes with safer alternatives. Other elements of green product design include resource efficiency (using less energy and raw materials in production *and* product use) as well as using recycled ingredients *and* ensuring that products can be recycled at the end of their useful lives. Green product design sometimes increases up-front costs for new equipment but balances this out through the reduced costs of using energy and materials more efficiently.

IMPLEMENTED BY:

RESOURCES:
DesignGreen, www.designgreen.org
GreenBiz: www.greenbiz.com

Product Stewardship

Product stewardship applies a life-cycle assessment to products, a cradle-to-grave approach to assessing and minimizing the environmental impacts related to products at every stage of life—from design to manufacture to regulation to use to disposal. This analysis seeks to remove toxins and waste from production processes and products and maximize use of recycled ingredients. The holy grail of product stewardship is cradle-to-cradle production, conceived and practiced by William McDonough and Michael Braungart, which creates a closed loop whereby all products become feedstock for the manufacturing stream after their useful lives, thereby achieving zero waste and sustainable production.

In the related concept of extended producer responsibility, manufacturers take responsibility for the entire life cycle of their products, whereas product stewardship encourages everyone in the value chain to contribute to product sustainability, from producers to regulators to retailers to consumers.

IMPLEMENTED BY:

RESOURCES:
Product Stewardship Institute, www.productstewardship.us
McDonough Braungart Design Chemistry Cradle to Cradle Certification, www.mbdc.com/c2c

Public Policy Leadership

The writing is on the wall that social and environmental issues are headed for stricter legislation and regulation. Many companies are responding by engaging in the public policy process to avoid becoming victims to laws or rules that adversely affect business or, worse yet, fail to achieve the desired social and environmental benefits through poor design. While business influence in the legislative and regulatory processes raises red flags for many environmentalists, as it often (if not almost always) signals attempts to weaken or circumvent limits or controls, the specter of climate change has created the interesting phenomenon where companies have been urging government to set limits on carbon emissions. Business has not suddenly become altruistic, but instead recognizes the reality of a carbon-constrained future, and seeks legislation and regulation to create certainty and a level playing field.

IMPLEMENTED BY:

RESOURCES:
Policy Innovations, www.policyinnovations.org

Recycling and Resource Conservation

"Reduce, reuse, recycle" is the environmentalist mantra, and the reduce component applies to resource conservation. Companies are operating more efficiently to save their own resources, which in turn conserves common resources such as water and energy. The recycling component of the mantra applies to many different areas of corporate life. Companies are using recycled content instead of raw materials, not only in their products but also in their production processes and operations—for example, by using heat generated from machinery to warm work spaces. They are also focusing on "recycled and recyclable," using recycled content in packaging, for example, and making the packaging itself recyclable.

As with energy efficiency, recycling and resource conservation can save money, as they reduce the need to purchase new resources. Companies can also sell items at the end of their productive lives to firms that recycle the content into new products. In the electronics sector, regulations such as the European Union's Waste Electrical and Electronic Equipment (WEEE) directive require recyclability to be designed into products, so for companies selling in EU markets, product recyclability is no longer optional, but rather mandatory.

IMPLEMENTED BY:

RESOURCES:
European Union's Waste Electrical and Electronic Equipment (WEEE) Directive, http://ec.europa.eu
Silicon Valley Toxics Coalition, www.etoxics.org

Safer Alternatives to Toxics

The spate of recalled toys tainted with lead paint starting in mid-2007 shone a spotlight on the risks inherent in globalized supply chains, as companies are hard pressed to police factories strewn throughout Asia, Africa, and Latin America. Analysis of the problem revealed not only that Chinese factories were using unauthorized paints in some instances but also that faulty designs by the companies themselves were to blame in other instances. So companies need to both monitor their supply chains more comprehensively and remove potentially toxic materials and ingredients from their product designs.

Product toxicity applies to much more than lead paint, however, encompassing potentially hazardous chemicals in products (such as bisphenol-A in plastic water bottles) as well as in production processes, such as the use of PFOA (an ingredient in Teflon). SC Johnson has perhaps the longest track record of incorporating safer alternatives into its products and processes through its Greenlist program.

IMPLEMENTED BY:

RESOURCES:
Investor Environmental Health Network (IEHN), www.iehn.org
SC Johnson Greenlist, www.scjohnson.com

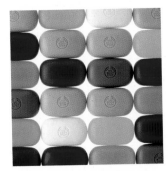

Supply Chain Accountability/Ethical Sourcing

In the age of globalization, supply chains encircle the world, making it increasingly difficult for companies to ensure the social and environmental responsibility of their first-, second-, and third-tier suppliers. Over the past decade or more, companies have developed ethical sourcing guidelines, and now monitoring organizations such as Verité regularly audit their supplier factories for compliance. The Gap made waves in 2004 when it disclosed supplier noncompliance with its standards, and more recently Nike set a precedent by publishing a comprehensive list of its factories.

In addition to policing their supply chains, companies are increasingly engaging their suppliers to support adoption of more environmentally responsible practices. For example, gaining Fair Trade or organic certification can be a complex and costly process, so companies are increasingly supplying the financial and technical support necessary for farmers to go green.

IMPLEMENTED BY:

RESOURCES:
Ethical Trading Initiative, www.ethicaltrade.org
Verité, www.verite.org
Social Accountability International, www.sa-intl.org

Sustainability Reporting

Sustainability reporting has grown from a handful of companies pioneering the practice in the 1990s to more than 4,000 companies around the world producing over 16,000 sustainability reports at the latest count. Data requests from socially responsible investors certainly fueled this trend, as has consumer demand. Companies have also discovered the usefulness of sustainability reports for communicating positive social and environmental initiatives and disclosing sensitive challenges and mistakes internally amongst their own worker body. The third generation of Global Reporting Initiative (GRI) guidelines (dubbed G3) has emerged as the gold standard in sustainability reporting.

In addition to corporate sustainability reports, a number of other reporting mechanisms are adopting sustainability factors. For example, investment analyst reports are increasingly incorporating environmental, social, and governance (ESG) factors into their analyses.

IMPLEMENTED BY:

RESOURCES:
Global Reporting Initiative (GRI), www.globalreporting.org/Home
CorporateRegister.com, www.corporateregister.com
ACCA-Ceres Sustainability Reporting Awards, www.Ceres.org

Sustainable/Green Investing

Mainstream financial institutions are slowly greening their investments across a broad spectrum of practices. On the retail side, companies are offering investment funds that apply environmental considerations to stock picking, such as the five climate change funds launched in late 2007 by the likes of Virgin Money, Deutsche Bank, and HSBC that seek to avoid climate-related risks and profit from opportunities from global warming mitigation and adaptation. On the sell side, brokerages increasingly analyze environmental, social, and governance (ESG) factors in the research reports they generate to sell stocks, since a 2004 United Nations project encouraging this practice.

However, the greening of investment is an arduous process, as many financial institutions that are taking positive strides in some areas of their business continue to vote against shareholder resolutions on environmental issues such as product toxicity or climate change on the proxies of companies they hold in mutual funds.

IMPLEMENTED BY:

RESOURCES:
SocialFunds.com, www.socialfunds.com
United Nations Principles for Responsible Investment (UNPRI), www.unpri.org
United Nations Environment Programme Finance Initiative (UNEP FI), www.unepfi.org

Sustainable Packaging and Shipping/Logistics

Sustainable packaging made headlines in 2007 when Wal-Mart's Packaging Sustainability Network compelled General Mills to straighten the noodles of Hamburger Helper in order to reduce the packaging. Shaving a little bit off each package adds up when dealing in truckloads, increasing the number of boxes fitting in a trailer and ultimately reducing the carbon footprint of each box of product. Sustainable packaging also seeks to use recycled and recyclable materials—for example, replacing petroleum-based plastics with bio-based plastics. Shareholder activists are convincing many companies, such as Sears and Target, to phase out the use of polyvinyl chloride (PVC—a toxic chemical) in packaging.

On the shipping/logistics front, 20% of U.S. energy goes toward moving goods and logistics, and 20% of that—or 4% of all energy—is spent on trains and trucks that are not even moving goods but rather idling. So sustainable shipping/logistics entails more than reduced packaging, encompassing increased fuel efficiency, the use of renewable fuels such as biodiesel, and the development of hybrid trucks. On the high seas, cargo ships' use of bunker fuel (literally, bottom-of-the-barrel fuel left behind after crude oil has been refined into gasoline and diesel for cars and trucks) contributes disproportionately to pollution and emissions, so sustainable shipping will require transitioning to better fuels, such as distillates.

IMPLEMENTED BY:

  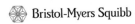

RESOURCES:
Sustainable Packaging Coalition, www.sustainablepackaging.org
Sustainable Shipping, www.sustainableshipping.com

Waste Management

A core sustainability challenge posed by the materialism encouraged by capitalism is this: what the heck to do with all the stuff we consume? The rise of sustainability has also fueled a stronger focus on waste management, in equal parts finding creative ways to reduce or make productive use of waste (for example, by harvesting energy from landfill methane) on the back end, and on the front end eliminating waste in the first place—with the ultimate goal of zero waste, where all waste reenters the industrial stream as feedstock.

IMPLEMENTED BY:

  HONDA Interface·

RESOURCES:
Zero Waste Alliance, http://zerowaste.org
The Story of Stuff, www.storyofstuff.com
EPA WasteWise, www.epa.gov/wastewise

Water Management

Water security and access to clean water rank alongside climate change as the most environmentally pressing problems facing us in the 21st century—and, in fact, global warming exacerbates water challenges. Companies respond to this rising crisis by reducing water use, increasing reuse of wastewater when possible, and developing solutions to water problems, such as cheap water purification and desalination systems for use in the developing world.

IMPLEMENTED BY:

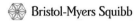

RESOURCES:
World Business Council on Sustainable Development (WBCSD), "Business in the World of Water," www.wbcsd.org
Pacific Institute, www.pacinst.org

Workplace Transformation

Employees spend much of their productive lives at work, enhancing the need to create sustainable workplaces. Companies are doing so by redesigning the physical layout of offices to encourage more interaction and collaboration, to support work-life integration (for example, by siting day care and workout space in the office place), and shifting to flexible schedules to meet diverse family needs.

IMPLEMENTED BY:

RESOURCES:
Center for Workplace Transformation, http://cwt-ru.org
General Services Administration (GSA), "Creating the Sustainable Workplace," www.gsa.gov/gsa

An Energy-Intensive Company Sees "No Option" but to Limit Greenhouse Gas Emissions

This maker of aluminum must grapple with the fact that the production of aluminum is one of the world's most energy-intensive businesses. More than 30 cents of every production dollar in the aluminum business are spent on energy, starting with the 950-degree heat and powerful electric currents needed to turn alumina into aluminum. When electricity prices rise, profits are squeezed. The solution? Alcoa has discovered that joining global initiatives to address climate change is a useful catalyst for conserving energy.

The road to profitability is paved with lower energy bills, which correspond to reduced greenhouse gas emissions. Promoting recycling is good for both the bottom line and the environment, since making products out of recycled aluminum feedstock uses only 5% of the energy of making them by smelting ore. Toward that end, Alcoa plans to double its use of recycled aluminum.

Alcoa has plenty of environmental challenges with 107,000 employees in 44 countries working in bauxite mines, refineries, smelters (which extract aluminum metal from its ore), and factories that mold aluminum into objects. It's been called one of the ten most toxic companies in America, has been the subject of protests, and has paid large fines for polluting. In Texas, Alcoa has been given special permission to avoid the state's clean-air standards. The company's annual report lists more than 100 locations that it is responsible for cleaning up. Some of these are federally designated Superfund cleanup sites—the worst-polluted sites in the nation.

But on climate change, the company's thorough and ambitious drive for improvement has made Alcoa a model and leader for other manufacturers. Alcoa pledged to reduce its direct greenhouse gas emissions by 25% in a decade. It reached this goal in only 4 years (the baseline was nearly 10 years earlier, so the cuts actually occurred over a 13-year period). The shrinking of Alcoa's carbon footprint was accomplished by measuring and tracking energy, then using it more efficiently in existing operations. This three-step approach led to savings of $20 million in 2005 alone.

A company's carbon footprint is the result not only of its manufacturing processes but also of its office facilities and even employees' actions. On the roof of its manufacturing facility in Visalia, California, Alcoa installed a

OPPOSITE: The Maranhão Aluminum Consortium in Brazil (Consórcio de Alumínio do Maranhão, also known as Alumar) is one of the world's largest aluminum and alumina production complexes.

pilot demonstration of advanced thin-film solar panels. In Australia, it collaborated with a nonprofit organization, Greening Australia, to help employees and their families understand, measure, track, and reduce household carbon footprints.

The search for low-cost, low-carbon energy sources led Alcoa to consider solar, hydro, and other clean energy at facilities around the world. The company's newest smelting facility was built in Iceland in order to make

The first shipment of alumina to Alcoa Fjarðaál in Iceland

use of that country's plentiful, clean hydroelectric power. Building a large smelter in a small country was not popular with some local residents; many Icelanders protested their government's decision to dam a river to benefit the Alcoa plant. In keeping with its strategy for renewable energy, Alcoa is now looking into using geothermal heat from Iceland's volcanic geology as an energy source for a second smelter.

With the easiest energy gains already captured, the company has been exploring new technologies that have the potential to take a big chunk out of its energy needs. The Environmental Protection Agency estimates that the aluminum industry can pare its energy use down to one-third from its current needs. But to reduce energy by such a large amount will require some major technological breakthroughs in the energy-intensive smelting process.

Smelting is still done in much the same way as when the process was first commercialized in 1886. Aluminum oxide, refined from bauxite ore and known as alumina, is dissolved in an electrolytic bath within a carbon or graphite-lined steel container known as a "pot." An electric current is passed through the pot on a carbon rod, or anode, and molten aluminum is then deposited at the bottom of the pot and siphoned off to become ingots. Carbon dioxide (CO_2), carbon monoxide (CO), and other emissions are either vented through the top or collected and treated through conventional pollution-control processes.

Alcoa is funding research on breakthrough smelting technologies that would greatly reduce emissions. One process is called inert-anode smelting. If a material could be found to replace the carbon in the anode, the smelting process would produce far less carbon dioxide.

Another promising technology is called carbothermic reduction. This chemical process, too complicated to explain here, has been researched since the 1950s, but various hurdles have kept it from becoming commercially viable. In recent years scientific advances, some the result of Alcoa research, have made carbothermic reduction seem more promising: if successful, the process would use only a quarter of the electricity of traditional smelting and emit only a third as much greenhouse gases per ton of aluminum.

Both of these new technologies may require years more research before they are commercially feasible. In the meantime, one carbon-reducing technique implemented by Alcoa in 2007 is already set to go: carbon sequestration in bauxite waste. This new technology, developed with the Department of Energy's National Energy Technology Lab, uses bauxite residue, sometimes called "red mud," as a carbon sponge. Because the residue is highly alkaline, it normally must be contained and monitored. When carbonated or treated with CO_2, the residue's pH level is reduced to the level of natural alkaline soils, so that it becomes safe to reuse as road or building materials. Alcoa estimates that in Australia alone, where the process will be piloted, it could keep 300,000 tons of CO_2 out of the atmosphere annually.

In addition to improving its profits, the company's work on greenhouse gas emissions has also earned it recognition and prizes. In 2005 Alcoa was named one of the three most sustainable companies in the world at the World Economic Forum in Davos, Switzerland. In 2007 *Ethisphere* magazine dubbed Alcoa one of the world's most ethical companies. Dow Jones has included the company in its Sustainability Indexes for six years. The Climate Disclosure Project's Leadership Index named it best in class for the way it analyzes, documents, and discloses information about energy use and carbon emissions, with independent third parties checking progress. Such accolades reflect the company's strong public position on climate change as well as its success in reducing its own carbon footprint.

As a founding member of the Global Roundtable on Climate Change and the U.S. Climate Action Partnership, Alcoa has joined other businesses and environmental organizations in calling for the U.S. government to develop a national climate change policy. Alcoa supports a mandatory federal cap on carbon emissions. The company's executives emphasize that fighting climate change can be an opportunity for companies, not just a burden or a cost.

As CEO Alain Belda said, "companies can grow and prosper in a greenhouse-gas-constrained world. Actually…there is no other option."

Building with a View of the Park (the Amazon National Park)

The architects of a new Alcoa mining facility in Juruti, Brazil, near Amazon National Park, designed a complex that takes inspiration from the building style in Yanomami Indian villages. The architects minimized the environmental impact by using local materials rather than transporting imported materials. Buildings in the new facility are faced with locally made, unfired bricks. They incorporate coverings, room dividers, and ceilings in the shape of traditional village structures, with large covered communal spaces between the buildings. The coverings and dividers have a modern twist, though: they are made of recycled plastic and aluminum toothpaste tubes. The neighboring region, including Amazon National Park, is an international "biodiversity hot spot," with a high number of rare and endangered species in a threatened habitat. Alcoa collaborated with the government of Brazil and Conservation International to build a lookout platform and nature trails—the first of many planned conservation works. The conservation projects provide employment for local residents.

Vital Statistics

Main site: New York, New York
Main product: Aluminum
Number of employees: 107,000
Green partners: U.S. Climate Action Partnership • Green Power Market Development Group • Pew Center on Global Climate Change • World Business Council for Sustainable Development • Rainforest Alliance Climate Change Program • Resources for the Future • Conservation International • Kew Gardens
Success: 25% reduction in GHG emissions compared to 1990 • Named one of the world's most sustainable corporations at the World Economic Forum
Challenge: Elimination of workplace fatalities • Availability and cost of energy • Reduction in use of fresh water
Awards: Global 100 Most Sustainable Corporations in the World—Corporate Knights and Innovest • Dow Jones Sustainability World Index • United Nations Environment Programme's Global 500 Roll of Honour • Top Company on Climate Change and Governance—Ceres

Laying off the Juice

For every kilowatt of power used in a typical data center, an average of 1.4 kilowatts of energy is wasted, a fact that Advanced Micro Devices, Inc. (AMD) is working hard to rectify. High-performance servers in data centers are a primary culprit, with additional inefficiencies coming from cooling, backup power systems, lighting, and power conversion. Microprocessor vendor AMD, based in Sunnyvale, California, succeeds in manufacturing more energy-efficient products that use less power. AMD's success in innovative product design, significant reductions in greenhouse gas emissions, and energy efficiency improvements at its manufacturing plants and other facilities landed it a spot, in 2007 and 2008, on the Global 100 Most Sustainable Corporations in the World list. Compiled by Innovest Strategic Value Advisors, a research firm, and Corporate Knights, a Canada-based media company, the list identifies companies that serve as role models for managing environmental, social, and governance risks.

More energy-efficient computers are becoming increasingly critical. An AMD-sponsored study conducted in 2006 showed that total power used by servers in the United States doubled between 2000 and 2005, a result of more servers being used to meet increased computing needs. An expert in server processor power efficiency, AMD led the way in recent years in shifting consumer thinking about how to evaluate a central processing unit (CPU). Until recently, most information technology departments made purchasing decisions based on a CPU's speed alone. In 2006, AMD's marketing materials began focusing on energy efficiency as a key differentiating factor, and its advertising campaign slogans included "It's time for you to lay off the juice." Now buyers are thinking

OPPOSITE: Die shot of AMD's native Quad-Core Opteron processor

about performance per watt, a concept that is similar to miles per gallon.

In late 2007, AMD introduced a new energy-efficient server chip, the Quad-Core AMD Opteron processor. Code-named Barcelona, it incorporates four processors on one piece of silicon. This means that signals travel shorter distances, allowing faster processing at lower energy levels. Several other features also help reduce energy consumption. Barcelona employs an energy-efficient memory system that uses up to 58% less power than previous memory systems, and AMD's CoolCore technology automatically turns off the parts of the CPU that aren't in use. The PowerNow! technology feature controls the transmission speed (measured in megahertz, MHz) used in each processor. In the past, all cores within the processor would run at the maximum speed required for a single core to complete its task even if the other cores were idle. PowerNow! technology allows each core to run at its own MHz load, which helps reduce power used and ties power used directly to power needed.

Whenever AMD designs a product, for applications ranging from handheld devices to supercomputers, company engineers address energy conservation. One innovation is DTX, a new industry-standard specification that allows for smaller desktop PC designs that consume less power and generate less noise, with lower system cooling costs. DTX is an open-standard specification, meaning that it can be used to design products made by different manufacturers, so that power savings can be realized regardless of the source of the system.

Other AMD product innovations include versions of its dual-core Athlon desktop processor, introduced in early 2007. It performs up to 154% better per watt than standard AMD desktop processors. AMD has also been refining its abilities to offer server virtualization. Virtualization partitions a single computer into several independent virtual machines that can run different operating systems and software at the same time, reducing the need for multiple servers and helping to decrease power usage.

AMD is focusing on its operations as well. The company set an EPA Climate Leaders goal of cutting normalized greenhouse gas emissions by 40% from 2002 to 2007, but by 2006 the company had already reduced its normalized emissions by over 50%. One way it accomplished its goal was by changing to more efficient, less polluting sources for the energy used in its manufacturing processes. Now, 60% of its energy comes from either highly efficient trigeneration systems or from renewable energy sources. AMD has set a new Climate Leaders goal to further reduce its normalized greenhouse gas emissions by another 33% by 2010 compared to 2006.

Trigeneration is different from conventional systems, where electricity, heat, and cooling are generated separately. Trigeneration uses the waste heat generated from electricity production for heating and cooling and is therefore much more efficient. In Austin, Texas, AMD purchases renewable energy through Austin Energy's program called GreenChoice. AMD has committed to using 100% GreenChoice energy at its new Lone Star campus in Austin. AMD is one of the largest purchasers of energy from GreenChoice, which offers customers the ability to buy electricity from renewable sources, including wind power and methane gas captured from landfills.

All of AMD's 2,600 Austin-area employees will work from the Lone Star business campus in southwest Austin.

AMD has also reduced perfluorocompound (PFC) emissions by 50% over its 1995 baseline. PFCs are used during the semiconductor manufacturing process. Most of the reductions come from the Dresden, Germany, wafer fabrication plant, where alternative materials with much lower global-warming potential are now being used to clean the process chambers in manufacturing tools.

A key aspect of AMD's approach to sustainability includes its collaboration with others to ensure that information technology becomes greener faster. AMD was a founding member in 2007 of the Green Grid, a nonprofit organization designed to share best practices on how to improve energy efficiency in data centers and business computing devices. Among the 150 companies in the Green Grid are such names as Dell, Hewlett-Packard, IBM, Microsoft, and Sun Microsystems. One issue that was facing AMD and the other members of the Green Grid is how to develop an industry-wide formula to compute useful work per watt. The performance of a CPU varies depending on how fully it is being used and the type of work it is doing, and in February 2008, the organization announced metrics designed to take these factors into account.

In 2006 and 2007, AMD sponsored the California Cleantech Open's Smart Power prize, given to new businesses developing technologies that allow users greater control over their own energy consumption.

Data Overload

Concerned about data-center energy consumption, AMD commissioned a study, the first of its kind, to calculate how much money was being spent to power servers, cooling equipment, and auxiliary infrastructure equipment in data centers. The results revealed that power consumption by servers in the United States doubled from 2000 to 2005. Jonathan Koomey, a staff scientist at the Lawrence Berkeley National Laboratory and a consulting professor at Stanford University, discovered that a spike in data-center servers was the cause of 90% of the increase, with the remainder coming from the development of less energy-efficient technology.

The power used in 2005 by computing equipment cost an estimated $2.7 billion and was about 1.2% of all power used in the country. At an industry conference in 2007, Randy Allen, corporate vice president of product marketing, said the numbers are a wake-up call showing that unchecked demand for data-center power will ultimately constrain economic growth. The executive suggested several ways that industry leaders and government agencies can curb data-center power consumption, including instituting an annual report on data-center business efficiency to measure progress, and developing a standard methodology so that businesses can measure the power efficiency of their data centers.

Vital Statistics

Main site: Sunnyvale, California
Main product: x86 CPU processors
Number of employees: 16,400
Green partner: Charter partner of the U.S. EPA Climate Leaders
Success: Goal of 40% reduction of normalized emissions by end of 2007, surpassed by 50% reduction by end of 2006 • Energy consumption goal to reduce normalized emissions by 30%, surpassed by end of 2007
Challenge: Aligning business model with full integration of corporate responsibility and environmental stewardship
Awards: Global 100 Most Sustainable Corporations in the World—Corporate Knights and Innovest

Let It Snow, Let It Snow…Please, Let It Snow: Aspen Skiing Company Turns to National Advocacy to Halt Climate Change

For the 2007–2008 season, Aspen Skiing Company's entire ad budget focused on ways to fight climate change, with celebrities such as snowboarding star Gretchen Bleiler, freeskier Peter Olenick, and extreme skier Chris Davenport serving as spokespeople. In addition, the company sent compact fluorescent lightbulbs to 40,000 of its most loyal customers, with a direct appeal to reduce their carbon emissions.

If climate change increases global temperatures as predicted, and the increase results in less snow and shorter winters, many major ski resorts will be in jeopardy. This means that the rich and famous and the young and daring who frequent Aspen and other resorts will have to find other ways to spend their time. More significant is that the reduced snowfall that could curtail skiing also means less water for the already strained Colorado River basin. Approximately 30 million people in seven states depend on water from the Colorado River. Seen in that light, the ski industry is the canary in the coal mine for climate change.

Aspen Skiing Company, a private operator of the Aspen and Snowmass ski resorts, has been whistling like a canary for more than a decade. In the Aspen area, snowfall has declined by 16% since 1981, and projections for the next 75 years across the West are dire (read more about the predictions at www.savesnow.org). Aspen began its sustainability efforts with a formalized recycling program in 1997. This initial effort led to the construction of dirt half-pipes built in the summer months instead of building the structures out of snow in the winter. When making snow today, Aspen uses specks of dust to seed artificial snowflakes. Both tactics reduce the use of natural resources and save the company money on both power and water bills. So does converting its 40 mountain-grooming snowcats to using clean, renewable biodiesel.

Over time, Aspen Skiing Company began to realize that its own environmental efforts, however laudable, are of little import in the grand scheme of global climate change, and it decided to take up the mantle of national leadership by educating consumers, politicians, and even chief justices.

"If you were Aspen and you really cared about the environment and climate change, how could you have the biggest impact?" asks Auden Schendler, Aspen's direc-

tor of environmental affairs. "The answer is by using the name Aspen to drive change. There are 55 million skiers in this country. We want to inspire a grassroots movement on climate change. Those 55 million skiers are affluent, they vote, they can drive change. We want to use Aspen as a lever. We want Aspen to be a thought leader—not just doing it, but talking about how we do it."

In 2006, Aspen filed an amicus brief with the U.S. Supreme Court, which was hearing a case brought by 12 states charging that CO_2 should be considered a pollutant. The Court eventually ruled in favor of the plaintiffs, and Schendler says it's the "biggest thing Aspen Skiing Company has ever done for the environment." In 2007, the company filed written testimony for the U.S. Congress's Committee on Natural Resources oversight hearing on energy policy and climate change on public lands, citing the possibility that by the end of the century Aspen will have the climate of Colorado Springs, a desert community with no ski business.

The initial spark behind Aspen Skiing Company's advocacy efforts came from former CEO Pat O'Donnell. "My mandate to Auden was to become an activist," O'Donnell recalled. "We have to get involved at the state and national levels. Otherwise, we'll be sitting around with a squeaky clean record and we'll say, 'We did everything.' And we'll be bankrupt, because of climate change."

The company faces two key challenges. The first is coming on too strong and turning away less engaged consumers. Activism can be a double-edged sword and can turn off as many consumers as it turns on, which is why Aspen Skiing Company was often alone in its initial proclamations. But now the National Ski Areas Association has partnered with the Natural Resources Defense Council to lobby Congress on behalf of climate change legislation. And Aspen Skiing Company's own surveys show that close to 40% of its customers say they are more likely to return to the Aspen slopes because of its activism.

The second challenge is in the court of public opinion. It's one thing to reduce the power and water used in artificial snowmaking, but why make snow at all if the only purpose is to make money? That charge, of course, could be levied against almost any business, except it's easier when the product is a nonessential luxury good. Schendler has an answer for that.

All Aspen/Snowmass snowcats run on a blend of clean, renewable biodiesel fuel.

"Our business is creating emissions—we fly people over here, we put them on lifts. The subtext is if you care about the planet, you should close down. But the solution is not to end capitalism. It's to make capitalism radically more efficient and less damaging to the environment. The corporate sector is part of the solution. In fact, by being leaders in ski area environmentalism and making a big deal out of it, Aspen Skiing Company has arguably forced the rest of the industry to change. If we stayed humble and quiet, other resorts wouldn't feel pressed to compete." Let the games begin.

Lowering the Lights—and the Heat

In order to reduce energy consumption, Aspen Skiing Company has undertaken an ambitious program of lighting retrofits that started in the year 2000. In its Little Nell Garage, the company swapped out 110 metal halide lamps with T-8 fluorescent fixtures. The retrofit prevents 300,000 pounds of CO_2 emissions annually and saves the company more than $10,600 each year. More recent retrofits, to replace halogen, incandescent, and halide lighting elsewhere with compact fluorescent lighting (CFL), save tens of thousands of pounds of CO_2—and more dollars. Another energy-saving piece of equipment is a new compressor on Aspen Mountain that curbs an additional 466,000 pounds of CO_2 emissions each year. Aspen Skiing Company now estimates it has reduced its CO_2 emissions from energy consumption by 2.1 million pounds a year, which saves the company $85,000 annually.

The Clubhouse is one of the greenest commercial buildings in Colorado, beating local energy codes by more than 60%.

Vital Statistics

Main sites: Aspen and Snowmass Village, Colorado
Main products: Skiing and hotels
Number of employees: 3,400
Green partners: Natural Resources Defense Council • Chicago Climate Exchange • City of Aspen • Community Office for Resource Efficiency • KPMG Performance Registrar, Inc. (ISO 14001) • Ceres • Colorado Office of Energy Management • Holy Cross Energy
Success: Pioneers in biodiesel in snowcats • Use of renewable power • Green building • Environmental philanthropy • Policy action
Challenge: Cutting CO_2 emissions at the scale necessary to slow climate change
Awards: 2007 World Travel and Tourism Council—Tourism for Tomorrow Conservation Award • 2007 EPA Climate Leader Award • 2006 EPA/DOE Green Power Partner of the Year

Selling Health and Beauty Products That Are Organic, Indigenous, Renewable

Some companies arrive at environmental awareness and action over a long period of time, taking measured steps until they recognize that "going green" also has a positive impact on the bottom line. Other companies are shocked into change by activists following a watershed event. Aveda, the Minnesota-based health and beauty products company, was founded by an entrepreneurial and forward-looking hairstylist, who first created a plant-based shampoo in his kitchen, before the first Earth Day.

Horst Rechelbacher's mission from the start, in 1978, was to "be an advocate for creating plant-based products, when our industry was promoting the use of petrochemical ingredients, [for] products [from] sustainable agriculture and [for] responsible packaging" (Aveda Ceres Report, 1999). "Aveda believes in conducting business in a manner that protects the earth, conserves resources, and does not compromise the ability of future generations to sustain themselves," says Dominique Conseil, president of Aveda since 2000.

Aveda, now owned by Estée Lauder, was the first privately held company to endorse the Valdez Principles, written in 1989 after the *Exxon Valdez* oil tanker spill in Alaska, and now known as the Ceres Principles. Aveda's primary manufacturing facility in Minnesota is 100% powered by wind energy: the company's funding of new wind energy turbines generates enough wind energy to offset 100% of the electricity used in manufacturing. More impressive, most of its ingredients are from plant-based or nonpetroleum mineral-based materials: 90% of its essential oils are certified organic. Aveda's containers and packages are made with up to 100% postconsumer recycled content (PCR). When Aveda updated the look of its shampoo bottles, it maximized the postconsumer resin content in the bottles to save about $1 million a year in packaging costs.

Aveda pioneered the development of the industry's first ever refillable lip case for its Uruku lip colors. The cases are made from 88% PCR resin and infused with 30% natural flax fiber that has a base comprised of up to 65% PCR aluminum. Each refillable lip case is used with an average of twelve lip color refills, which avoids disposal of approximately three tons of excess lip-color packaging materials each year. The outer clamshell packaging

OPPOSITE: At Blaine Corporate Headquarters, Aveda integrates previously outsourced manufacturing, thus creating value and jobs at Aveda and in the community. (Rick Peters for InsideOut Studios)

of Uruku lip colors contains 100% PCR newsprint and includes a sleeve made with 100% PCR material.

The company's overall mission and strategy are encapsulated in its cornerstone Soil to Bottle approach and "traceability" of ingredients. Aveda has established a process in which it carefully monitors its products through growing, harvesting, and manufacturing. Aveda uses many certified organically grown and harvested plants, many of which are from indigenous or traditional farmers—babassu nuts and lippia from Brazil, rose and lavender from Bulgaria, Brazil nuts from Peru, and urukum from the Amazon—thus practicing a form of inclusive capitalism that places a high value on producers in its supply chain.

Aveda started using Forest Stewardship Council (FSC) wood pallets in 2002. (Rick Peters for InsideOut Studios)

Sustainability also extends to shipping. In 2002, Aveda began using pallets made of wood certified by the Forest Stewardship Council (FSC) for outgoing North American and international shipments of finished goods manufactured in Minnesota, and also switched shipment of two of its most-used products from nonrecyclable drums to reusable totes. Since 2003, Aveda has also encouraged use of FSC-certified wood in pallets by its component and raw materials suppliers. In its stores, reclaimed wood is used for the makeup display/merchandising units, sunflower seed husks are incorporated into building materi-

als used in the cash wrap areas, and wheat straw is used to make some of the cabinets and counter spaces in the backroom areas. Aveda has created a Materials Use Toolkit to guide the purchase and use of environmentally sustainable materials throughout operations.

Aveda's explanation of its mission reflects its long-term commitment to the earth and its communities: "We support values that cultivate sustainable economies and cultures. We see environmental issues as being inextricably tied to the economic conditions of the communities from which industrialized countries derive the raw materials used to manufacture finished products. Aveda has been directing a significant portion of its…grant making to indigenous cultures and community groups to create sustainable economic activity that results in the protection of cultural traditions, rituals, and knowledge as well as improved environmental quality and community health."

Switching from 55-gallon single-use drums to 250-gallon reusable totes for two of its most-used materials saves Aveda $25,000 per year in disposal, labor, and testing costs. (Rick Peters for InsideOut Studios)

Eureka! Urukum!

The small village of Nova Esperança sits on a red-dirt cliff on the banks of the Gregorio River in Brazil's Amazon basin. It is surrounded by vibrant rain forests that support the urukum plant, a bushy tree that stretches nine feet tall and produces spiky red or green pods. Squeeze the seeds in your hands and your fingers become paintbrushes, giving brilliant color to whatever you touch. Aveda uses urukum in several of its products: Control Paste, Firming Fluid, Pure Abundance Volumizing Shampoo, Uruku Eye Accent, and Uruku Lip-Cheek Crème.

The indigenous Yawanawa people traditionally lived in the thick rain forest that nurtures these urukum trees, but from the late 1800s until the 1980s, a commercial rubber monopoly dominated the local economy and the Yawanawa were dependent on the rubber economy for their livelihood. People were dispersed to provide labor on plantations, the traditional society broke down, and their cultural survival was threatened. Following the demise of the commercial rubber industry in the 1980s, local leaders initiated the Yawanawa Bixa project to develop commercial production of the traditional urukum (*Bixa orellana*). In 1992, Horst Rechelbacher met Yawanawa leaders at the Earth Summit in Brazil and the following year a partnership was established between Aveda and the community. With the help of Aveda, the new village of Nova Esperança (New Hope), was established and an expanded urukum plantation was created.

The partnership continues to create revenue and a means of cultural survival for the community, while preserving the beauty of their land from the threat of loggers, ranchers, and exploration for gas and oil.

The Yawanawa have recently achieved a major milestone—obtaining official government demarcation of their traditional lands, including ancient burial grounds and hunting areas. Aveda has also helped the community build a solar energy system, a school, and a dispensary to treat malaria. Aveda helped the Yawanawa gain organic certification and also develop partnerships with a pharmaceutical facility that processes their urukum. The community—with this help from Aveda and others—has tripled in size and grown even more substantially in confidence, pride, and hope for the future. The Aveda-Yawanawa partnership is a shining example of what Aveda president Dominique Conseil calls "ethical capitalism."

Vital Statistics

Main site: Blaine, Minnesota
Main product: Hair and skin care
Number of employees: 2,407
Green partner: Global Greengrants Fund • Ceres
Success: Giving for environmental causes rose from $300,000 in 1999 to $2.1 million in 2007
Challenge: Maintaining sustainable supply chain
Awards: Ameristar Award for Excellence and Innovation in Environmentally Sustainable Packaging for Light the Way candle

Greener Money

Bank of America 🏦

Very near to the neon glare of Times Square in New York City, where the lights are bright enough to read the newspaper movie listings on the sidewalk at 10:00 p.m., is one of the most energy-efficient skyscrapers in the United States. It belongs to Bank of America, which is betting that the nearly $1 billion, 55-story tower (the second highest building in New York, after the Empire State Building) will be worth every penny.

Toilets that flush without water, air-conditioning fueled by giant ice blocks, and exterior walls made of low-iron glass that lets in more light than normal glass will save on energy costs and serve as concrete testimony to Bank of America's commitment to the environment.

The bank, which is one of the world's largest financial institutions, also announced in 2007 a $20 billion commitment to climate change business solutions. The initiative includes new consumer products that encourage customers to reduce energy consumption and greenhouse gas emissions, such as mortgages that reward homeowners for installing energy-saving features, as well as lending and investment opportunities aimed at corporate clients.

As part of this initiative, Bank of America also made a formal commitment to shift the financing in its utilities portfolio to support low-carbon sources—an industry first. The pledge involves reducing GHG emissions from its utilities portfolio by 7% by 2008 from a 2004 benchmark. In a 2008 Ceres report, Bank of America was ranked as one of the top two U.S. banks on climate action.

The bank has also announced plans to include carbon-emitting costs—in the range of $20 to $40 per ton—in evaluating loans for utility customers—another industry first. "We have a tremendous opportunity," said Kenneth D. Lewis, chairman and CEO, "to support our customers' efforts to build an environmentally sustainable economy—through innovative home and office construction, new manufacturing technology, changes in transportation, and new ways to supply our energy." The bank serves more than 59 million consumers and small businesses in the United States, and also lists 99% of the Fortune 500 as clients. Globally, it does business in 175 countries.

The Bank of America building in New York City, which is scheduled for occupancy in 2008, will use about half

OPPOSITE: Bank of America is helping to support sustainable growth in the Usal Redwood Forest, north of Fort Bragg in Northern California.

of the electricity and water of a conventionally built office building. The 9½-foot-tall windows insulate as well as regular windows but let in more light, allowing sensors to switch off the ceiling lights when daylight floods into offices. The tower's own power plant, which runs on natural gas, is 77% energy-efficient, versus the 30% energy efficiency in buildings with more traditional power setups. Ice tanks in the basement make ice at night, when power is cheaper, to be used in the air-conditioning system during the day. Rainwater is collected to run the air-conditioning system and irrigate the green roof. Waterless urinals for men will save 3 million gallons of water a year.

The bank hopes that when the building is completed, it will get "green" certification by the U.S. Green Building Council—the Washington, D.C., trade association that has taken on overseeing green building. USGBC's Leadership in Energy and Environmental Design (LEED) system is the benchmark for designating buildings with reduced footprints. Bank of America wants its new tower to obtain the highest LEED ranking, Platinum, which so far only a small fraction of LEED-certified buildings have been able to achieve.

The new green tower is a physical symbol of other equally important initiatives. Consumers have several new opportunities to contribute to the environment when they do business with the bank. The newly launched Brighter Planet Visa credit card earns customers one point for every dollar they spend. The points are automatically redeemed by Bank of America to support renewable energy projects. Executives estimate that 1,000 points will offset 1 ton of carbon dioxide, which has the same benefit to the environment as taking a car off the road for two months.

Another new product is the Energy Credit mortgage, which offers a $1,000 credit toward closing fees for homes that qualify for certification under the federal government's Energy Star program. To qualify, homes must meet certain standards for items such as insulation, windows, and energy-efficient heating and lighting systems. The product is a win-win-win for the bank, the consumer, and the environment. The bank can extend more credit to the homeowner, knowing that lower utility bills will keep monthly expenses down. The homeowner benefits from both more cash available from the bank and from lower

expenses, while the environment benefits because less energy is used. Government figures indicate that residential homes account for about 20% of the greenhouse gas emissions in the United States.

Ninety percent of the bank's $20 billion climate initiative, $18 billion, is being directed toward commercial clients. The bank will provide the financing necessary to encourage the development of new green products and

Opposite Bryant Park in Midtown Manhattan, construction on the environmentally friendly Bank of America tower is expected to be completed in 2008. (Cook & Fox Architects LLP)

technology and accelerate the implementation of existing low-carbon solutions. In commercial real estate, corporate and investment banking, and lending, new products and services will meet a wide variety of needs. For example, Bank of America is working to develop financing tools specifically for building projects with LEED certification. Also, clients who are creating and implementing sustainable products and services will be given favorable consideration when applying for loans.

In 2007, the bank became a member of the Chicago Climate Exchange (CCX), the world's first voluntary emissions exchange to expand customer access to the growing voluntary carbon marketplace. It plans to develop and market new environmentally focused products using the credits. Bank of America's membership and investment in CCX will help the fledgling emission trading industry grow.

Bank of America is looking to improve its own internal operations as well. In 2005, Bank of America won the Clean Air–Cool Planet Climate Champion Award for, among other reasons, setting a goal of reducing heat-trapping gases caused by its own operations by 9% by 2009. Paper usage per employee fell by 40% between 2000 and 2006. And in 2007, the bank extended its offer of a $3,000 reimbursement for a hybrid vehicle to over 185,000 employees located in the United States.

Solar-Powered Schools

Thanks to Bank of America and Chevron Energy Solutions, the largest solar-powered school district in the United States will soon be in operation. The San Jose Unified School District in California will run the extremely energy-efficient system using photovoltaic arrays that generate 5 megawatts of power. Chevron will build and operate the system, while Bank of America will own the equipment and sell the power to the school district at contract rates lower than regular utility rates.

The unique arrangement will result in an estimated 25% reduction in the school district's demand for utility power. The school district is large, with 31,000 students in 39 schools. Carbon emissions will be reduced by 37,000 tons, and over the lifetime of the equipment, energy savings are expected to total $25 million. Because the San Jose district didn't have to buy the system, no capital outlay was required, and the pricing contract with Bank of America protects the schools from unpredictable utility rate swings.

Vital Statistics

Main site: Charlotte, North Carolina	
Main products: Banking • Investing • Asset management • Other financial products and services	
Number of employees: 200,000	
Green partners: Ceres • The Nature Conservancy • Conservation International • Pew Center on Global Climate Change	
Success: Provided long-term financing for Redwood Forest Foundation's preservation efforts • Helped San Jose become largest solar-powered school system in America • Established GHG-reduction targets in its lending and applying cost of carbon in lending decisions	
Challenge: Expanding environmental products and services to develop opportunities for consumers to address climate change	
Awards: Clean Air–Cool Planet Climate Champion Award • Global Green USA Green Building Design Award	

Making Energy Conservation
a Cornerstone of Sustainability

Baxter

As a global manufacturer of medical devices, pharmaceuticals, and biotechnology that help sustain human health—including the first commercial artificial kidney, the first therapeutic treatment for hemophilia, and the first commercially produced intravenous solutions—it is not surprising that Baxter International has garnered widespread recognition as a leading corporate sustainability practitioner.

The top sustainable and responsible investing (SRI) rating firms in the world, including Sustainable Asset Management (SAM), Innovest Strategic Value Advisors, and KLD Research & Analytics, have consistently ranked Illinois-based Baxter among the top corporate sustainability performers.

These firms base their rankings on in-depth research of actual company policies and practices on social and environmental issues, such as carbon emissions reductions, energy efficiency, and product safety, among many other criteria. Such rankings also underpin investment decisions, with an underlying correlation between sustainability best practices and strong financial performance.

"At Baxter, sustainability is a business priority," said CEO Robert Parkinson in his keynote address at the Ceres annual conference in 2007. "Sustainability and profitability are not mutually exclusive. In fact, they are closely intertwined and reinforcing. The sooner we all recognize this, the better—for business and society."

In the mid-1990s, Baxter pioneered environmental financial reporting—monitoring costs and savings associated with water usage, waste reduction, and air emissions—by applying the same rigor to these environmental aspects as it does to other parts of its business. Baxter's Environmental Financial Statement demonstrates the value of proactive environmental management to senior leadership and external stakeholders. Baxter published its first Corporate Environmental Report in 1993 and a more comprehensive sustainability report in 1999.

Baxter attributes the vast majority of the gains, $76 million, reflected in the Environmental Financial Statement for 2006, to cost avoidance from initiatives it started during the previous six years. Baxter uses a rolling six-year period to track cost avoidance in the current reporting year. The returns suggest that a long-term view of environmental sustainability initiatives, such as water and energy conservation, has a cumulative and positive impact on a company's bottom line.

OPPOSITE: Baxter corporate headquarters in Deerfield, Illinois, became a carbon-neutral facility in 2007.

Baxter's focus on managing its environmental footprint and improving its operations is not new. The company has set environmental goals for the past 20 years. More recently, in 2005, Baxter set new five-year environmental goals, including: waste, 30%; water usage, 20%; energy usage, 20%; GHG emissions, 20%. All reductions are indexed to revenue. In the first year of measuring this performance, 2006, the company realized a 9% reduction in water usage, and a 5% reduction in energy, both per unit of sales. But it showed virtually no progress on waste reduction, a trend Baxter must improve on to achieve its 2010 total waste-reduction goal.

"Climate change is the most pressing global environmental challenge of this generation, and a critical sustainability issue," Baxter states in its sustainability report. "Baxter's approach to climate change is multifaceted, with energy conservation as the cornerstone."

For example, Baxter has a plant in North Carolina where the energy for steam used to sterilize its products comes from wood chips from area furniture mills that might otherwise go to landfill. Across its operations more broadly, Baxter employs facility-based energy efficiency projects that include the use of intelligent controls for motors with varying loads, which has improved efficiency by 5% to 60%, and optimized the generation and distribution of compressed air in manufacturing operations. Over the last three years, Baxter has saved from $6 million to $9 million a year through energy conservation.

On the renewable energy front, Baxter employs renewable energy directly to power its operations where feasible—for example, its manufacturing plant in Malta has the largest solar grid–connected system in that country. Where it is not economically or technically viable to directly use renewables, Baxter is buying carbon offsets to neutralize its carbon emissions.

In his Ceres keynote address, CEO Parkinson announced that Baxter's Deerfield, Illinois, corporate headquarters had gone carbon-neutral, offsetting 15.5 million kilowatt hours of annual electricity use through Green-e certified renewable energy certificates (RECs) that will help support wind energy production. By purchasing the RECs, the company prevents nearly 12,000 tons of carbon dioxide emissions annually. This amounts to the electricity needed to power more than 1,257 average

American homes annually, or the emissions of 2,172 passenger cars per year, according to the U.S. Department

More efficient lighting systems, such as those installed at Baxter's plant in Marion, North Carolina, are among the technology upgrades Baxter is implementing to reduce energy consumption in its facilities worldwide.

of Energy. Baxter is extending its action on this front to include carbon neutral products, such as its AVIVA IV solution container, the first product of its kind in the medical industry to earn Green-e certification for being made with 100% renewable electricity.

Such actions contribute to Baxter's participation in the U.S. Environmental Protection Agency's Climate Leaders program, which recognizes companies for measuring their GHG emissions, setting aggressive reduction goals, and annually reporting their progress to EPA. The company also works with EPA and the Department of Commerce in the Green Suppliers Network to identify suppliers committed to minimizing their environmental impacts.

In addition to enforcing its codes of conduct on its vast supply chain—50,000 suppliers providing $4 billion worth of goods and services annually—the company now also encourages its suppliers to submit to the network's review to support their greening. By March 2006, Baxter had recruited 4 suppliers to complete the review process, resulting in reduced water use by 5.7 million liters annually, decreased waste generation by 91 metric tons, and significantly lower energy use, leading to estimated annual cost savings of over $8 million.

Baxter's systemic approach to environmental stewardship extends to addressing product toxicity by shifting to better alternatives. As part of the company's product development process, Baxter applies a product sustainability review to all new medical devices, assessing environmental impacts across the product life cycle, including those related to materials selection and use. This includes a screen for toxic chemicals, and the company eliminates these chemicals whenever feasible.

Baxter continually evaluates a variety of materials and allocates significant funding for the research and development of biomaterials. The company pioneered the industry's first flexible container for intravenous medications, and has pioneered an assortment of non-PVC products for use in many medical applications. Over time, the company's leadership in environmental product stewardship has increasingly supported broader business objectives and represents a source of competitive advantage.

Baxter Phases Out Hazardous Substances Ahead of Legal Obligation

In 2007, Domini Social Investments filed a shareholder resolution on safer chemical use at Becton, Dickinson and Company, a medical devices manufacturer. The resolution cited Baxter, its competitor, as a model of best practice in safer chemical use. Specifically, the resolution cited Baxter's voluntary compliance with the RoHS (restriction of the use of certain hazardous substances in electrical and electronic equipment) directive banning toxic components such as lead, mercury, cadmium, and bromated fire retardants (BFRs). While the measure took effect in the European Union (EU) in 2006, it exempts medical device manufacturers from mandated compliance.

Baxter sees the writing on the wall that the EU will eventually lift the exemption—in a May 2006 meeting, the European Commission discussed 2012 as a possible date—and so it is developing a global strategy to eliminate hazardous substances listed under RoHS by securing information about product content from its suppliers. Baxter's foresight not only prepares it for future compliance with RoHS but also avoids current risks associated with shareholder resolutions, such as negative impacts on reputation.

Vital Statistics

Main site: Deerfield, Illinois

Main product: Products to treat hemophilia, immune disorders, infectious diseases, cancer, kidney disease, trauma, and other medical conditions

Number of employees: 45,000

Success: Founding member of Chicago Climate Exchange • Charter member of U.S. EPA Climate Leaders Program • Pioneer in environmental financial reporting

Challenge: Expanding access to health care • Maintaining high product quality • Supporting public health • Responding to global sustainability challenges

Awards: Global 100 Most Sustainable Corporations in the World—Corporate Knights and Innovest • Dow Jones Sustainability World Index • Named to Carbon Disclosure Project's Climate Disclosure Leadership Index • EPA Fortune 500 Challenge Top 25 Purchaser of Renewable Energy • EPA Climate Protection Award

Making Delicious Ice Cream Is Only Part of Its Mission

The name Ben & Jerry's is virtually synonymous with environmental and social responsibility. Ben & Jerry's, the iconic Vermont-based ice cream maker known for flavors such as Cherry Garcia, Phish Food, World's Best Vanilla, and other "euphoric concoctions," was the first public company to sign on to the Ceres Principles in 1992, and its 2001 Environmental Report won the first award for Outstanding Sustainability Reporting from Ceres.

Ben & Jerry's commitment to environmental responsibility goes back to its origins in 1978, when founders Ben Cohen and Jerry Greenfield used recycled materials to patch the roof on their first Scoop Shop, a renovated gas station in Burlington, Vermont. The company's long list of innovative and progressive social and environmental actions have caught people's attention: American consumers rated Ben & Jerry's the most socially responsible company in the United States in 2006, according to Golin-Harris's fourth national survey of corporate citizenship.

Ben & Jerry's environmental tracking system, which dates to 1994, measures key indicators, such as energy use, carbon dioxide emissions, recycling, solid waste, wastewater, composted waste ice cream, water use, and wastewater parameters. All of these indicators are normalized (other companies call it "indexed") to gallons of production. The company's most recent emissions goal was modest: to reduce CO_2 emissions to 10% below 2002 levels by 2007. By the end of 2006, Ben & Jerry's CO_2 emissions were 32% below 2002 levels (on a normalized basis), even though production volume was up almost 50% over the same period. Or, put another way, although Ben and Jerry's was producing 50% more ice cream by 2006, its CO_2 emissions rose only 2%. But, said the company, even that 2% must go!

In its 18th annual environmental report in 2006, Ben & Jerry's, acquired in 2000 by Anglo-Dutch multinational Unilever (Dove soap, Lipton tea, and Hellman's mayonnaise are among Unilever's 1,500 brands), announced it was using a new analytical technique to measure its environmental impact, the Global Warming Social Footprint. The company wanted to know the amount of CO_2 emissions the company needed to cut from its operations to make an appreciable difference.

In consultation with the Center for Sustainable Innovation (CSI), Ben & Jerry's used the WRE350 Plan to measure its global environmental impact. The plan,

OPPOSITE: Ben & Jerry's ice cream cart

developed at the National Center for Atmospheric Research in Boulder, Colorado, establishes annual limits on the amount of carbon dioxide humans can emit globally over the next 150 years in order to stabilize concentration in the atmosphere at a safe level of 350 parts per million (ppm). Current levels are about 385 ppm. Some scientists think 450 ppm is a key threshold that cannot be exceeded in order to avoid potentially catastrophic climate change impacts around the world.

The CSI audit found that Ben & Jerry's manufacturing plants emitted 6,279 net tons of carbon dioxide from 2001 to 2006, which is just 133 tons more carbon than its share of the WRE350 Plan allows (or 2.2% more than its plan allotment during 2001–2006). Ben & Jerry's has yet to determine how to reduce its emissions to the levels recommended in the WRE350 Plan but knows it needs to achieve efficiency gains, switch to lower- or no-carbon energy sources, or purchase more carbon offsets to do so. In 2006, Ben & Jerry's offset 5,160 tons of CO_2 emissions with NativeEnergy, by investing in the Rosebud St. Francis wind turbine project in South Dakota. The offsets were equivalent to eliminating over 10 million car miles (equivalent to driving around the world 415 times, or removing 860 cars from the road for a year), according

Ben & Jerry's chocolate chunks are made with fair trade cocoa from Ghana.

to the company. It was the fifth year in a row that Ben & Jerry's offset 100% of its carbon emissions from its manufacturing operations and employee air travel.

Ben & Jerry's is also tackling sustainability through its supply chain. Values-led sourcing has been a core corporate principle from the start, when the company bought hormone-free milk and cream from the St. Albans Cooperative Creamery in St. Albans, Vermont. It now buys fair trade coffee from Mexico, fair trade cocoa from Ghana, and fair trade vanilla extract from Indonesia. However, only half of Ben & Jerry's spending on raw materials in 2006 was with values-led suppliers, and the company realized it needs to do better. Starting in 2007, for example, the company began a four-year transition to buy all eggs only from free-range chickens.

Despite its progressive record on sustainability matters, Ben and Jerry's has faced challenges meeting its own high standards for eco-friendly operations. For example, Ben & Jerry's recently had to abandon its unbleached Eco-Pint containers, which were made without chlorine, as supplies were increasingly difficult to find. In the fall of 2006, the company transitioned to a pint container made from a bleached paperboard that is more readily available and has superior forming characteristics. Despite the use of chlorine, the new supplier has an excellent track record of sustainable forestry practices.

When Ben & Jerry's founders sold the company to Unilever, there was concern that the company's commitment to social and environmental responsibility would waver. So far, the worst of those fears have not materialized, but the company admits, in its 2006 social and environmental assessment on its website, that it has been "strained by restructuring" in the last few years and that its "Social Mission projects have lost some momentum." For example, the Humane Society of the United States informed Ben & Jerry's that its eggs did not live up to the company's values, a problem the company itself likely would have identified in times past. But Ben & Jerry's also says it has made headway integrating its "progressive ideals" into Unilever's larger, more complex multinational structure, where many operations are outsourced.

To reenergize the company and its employees, two Ben & Jerry's employee workgroups (Fairness and Sustainability) spent 2007 putting together an action plan for management. As CEO (Ben & Jerry's abbreviation for Chief Euphoria Officer) Walt Freese puts it: "Our Social Mission calls us to 'initiate innovative ways to improve the quality of life' where we do business, not merely to maintain and expand the successful projects of the past. We are called to do more with our business to make the world a better place." Despite some missteps in recent years, Ben & Jerry's corporate heart is still in the right place.

Dairy Farmers Act Local, Think Global

In 2002, to support its expansion into Europe after the sale of the company to Unilever, Ben & Jerry's started producing ice cream at a Unilever facility in Hellendoorn, the Netherlands. Because of Ben & Jerry's environmental commitment, Hellendoorn was the first industrial facility in Holland to meet all its electricity needs with 100%

renewable energy. Ben & Jerry's also helped implement management programs that will drive continuous improvements in energy efficiency through monitoring systems and movement detectors on lighting systems.

In 2003, Ben & Jerry's started a sustainable dairy farming initiative. Both the U.S.-based Dairy Stewardship Alliance and the Dutch Caring Dairy are collaborative efforts that work directly with dairy farmers to develop sustainable farming practices. In 2006, the Dutch farmers visited farmers in Vermont who participate in the Dairy Stewardship Alliance, and in 2007, the U.S. farmers paid a return visit.

Vital Statistics

Main site: South Burlington, Vermont
Main products: Ice cream, frozen yogurt, and sorbet
Number of employees: 520
Green partners: NativeEnergy • SaveOurEnvironment.org
Success: Developing values-led business decisions that create positive social, economic, and environmental change
Challenge: Continuing to expand VLB (Values-Led Business) decisions to greater parts of business by choosing ingredients from manufacturers with social consciences

Coconut Body Butters to Lipsticks: The Body Shop Makes Community Trade Look Beautiful

Launched in 1976 by entrepreneur Dame Anita Roddick, The Body Shop International PLC has been firmly committed to community—local and global—from its inception. Today, the international powerhouse has upward of 2,000 stores in over 55 countries and manufactures and sells more than 1,200 products—none of which has ever been tested on animals. Thanks to its longtime fair trade program, The Body Shop's products are part of a chain of sustainable relationships between communities of all kinds all over the world.

Roddick founded The Body Shop when she was inspired to examine conventional retail assumptions. "Why buy more of something than you can use?"

Roddick explained. "The foundation of the environmental activism of The Body Shop was born out of ideas like these." Roddick began mixing beauty products in her home more than thirty years ago with the prescient notion that her company—no matter what heights of success it achieved—would look outward at the rest of the world.

The U.K.-based company's five core principles—Support Community Trade, Defend Human Rights, Against Animal Testing, Activate Self-Esteem, and Protect Our Planet—have inspired positive social and environmental change across a number of industries. From the beginning, Roddick was a firm believer in corporate transparency, providing consumers with the practical information they need to make informed decisions about products they are purchasing.

The Community Trade program was established in 1987 and is one of the largest intiatives of The Body Shop. When Roddick witnessed a gathering of Amazonian Indian tribes protesting a potentially harmful hydroelectric project in their rain forest, she decided to take

OPPOSITE: Women involved in The Body Shop Community Trade program from the Eudafano Women's Cooperative in Namibia are producers of marula oil, used as a moisturizing ingredient across many products in The Body Shop's makeup products.

action. The company's popular Brazil-nut-based products were the result. Currently, The Body Shop is the only cosmetics company with such large-scale commitments to fair trade sourcing from local communities. The Body Shop trades with suppliers in more than 20 countries, providing life-affirming income to more than 25,000 individuals worldwide. Raw materials such as cocoa butter, shea butter, olive oil, and sesame seed oil enable The Body Shop to extend its reach far and wide.

The Body Shop garnered international attention when it launched its Against Animal Testing campaign in its native England. The campaign resulted in the banning of animal testing of cosmetic products and ingredients in 1998, thanks in part to the largest-ever petition to the European Commission, submitted two years prior. The Body Shop was also the first international cosmetics company to join the Humane Cosmetics Standard, a benchmark for major international animal protection groups.

Although The Body Shop is wholeheartedly committed to social and environmental change, the company admits there are areas where it could improve, especially in regard to climate change. In the words of chairman Adrian Bellamy and CEO Peter Saunders, "In the past, The Body Shop has campaigned on renewable energy and invested in wind farms, but we know this is an area where we have some catching up to do if we are really to make a difference to global warming."

In 2001, The Body Shop launched a campaign with Greenpeace International to showcase the importance of renewable energy. The company has also invested in a wind farm in Wales. But it was not until 2006 that it committed to becoming carbon-neutral, a goal with a deadline of 2010. To reduce energy consumption, The Body Shop hopes to transform the way it transports goods and lights and heats its stores. It will make its offices, warehouses, stores, and all business travel carbon-neutral and work with franchisees to reduce carbon emissions. The next steps toward carbon neutrality will be achieved by purchasing carbon offsets.

Packaging is another priority area. Although the company uses the minimum packaging required to maintain its products' integrity, some of its efforts to reduce packaging costs have been unsuccessful. The option to refill containers was an early innovation at The Body Shop stores, but interest in it declined. In the United Kingdom,

All soaps from The Body Shop now contain sustainable palm oil sourced from a plantation in Colombia.

less than 1% of The Body Shop customers chose to use it. In 2001, the practice was stopped. The Body Shop introduced cartons and bags that can be used more than once, and indefinitely in the case of the company's Bag for Life shopping bag. All The Body Shop's polyethylene terephthalate (PET) bottles contain a minimum of 30% recycled material, and by the end of 2008 this is set to double.

In 2006, The Body Shop was bought by the L'Oréal Group. It continues, however, to operate independently so as to retain its unique identity as a force for change in an industry all too often preoccupied with the superficial.

Knights of the (Sustainable Palm Oil) Roundtable

Palm oil is an invaluable ingredient for millions of people—it is the second most used vegetable oil in the world. However, its production is often associated with deforested land, compromised ecosystems, wildlife endangerment, and human rights abuse in factories and warehouses. The Body Shop is tackling this issue and has been a leader in the Roundtable on Sustainable Palm Oil, along with organizations such as Oxfam, to transform the way oil palm trees are grown and palm oil plantations are operated. More than 40% of the world's palm oil producers are participating in the initiative, along with some of the world's major name-brand retailers. The Body Shop has also taken a leadership role to ensure that small local farms can maintain the roundtable standards while remaining healthy and productive. With the help of the Body Shop, which now sources all traceable palm oil for assurance of sustainability, the roundtable expects fully certified palm oil to be widely available by the end of 2007.

Vital Statistics

Main site: Littlehampton, United Kingdom
Main product: Beauty and cosmetics products
Number of employees: 7,000
Success: Forming a wide net of sustainable relationships with suppliers worldwide
Challenge: Achieving concrete results in counteracting global warming

Can Big Oil Shift to Alternatives? BP Turns Its "Beyond Petroleum" Slogan into Action

When Lord Browne, former group chief executive of BP, said in 1997 in a speech at Stanford University that climate change and global warming were issues of global concern, another industry executive noted with disdain that British Petroleum, as it was then called, had "left the church."

Browne's remarkable acknowledgment made BP the first energy company to recognize its "shared responsibility" to address the global threat caused by climate change. Many consumers and newspaper reporters took his words as those of a self-serving industrialist out to boost the company's reputation among consumers. But over time it became clear that while Browne may have left one "church," he had found religion. Under his tenure, BP became recognized as a pioneer in the oil and gas industry for both reducing greenhouse gas emissions and investing substantially in alternative and renewable businesses.

Ten years later, in April 2007, when Browne spoke again at Stanford, he could point to concrete actions BP had taken in response to his clarion call on climate change. Notably, BP had reduced operational emissions to 10% below 1990 levels by 2001, nine years ahead of its own goal, and now deploys infrared cameras to detect invisible gas leaks at production facilities. And BP had well-developed wind, solar, and hydrogen projects through its BP Alternative Energy. Finally it was funding research on biofuels in partnership with DuPont, and had formed a hydrogen research project with General Electric. In 2006, the California Climate Action Registry awarded BP one of its three Climate Action Champion Awards for long-term commitment and execution to reduce emissions and develop alternative energy sources.

Nevertheless, BP is one of the world's biggest oil companies, and that creates problems, both real and perceived, for its "low-carbon" platform. During that ten-year period, BP went from being a $50 billion regional company to being a $265 billion global company, acquiring Amoco, Arco, Castrol, and Sohio. In 2002, in conjunction with a name change from British Petroleum to BP, the company unveiled its yellow-green sunburst logo with a "beyond petroleum" advertising campaign. Billboards touted that "BP believes in alternative energy: like solar and cappuccino," an advertising campaign perceived by many as a PR stunt, albeit one so effective in consumer polling that many global companies wished they had embraced a similar campaign.

Then BP hit a gusher of trouble. In 2004, BP traders

OPPOSITE: Drilled in some of the deepest waters to date in the Gulf of Mexico—4,000 to 7,000 feet—BP's drilling platform Atlantis's field size, water depth, and reservoir structure make it among the most technologically challenging developments undertaken by the company.

BP employees use a process safety management approach in all aspects of oil production.

were accused of price fixing. In 2005, 15 BP workers were killed and 170 injured at its Texas City, Texas, refinery in an explosion. In 2006, a burst pipeline resulted in the largest spill ever (207,000 gallons) in Prudhoe Bay on the North Slope of Alaska. That was followed five months later by discovery of dangerous corrosion on a 16-mile stretch of Alaska pipeline, which crimped oil supplies in the United States and raised oil prices while a mechanical "smart pig" squirted through the line looking for faults. BP's image as a socially and environmentally responsible company took a huge hit. "Green Logo, but BP Is Old Oil," read a 2006 *New York Times* headline.

BP made record profits of $22.3 billion in 2006, thanks to high prices for oil and gas, but took full responsibility for its disastrous miscues, and is now getting back on track to fulfill its decade-old commitment to the environment, with recently installed group executive Tony Hayward at the helm. The effort is two-pronged: (1) innovate to reduce CO_2 emissions from the use of fossil fuels, which will continue to be a linchpin to global energy supply over the next 20 to 30 years; and (2) develop and commercialize renewable low-carbon energy sources.

Since 2001, BP has aimed to use operating efficiency to offset half of the greenhouse gas (GHG) emission increases resulting from growth in its businesses. In the last five years, the company estimates that emissions growth of some 11 million tons has been offset by around 6 million tons of sustainable reductions. Overall, emissions in 2006 were 2.4 million tons less than in 2005. Oil spills were reduced from 578 in 2004 to 417 in 2006. BP's Hayward estimates the new efficiencies have created $2

billion worth of value for BP shareholders in a decade.

Going forward, BP's new practice of "environmental requirements for new projects" (ERNP), which started in 2004 for new work in environmentally sensitive areas (such as "International Union for Conservation of Nature" areas), now applies to all projects in all areas. The practice includes a set of environmental impact processes, and a set of performance requirements, many of which were developed in consultation with institutional investor F&C Asset Management. "The guidelines should give reassurance to investors that BP understands the emerging risks associated with biodiversity and ecosystem management," reports Dr. Robert Barrington, director of governance and sustainable investment at U.K.-based F&C.

BP has also made a serious commitment to renewable energy. Launched in 2005 with the promise to invest $8 billion over 10 years, BP Alternative Energy is a rapidly growing business. Globally, the power sector is the biggest source of greenhouse gas emissions, responsible for about twice the emissions of transportion.

BP Solar, in particular, shows near-term promise. Started 25 years ago, it is now a profitable entity with manufacturing plants in Australia, India, Spain, and the United States, and ranks as the third-largest solar supplier in the world, with operations in 106 countries. BP's main goal is to achieve grid-peak parity with conventional electricity rates. Currently, solar systems generate electricity at a cost of about 20 to 30 cents per kilowatt-hour (kWh). BP Solar hopes that it can eventually produce solar systems that generate electricity at about 13 to 18 cents per kWh by 2010, matching the average cost of electricity in the United States. By 2015, prices are projected to fall to 10 cents per kWh. As part of the Solar America Initiative, partly funded by the Department of Energy, BP is working with other suppliers, manufacturers, and several universities to refine and commercialize its Mono2 manufacturing process, which produces a high-performing silicon wafer at significantly lower production costs. "As the cost of solar comes down and demand rises, we'll have to reach a scale of production about three orders of magnitude more than where we are now," says John Wohlgemuth, BP's Solar America Initiative director. "Output will have to increase from hundreds of solar cells per hour to hundreds per minute."

In the United States, parity with the electricity grid at peak charging rates has already been achieved in Northern California and Hawaii. In Australia, BP is part of a consortium working on the Solar Cities Initiative for the government. And in Germany, BP signed a cooperation agreement with the Institute of Crystal Growth to develop a process for depositing silicon glass that has the potential to reduce the amount of silicon feedstock used in cell production.

In wind power, BP operates two wind farms in the Netherlands and has aggressively expanded its portfolio of U.S. wind farms, buying leading developers Greenlight Energy and Orion Energy and forming a strategic alliance with Clipper Windpower. BP now has interests in projects with a potential total-generating capacity of 15,000 megawatts in the United States. In 2007, BP began construction on five wind power projects in the United States, in California, Colorado, North Dakota, and Texas.

Looking to the future, BP has partnered with General Electric for hydrogen research, and plans to open the world's first hydrogen power plant in Carson, California, backed by $90 million in investment credits from the U.S. government.

In 2006, BP launched a dedicated biofuels business and announced a $500 million investment over 10 years in a university-based Energy Biosciences Institute at the University of California at Berkeley. The biofuels research is part of BP's sustainable transport initiative.

While these projects are encouraging, BP can expect strong criticisms for its latest expansion into the tar sands oil project in Alberta, Canada, where it takes two tons of oil-laced tar sands and two to four barrels of water to produce just one barrel of oil. Extracting tar sands oil produces triple the carbon emissions of conventionally extracted oil. This costly undertaking poses a substantial risk to BP's reputation and aspirations as a climate leader.

Advances in Alternatives

Alternative energy is a small piece of BP's activities, but research into future sources of power is a necessary hedge against higher oil prices that may yield dividends for energy consumers.

Solar. BP is working to refine and commercialize its Mono2 manufacturing process, which produces a high-performing silicon wafer at significantly lower production costs. In Germany, BP signed a cooperation agreement with the Institute of Crystal Growth to develop a process for depositing thinner films of silicon on glass that has the potential to reduce the amount of silicon used in cell production.

Hydrogen. BP has partnered with General Electric for hydrogen research and plans to open the world's first hydrogen power plant (with carbon capture) in Carson, California, backed by $90 million in investment credits from the U.S. government.

Biofuels. In 2006, BP launched a dedicated biofuels business and announced a $500 investment over 10 years in the Energy Biosciences Institute at the University of California at Berkeley and University of Illinois at Urbana-Champaign. BP launched a partnership with DuPont to develop an advanced, low-cost biobutanol for transport use.

Vital Statistics

Main site: London, England
Main product: Gasoline
Number of employees: 100,000
Success: Reduced carbon emissions from 1990 levels in three years
Challenge: To continue to reduce carbon emissions
Awards: Dow Jones Sustainability World Index • FTSE4Good, Tata BP Solar, Good Green Governance Award 2006 (Srishti Publications), Climate Action Champion Awards (California Climate Action Registry)

Saving Lives and Spotted Owls

 Bristol-Myers Squibb

Exotic and even common plants form the building blocks of many important medicinal drugs, such as Taxol, a potent chemotherapy agent made from the bark of the Pacific yew tree. Bristol-Myers Squibb, a leading global pharmaceutical company, recognizes the importance of biodiversity and ecosystem preservation for today and for future generations. Accordingly, the company has integrated biodiversity and land preservation in its Sustainability 2010 Goals, a set of aspirations established a decade earlier to map the company's progress on social and environmental targets.

The spotted owl, a poster child for environmentalism, exemplifies the complex interconnectedness of pharmaceuticals and biodiversity preservation. The Pacific yew tree was not only a key ingredient of Bristol-Myers Squibb's Taxol but also a key habitat for the spotted owl, a federally protected and endangered species. Traditional methods of harvesting Pacific yew bark kill the tree, thus threatening the spotted owl's habitat (and very existence) as well as compromising the long-term availability of the key Taxol ingredient.

With the projected demand for Taxol far exceeding the supply available from the tree bark, the company needed to develop a new process in order to manufacture the drug. Cells were extracted from yew needles and then reproduced to create Taxol. This method also improves the consistency and quality of the raw material in addition to protecting the habitat of the spotted owl.

Recognizing that species preservation goes hand in hand with habitat preservation, Bristol-Myers Squibb set out to sponsor local endangered or threatened species (or partner with an organization that protects these species and their habitats) in countries and states where it operates. For example, the company facility in Bangkok, Thailand, adopted elephants, and in October 2006, employees there participated in a project to replenish a mangrove forest in Samutsongkram province. Bristol-Myers Squibb is well on its way to meeting its 2010 goal to adopt endangered species in each of the states and countries where it operates.

Land preservation is also directly covered in its Sustainability 2010 Goals, which call for conserving

OPPOSITE: Bristol-Myers Squibb's biodiversity program helps to preserve the coral reef around Komodo Island in Indonesia that is home to a variety of tropical fish and other organisms.

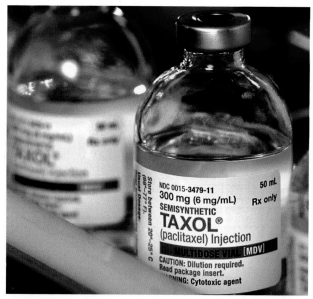

A vial of Taxol (paclitaxel), a cancer treatment manufactured by Bristol-Myers Squibb

ecologically significant areas equal to Bristol-Myers Squibb's total global property footprint. To ensure a future in otherwise threatened areas, the company partners with government agencies and professional organizations that work with existing preserves, providing financial assistance and human labor to help conservation efforts.

For example, Bristol-Myers Squibb joined forces with the Wildlife Habitat Council, a nonprofit group of corporations, conservation organizations, and individuals that protect and enhance wildlife habitats, and the company has earned certification for wildlife habitat projects at several of its facilities. Through such initiatives, the company has increased its ecological conservation projects from 1,336 hectares in 2000 to 1,598 hectares of biologically diverse habitats in Australia, Brazil, Indonesia, Ireland, Mexico, China, and the United States by 2006.

In 2002, the Bristol-Myers Squibb Foundation made a $100,000 grant to the Nature Conservancy to map the biodiversity of and develop an eco-regional plan for Puerto Rico, home to several of the company's major manufacturing facilities.

"This eco-regional plan will provide us with a better idea of what's left on Puerto Rico and in what condition so that we can start to work with local communities and partners to conserve those remaining special places," said Steve Volkers, director of corporate programs for the Nature Conservancy. "By supporting the development of

such a plan, Bristol-Myers Squibb is making a tangible difference for all of the island's species," many of which are threatened or endangered and found nowhere else in the world.

Bristol-Myers Squibb and the Nature Conservancy also collaborated to promote environmental education in Puerto Rico, creating a set of classroom materials on marine conservation for students from kindergarten to eighth grade, with a teacher's guide, in Spanish and English.

The company's Sustainability 2010 Goals also include shrinking the company's energy and carbon footprints 10% below 2001 baseline levels (measured in relation to sales). By 2006, the company had reduced both its indexed direct and indirect energy use 8% below the baseline. And its overall indexed greenhouse gas emissions fell 13% below the 2001 baseline by 2006, four years ahead of schedule.

To further reduce energy use, the company's Wallingford, Connecticut, facility is voluntarily participating in a federally sponsored program, Labs 21, which seeks to improve laboratory energy and water efficiency and encourages the use of renewable energy sources. A 1-million-square-foot pharmaceutical research and development center covering 180 acres, the Wallingford facility uses large amounts of energy. A key strategy is using a combined heat and power (CHP) plant that uses clean-burning natural gas and a heat recovery system in the form of a waste heat boiler.

The CHP system operates at approximately 72% efficiency, more than double the estimated 32% efficiency rate of the entire U.S. electric system, according to a 2004 World Resources Institute (WRI) report on the Climate Northeast partnership that WRI coordinates and Bristol-Myers Squibb participates in. This system, which recovers heat from the gas turbine to make steam for the complex and for heating during the winter months, has reduced GHG emissions generated "inside the fence" at the Wallingford facility by approximately 20%—or about 6,600 tons per year.

The company's Sustainability 2010 Goals also call for reducing water consumption at all of its facilities 10% below the 2001 baseline in relation to sales. Bristol-Myers Squibb is developing projects and conservation practices site by site, for example, by assessing the water usage of various manufacturing procedures, upgrading equipment efficiency, and implementing water recycling programs. By 2006, the company had already surpassed its goal, reducing indexed water use by 16%—and the company continues to implement conservation projects to further its efforts.

Areas where water resources are scarce present a greater challenge, and the company has an ambitious goal of 20% water usage reduction from a 2002 baseline year for those areas. In 2006, the combined water use of its facilities in Mexico, Egypt, Pakistan, and the Philippines (4 of the 10 water-stressed countries it operates in) had achieved its 2010 goal.

Cures from a Coral Reef?

Bristol-Myers Squibb is collaborating with the University of the South Pacific, Georgia Tech, and the Scripps Institution of Oceanography in a project to isolate natural products from marine organisms found in Fiji and to test them against a host of diseases, including cancer, malaria, HIV/AIDS, and tuberculosis, and infectious disease-causing organisms such as drug-resistant *Staphylococcus aureus*. The team prepares extracts from the marine organisms that are collected and sends them to Bristol-Myers Squibb, where they are screened for therapeutic activity against cancer.

The potential benefits are multiple. The project helps build local institutions and attitudes to conserve the complex and fragile biodiversity of the South Pacific and of coral reefs in particular. To ensure that Fijian villagers and the Fijian government will benefit financially from the discovery of a new drug that is developed from the compound (a process that can take 10 years or more), an agreement is already in place.

Vital Statistics

Main site: New York, New York
Main product: Pharmaceuticals and related health care products
Number of employees: 42,000
Green partner: GEMI (Global Environmental Management Initiative)
Success: Sustainability 2010 Goals • Biodiversity and ecosystem preservation
Challenge: Increasing water and energy conservation
Awards: Ceres-ACCA North American Awards runner up for Best Sustainability Report in 2007

A Big-Time Carbon Buster: BT Uses Its Own Information Communications Technology Services to Reduce Its Footprint

BT is calling attention to the carbon impact of information communications technology (ICT) while at the same time lauding ICT's ability to reduce carbon emissions and business travel for multinational companies. To show the way, BT presents itself as a model. BT Group, the former state-owned telecommunications provider in the United Kingdom once known as British Telecom (founded in 1846 as the Electric Telegraph Company), has a vision: to tackle climate change through the innovative use of communications products. Since 1996, BT has achieved a 60% reduction in its U.K. carbon footprint—and is now pledged to an 80% reduction from 1996 levels by 2016. To achieve this lofty goal will require reduced emissions and conversion to renewable energy as well as greater use of its own technology.

Five years ago, BT—primarily a telephone operating company—decided to stake its future on meeting the growing demand for ICT infrastructure and networking solutions among global companies as well as the rapid expansion of broadband in the United Kingdom. This growing "new wave" business (including broadband, mobility, and networked IT services) now makes up over 36% of BT Group's revenue.

BT is using its new business initiatives to address environmental sustainability issues for itself and its clients, and has launched a carbon assessment service in the United States and United Kingdom to measure the gains. BT's teleconferencing services, for example, have greatly reduced the need for employee travel among some of Britain's largest employers. Tesco, a major U.K. retailer, was able to cut carbon emissions related to employee travel by 2,500 tons annually by relying instead on teleconferences, saving $20 million in the process.

With 106,000 employees in 50 countries and revenues of $40 billion in fiscal 2007, BT also promotes flexible work hours and telecommuting. Up to 80% of BT staff work from home at least one day a week. BT

OPPOSITE: The landmark BT Tower looms over London at 620 feet.

estimates the annual carbon savings from telecommuting among its employees at 97,000 tons and the financial savings to the company at $75 million. "Broadband technology is already cutting the need to travel, through home working and videoconferencing," says BT Group finance director Hanif Lalani. BT estimates a 25-to-1 return on investment for spending on telephone, Internet, and videoconferencing services over the lifetime of the network.

Chair of BT's Ethnic Minority Network, Malcolm Weston, receives the U.K.'s Business in the Community award, presented to him by His Royal Highness Prince Charles and, not pictured, U.S. Vice President Al Gore.

"BT can credibly and demonstrably help a customer understand the role networked IT services play in both producing and reducing carbon footprint," says Scott Cain, head of IT transformation, BT Global Services.

The carbon impact assessment service could be dismissed as mere marketing, except that BT backs it up with action. A month after announcing its carbon impact assessment service, BT announced plans to develop wind farms aimed at generating up to 25% of its existing U.K. electricity requirements by 2016. BT is one of Britain's biggest consumers of electricity, accounting for about 0.7% of the United Kingdom's overall consumption—and since 2005 has purchased 99% of its U.K. electricity from renewable or low-carbon sources. BT is now identifying high-yield wind sites on or adjacent to BT-owned land, with the aim of generating wind power from 2012 onward. On a global scale, only 39% of BT's energy consumption is from renewables, with another 52% from low-carbon sources.

"Although an outperformer in most sustainability criteria, BT particularly excels in the environmental and social dimensions," noted the Dow Jones Sustainability World Index upon BT's seventh consecutive inclusion in the telecommunications sector index. "The company's sustainability efforts are very much aligned with the group's wider corporate strategy." In 2005, *BusinessWeek* and the Climate Group ranked BT number four in the Top Companies of the Decade in battling climate change. In 2007, the *Independent,* a prominent U.K. newspaper, ranked BT number two in Britain and number nine in the world on its Green Leaders guide to the world's greenest companies.

One of the most impressive aspects of BT's green alignment is the pressure it exerts on suppliers to adopt sustainability policies. This is part of its three-pronged strategy to cut its own carbon footprint, to engage employees to reduce their personal footprints (by encouraging them to turn off PCs and lights in the office and at home, and to work from home whenever possible), and to influence customers and suppliers to reduce their footprints. During Environment Week 2007, BT launched its Carbon Clubs initiative, which encourages BT employees to engage with their local communities to tackle carbon emissions. In all new contracts with suppliers, BT considers the energy consumption and environmental impact of a product or service as mandatory criteria—and the consumption and impact of any replacement product or service must be less than that of its predecessor.

One of the downsides to BT's quest for more broadband Internet and conferencing services is that new data centers demand more power to support the new infrastructure, which in turn requires more powerful cooling systems. A market report by information technology analyst IDC, for example, notes that U.S. companies spent $5.8 billion powering servers in 2005, and another $3.5 billion cooling them. Twenty years ago, chips consumed no more than 8 watts of power; today, 110 watts is typical, according to BT's white paper "A Realist's Guide to Green Data Centers." This puts a strain on corporate data centers, not to mention the bottom line, as companies spend more on energy to store and transmit data. To help address this problem, BT's 21st Century Network initiative (21CN)—a broadband IP voice-and-data network—

has reconfigured data centers supporting the network to consume 40% less energy than the conventional data center by using innovations such as fresh-air cooling, raising the operational temperatures within the center, and moving from AC to DC power (rather than losing power during the conversion).

Unlike many companies that meet carbon reduction goals by purchasing renewable-energy offsets, BT is aggressively tackling the problem head-on. "Our strategy is to cut carbon first and foremost and that is our top priority," says a company report. "BT is investigating offsetting, but has not made a decision on the extent to which this will be part of our strategy." Translation: BT believes that reducing carbon is the most important element in reducing the effects on climate change, and it hopes that other companies will follow its lead.

Shining Light on ICT's "Dirty Little Secret"

Information communications technology (ICT) is a major generator of CO_2 emissions. According to research conducted for BT by the Gartner Group, ICT accounts for approximately 2% of all global CO_2 emissions. That's roughly equivalent to the amount currently generated by the airline industry. This, says BT, is ICT's "dirty little secret." You can easily see why BT encourages its employees to turn off their PCs and other equipment at night when you consider the percentage of ICT carbon emissions produced by various types of ICT equipment:

- Printers: 6%
- LAN and office telecoms: 7%
- Mobile telecoms: 9%
- Fixed-line telecoms: 15%
- Servers: 23%
- PCs and monitors: 39%

Vital Statistics

Main site: London, England

Main product: Communications solutions and services

Number of employees: More than 100,000

Success: Reduced carbon emissions by 60% since 1996 • One of the world's largest purchasers of green electricity (98%)

Challenge: Sustainable development • Managing social and environmental issues over and above minimum regulation while growing shareholder value

Awards: Dow Jones Sustainability World Index • Queen's Award for Sustainable Development • Global 100 Most Sustainable Corporations in the World—Corporate Knights and Innovest

Banking on Green:
Citi's Commitment Includes Investments, Building Retrofits, and Client Services

Citi has read the climate science reports and doesn't like what it sees—for itself or many of its clients. So it's bringing its vast global resources to bear on finding and developing long-term solutions to reducing energy use and global warming emissions. In 2007, Citi announced a $50 billion commitment over 10 years to address global climate change through investments and the financing of alternative energy, clean technology, and other carbon emission reduction activities. "The comprehensive program we are announcing today is not a wish list, but a realistic achievable plan that serves a critical global need and responds to an emerging investment opportunity," said former CEO Chuck Prince. Why did Citi make this a major commitment? Citi, like many other financial institutions that measure long-term risk in their portfolios, sees looming problems for itself and its clients. In its Carbon Disclosure Report, for which it was ranked number one among global banks, Citi cites compelling evidence of global warming in the 2007 Intergovernmental Panel on Climate Change (IPCC) reports compiled by hundreds of the world's leading climate scientists.

Specifically, Citi feels that if atmospheric concentrations of carbon rise significantly, the company and its clients would be adversely affected, requiring a "dramatic adaptation" of its core business model. Clients in energy- or emission-intensive industries (such as power, oil and gas, cement, metals and mining, manufacturing, and transportation) will be directly impacted by emerging carbon-reducing regulations, thus creating potential credit risks for Citi.

OPPOSITE: Citi's LEED Gold–certified office tower in Long Island City, New York

The bank's $50 billion commitment includes $10 billion in activities already under way, including measuring and reducing its own footprint, and advising clients on business risks and opportunities. Three-quarters ($7.5 billion) of the $10 billion invested is directed toward developing products and services for clients in the renewable and energy efficiency space. At the same time, Citi has developed new guidelines that can be applied to portfolios of electric utilities or power producers' assets to analyze carbon exposure and the impact of forthcoming climate legislation. The guidelines may push more clients away from coal-fired power plants and other carbon-intensive projects.

The biggest chunk of the $50 billion is a projected $31 billion in new investments by the Citi Markets and Banking group in clean energy and alternative technologies. This builds on the clean energy work already in progress, and will be invested primarily in alternative energy companies working in solar, wind, hydro, and geothermal projects. This will also include investments made in new technologies that retrofit aging infrastructure to reduce energy usage.

Pamela P. Flaherty, president and CEO, CitiFoundation, and director, Corporate Citizenship (OlsenCorp.com)

Citi's Corporate Realty Services group has taken an inventory of energy use of the 92 million square feet in Citi's global real estate holdings, including ATM machines. The audit found that 80% of the energy expended came from 10% of the buildings, mostly large data centers or major office buildings. Citi estimates that it can save $1 for every square foot by making its offices more energy-efficient. In addition, Citi is buying "green power" for its buildings by partnering with Constellation NewEnergy, an energy services company. In 2006, Citi upped its procurement of green power by 400% from 2005. The company is also aiming for LEED certification of its new office buildings, such as Citi's new 15-story building in Queens, New York, which achieved LEED Gold certification. Some existing facilities, specifically office buildings in Dallas and New York City, are in the process of achieving LEED status through retrofits and redesigns, as well as its procurement and energy use.

Citi was the top-scoring U.S. bank in a January 2008 Ceres report that analyzed 40 leading global banks on their climate change governance practices. In addition, Citi released a new set of Carbon Principles along with JPMorgan Chase and Morgan Stanley. The principles provide an enhanced due diligence process for analyzing carbon exposure and the impact of climate regulations on the utility sector. "We're interested in climate change because it's an issue that impacts all our clients," said Pam Flaherty, director of corporate citizenship and president and CEO, Citi Foundation. "If you're not addressing the issue, you'll have more risks and you may not be taking advantage of opportunities."

Citi has long been active on environmental policy issues, including initial leadership in the development of the Equator Principles (2003), which established best practices for assessing and mitigating environmental risks in project financing. Citi has also called for market-based policies in the United States and abroad that will help reduce GHG emissions. Lastly, it released a research report in fall 2007 supporting higher fuel-economy standards when a CAFE (Corporate Average Fuel Economy) proposal was under debate in Congress. "When you have the world's number one bank, which has financial ties to many major automakers, saying fuel economy standards are a good economic play, it drives a stake through the heart of the auto industry's scare tactics," said Ed Markey (D-Mass.), a leading House advocate for achieving the 35-mile-per-gallon CAFE standard that was passed into law in December 2007.

While Citi and other banks have pledged more than $100 billion to develop climate change solutions, critics such as the Rainforest Action Network have asked banks to stop financing new coal-fired power plants and have demonstrated outside Citi offices in San Francisco.

"All the operational changes in the world aren't going to make up for the carbon from the plants they are funding," says Rebecca Tarbotton, who helped organize the protest.

Bottom-Up Initiatives

As part of the Clinton Climate Initiative, which partners with large municipal governments to reduce GHG emissions, Citi pledged $1 billion to implement a new Energy Efficiency Building Retrofit Program. The landmark program aims to reduce energy use in public and private buildings, which are responsible for more than half of GHG emissions in large cities.

CitiCapital will work with cities and building owners to retrofit existing buildings with new technologies, which can reduce energy use by 20% to 50%. As the market leader in municipal bond underwritings, CitiCapital has financed retrofit projects for 25 years, for municipalities and not-for-profit organizations in cities such as New Orleans and Salt Lake City.

In India, the Citi Foundation is focused on the link between microfinance and energy, and hosted a conference on the topic in India in 2007. "One of the great challenges is how to get clean energy to countries across the world where the demand and consumption is fast rising with increasing numbers of people moving out of poverty," says Flaherty.

Vital Statistics

Main site: New York, New York
Main product: Diversified financial services
Number of employees: 300,000
Green partners: United Nations Environment Programme Finance Initiative • Ceres • World Resources Institute • Pew Center on Climate Change
Success: Incorporated sustainability initiatives into key business units • Led development of industry environmental standards such as the Equator Principles and the Carbon Principles
Challenge: To find sustainability solutions that can be scaled up for greatest impact
Awards: Named top bank in Carbon Disclosure Project • Named leading U.S. bank in addressing climate change in Ceres/RiskMetrics report "Corporate Governance and Climate Change: The Banking Sector"

Getting the World in Shape

Like so many successful, iconoclastic companies, Clif Bar & Company came to be thanks to a highly personal vision. In 1990, Gary Erickson—bakery owner, serious recreational athlete, and former designer of bicycle saddles—realized partway through a 175-mile bike ride that the energy bars he had packed were woefully lacking in taste and nutritional value. Unfortunately, they were the only option at the time; there was no comparable product on the market.

Erickson's bakery, Kali's Sweets and Savories, used only high-quality, all-natural ingredients in its pastries and calzones. Convinced he could create a better-tasting energy bar while maintaining his standards, Erickson combined whole grains, fruits, and essential vitamins and minerals, and named the final product—and the company—Clif Bar, after his father, Clifford. Clif Bars were launched in 1992 at bike shops and natural food stores and were an instant hit with climbers and cyclists. Word

of mouth increased their popularity, and other outdoor adventurers were soon hooked. By 1997, Clif Bar had national distribution at grocery and convenience stores, and the little bakery that could was one of the nation's fastest-growing private companies. Today, the California-based company is the country's leading manufacturer of all-natural, organic energy and nutrition food and beverages and has grown 26% each year since 2005. It produced the first major energy bar to get organic certification and purchases more than 20 million pounds of organic ingredients each year. Currently, all Clif Bar products contain organic ingredients—of the 22 brands, 20 contain 70% organic ingredients or more.

While "all natural" and the great outdoors have always been synonymous with Clif Bar, the company decided to formalize its commitment to sustainability, and in 2001 launched an environmental program that was to become a company hallmark. By assessing the company's sustainability and making company-wide changes, Clif Bar has worked to reduce its ecological footprint. Staff ecologist Elysa Hammond explains, "The most important thing to us is that we run our business in harmony with the environment, with the least environmental impact possible." As a company that provides nutritious food products, it has a very direct connection to agriculture and the environment. With balance and well-being as core components of the company's mission, Clif Bar is committed to

OPPOSITE: Clif Bar employee Eric Walle takes part in the Clif Bar 2 Mile Challenge, which inspires people of all ages to put the brakes on climate change and lessen their dependency on petroleum fuel and automobiles by using natural energy to ride their bikes for trips of 2 miles or less.

contributing to the health of its consumers, as well as the health of the environment.

Changing the way one does business is the most direct way of reducing one's environmental footprint. Resource conservation in package design is an ongoing challenge for any consumer product company, and Clif Bar continues its research to find more sustainable packaging. The company has committed to using only 100% recycled paperboard (50% postconsumer) to manufacture its shipping cartons—eliminating 90,000 pounds of shrink-wrap, saving 7,500 trees, and conserving 3.3 million gallons of water—thereby avoiding the production of 660,000 pounds of greenhouse gases each year. At Clif Bar offices, only 100% postconsumer recycled paper is used, and unbleached, recycled paper and nontoxic inks are used for printing promotional materials.

Clif Bar's Eco Posse leads a variety of "green-up" projects that aim to help the company recycle everything it uses.

In an effort to achieve its goal of zero waste—diverting 90% or more of all solid wastes from landfills or incineration—Clif Bar recycles or composts over 70% of all waste generated at its Berkeley, California, headquarters. With the help of its in-house Eco Posse, which leads a variety of "green-up" projects, the company is nearing its goal of recycling everything it uses. And in the next few years, Clif Bar plans to relocate its headquarters. Aiming for LEED certification, the new green building will incorporate state-of-the-art sustainable building materials and will be powered by clean, renewable energy.

Back in 2003, the company estimated its carbon footprint by assessing the amount of energy it used in its offices, bakeries, and business travel. In response to this assessment, Clif Bar formed a partnership with NativeEnergy, a privately held Native American energy company that helps businesses, organizations, and individuals reduce their carbon footprint by purchasing renewable energy credits and offsets that fund renewable energy projects. This partnership with Clif Bar enables NativeEnergy to help build wind power projects that create sustainable economic benefits for Native Americans, Alaskan Natives, and other local communities in need. Clif Bar purchases enough renewable energy credits to offset its CO_2 emissions, and, through NativeEnergy, allows consumers to buy Cool tags, renewable wind energy credits, online and at Clif Bar–sponsored events. For each $2 Cool Tag sold, Clif Bar invests $2 in NativeEnergy's WindBuilders program, which helps the Rosebud Sioux tribe build the Rosebud St. Francis Wind Farm in South Dakota. The $2 price tag neutralizes the CO_2 emissions generated from traveling 300 miles in the average car.

Creating simple tools to help consumers take action is a big priority, and Clif Bar uses the Cool Tag program to help educate consumers and make the events it sponsors carbon-neutral. Clif Bar does this by forming partnerships with cycling events, triathlons, music festivals, ski resorts, and other outdoor venues in order to reduce their CO_2 output. Clif Bar then purchases enough renewable wind energy to offset the emissions caused by the event and helps to ensure that the sites are left in immaculate condition. These events also provide a platform for the company to promote more healthful and efficient living and to illustrate how easily environmental change can be effected.

Clif Bar's biodiesel-powered trucks carry the field-marketing team more than 120,000 miles a year.

The company is also spurring change through its 2 Mile Challenge, launched in 2007, that asks people of all ages to ride bikes for trips of two miles or less. The company plans to take the 2 Mile Challenge on a nationwide tour in a biodiesel bus complete with exhibits, videos, and commuter bikes designed to showcase the ease and advantage of biking for short excursions, as well as the benefits to the environment. "Forty percent of urban trips in the United States are two miles or less, but people use their cars nearly ninety percent of the time for those short jaunts," Erickson explained. "If we simply rode bikes for those two-mile trips, we'd get in shape, un-clog our roads, and spare the planet from millions of tons of carbon emissions, the leading cause of global climate change."

Erickson and his wife, Kit Crawford, with whom he owns the company, have devised a business model designed to make social and environmental responsibility an integral part of every aspect of the business. The company's Five Aspirations—Sustaining Our Business, Sustaining Our Brands, Sustaining Our People, Sustaining Our Community, and Sustaining the Planet—reflect the way they do business every day.

Being a Cool Commuter

In an effort to encourage commuters to find alternative modes of transportation or switch to more fuel-efficient vehicles, Clif Bar and American Forests partnered to introduce the Cool Commute program in 2004. Cool Commute rewards its most active walkers, bicyclists, and users of public transportation with rewards of up to $700 each year for staying out of the car. Employees who carpool are also rewarded for their participation in ride sharing. To make greener commuting more accessible, the company also features America's first-ever biofuel incentives for its employees, offering loans of up to $5,000 to help employees purchase a hybrid or biodiesel car as well as offering retroactive loans for those who already drive hybrid or biodiesel-powered vehicles. To further reduce its overall impact, the company plants trees through American Forests' Global ReLeaf program to offset the carbon emissions from its commuting employees. To date, 8,000 trees have been planted.

Vital Statistics

Main site: Berkeley, California	
Main products: Clif Bar, Nutrition for Sustained Energy; Luna, Whole Nutrition Bar for Women	
Number of employees: 206	
Green partners: Organic Farming Research Foundation • American Forests • Leave No Trace	
Success: Transitioning to organic ingredients • Cool Tags—offsetting more than 6.5 million pounds of CO_2 • Employee volunteerism	
Challenge: Sustainable packaging	
Awards: Stop Waste Business Efficiency Award—StopWaste.org • Climate Action Champion Award—California Climate Action Registry	

Replacing Every Drop

Coca-Cola

"Water is the main ingredient in every product our industry offers. It is also a limited resource facing unprecedented challenges from overexploitation, increasing pollution, and poor management. Our company and the beverage industry are in an excellent position to share the water expertise in the communities we serve—in resource management, wastewater treatment, rainwater harvesting, and even desalination. As demand for water continues to increase around the world, we expect cooperation will be critical."

That statement, from the "challenges and risks" discussion of the Coca-Cola Company's 2003 10-K Report to the Securities and Exchange Commission, can be seen as a call to action for responsible water conservation. Yet despite the company's focused commitment, in 2004 several Coca-Cola bottling plants in India were shut down due to drought-induced water shortages. A court later ruled that Coca-Cola was not liable and the plants were reopened, but the controversy ignited an internal and external dialogue surrounding the fundamental sustainability of the company's water-intensive business model.

On June 5, 2007, at the World Wildlife Fund (WWF) annual meeting in Beijing, Coca-Cola chairman and CEO Neville Isdell answered the company's critics with a pledge to "replace every drop of water we use in our beverages and their production." Mr. Isdell also announced that the water pledge would be supported by a separate, "transformational partnership" with WWF.

"We are focusing on water because this is where Coca-Cola can have a real and positive impact," Isdell declared. Carter Roberts, president of WWF-US, said, "The water crisis is as important as climate change. Thousands of people die each day from polluted water. Freshwater species are more at risk for extinction. These conditions will only get worse with climate change. The Coca-Cola Company's commitment to water neutrality is a first."

Access to clean, fresh water is clearly in Coca-Cola's interest as well as that of the planet. In 2006, Coca-Cola used 288 billion liters of water for beverage production, with 60% used in manufacturing processes such as rinsing, cleaning, heating, and cooling and 40% going into the beverages themselves.

The company's water pledge has three components.

OPPOSITE: Coca-Cola partnered with USAID/Indonesia to launch the Cinta Air program, which implemented a number of improvements to the community, including hand-washing stations, latrines, and wells.

The first two of the three R's—reduce, recycle, and re-plenish—are straightforward enough. "Reduce" refers to water-use ratio, which is a measure of water efficiency. From 2002 to 2006, the company's water-use ratio declined from 3.12 liters of water per liter of product to 2.52, an efficiency improvement of 19%. "Recycle" refers to wastewater treatment. While all manufacturing facilities comply with local regulations, company standards sometimes exceed local regulations. Today approximately 85% of the Coca-Cola system's manufacturing facilities already treat—or "recycle," in the company's phrasing—wastewater to a level capable of meeting the company's strict standards. All manufacturing facilities will be required to meet the standards by the end of 2010.

"Replenish," however, is virgin territory in the arena of environmental stewardship. " 'Replenish,' " Isdell said, "means that on a global basis we will give back by supporting healthy watersheds and sustainable community water programs to balance the water used in our finished beverages. We will do this by working on a wide range of locally relevant initiatives, such as watershed protection, community water access, rainwater harvesting, reforestation, and agricultural water-use efficiency."

In his Beijing speech, Isdell stipulated that the water replacement goal is "admittedly aspirational." Notably, he avoided the term "water neutrality." Indeed, the company says, "Unlike carbon, the concept of balancing water use is not well defined, and WWF, Coca-Cola, and its bottlers will work together to measure the impact of these activities on water sustainability." The company will begin to identify its replenishment activities and their associated metrics in 2008.

In the shadow of Coca-Cola's "water neutral" aspiration is the contradictory and inadequately addressed issue surrounding the sourcing and packaging of the company's Dasani bottled water. "The reality is corporations, like Coke, create a market for their products by casting doubt on the quality of tap water. Bottled water is subject to less regulatory scrutiny and in the case of Dasani, comes from the same source," observes Tony Clarke, director of the Polaris Institute and co-author of *Blue Gold,* a book detailing the crisis in the world's water supply.

Coca-Cola is, however, looking upstream to its own

This pump in a village in Huailai, China, is one result of the Coca-Cola-sponsored drilling of five deep water wells and the planting of 824 trees for fighting annual sandstorms. It has made water available to the village for the first time and is shared by several families and their animals.

supply chain, the producers of commodities such as sugar, citrus, and coffee, whose use of water is, in the aggregate, much greater than Coca-Cola's. "We realize that becoming 'water neutral' in our operations does not address the issue of embedded water in our agricultural ingredients and packaging materials," says Chairman Isdell. "Working with WWF, we will seek opportunities to reduce water use in our supply chain beginning with sugar, where we will expand our existing collaboration on the Better Sugarcane Initiative." This is an ongoing effort by a group of progressive sugarcane retailers, investors, traders, producers, and NGOs to develop an international definition for what constitutes sustainable sugarcane.

Coca-Cola is demonstrating solid environmental responsibility in other areas as well. In 2007, the company announced the world's largest bottle-to-bottle recycling plant, producing approximately 100 million pounds of food-grade recycled PET (polyethylene terephthalate) annually, the equivalent of 2 billion 20-ounce Coke bottles, its first PET plastic-bottle recycling plant in the United States. When it becomes fully operational in 2009, the Spartanburg, South Carolina, facility will be the Coca-Cola system's first recycling plant in the United States and its sixth worldwide. The plant will also be instrumental to the company's goal of recycling or reusing 100% of its plastic bottles in the United States.

The Coca-Cola system has also made progress in increasing energy efficiency and reducing its climate impact. By focusing on manufacturing, the Coca-Cola system's energy-efficiency ratio improved 16% from 2002 through 2006. In refrigeration technology, which accounts for its largest climate impact, the company completed the transition to hydrofluorocarbon-free insulation for new purchases of cooling equipment. The company also identified carbon dioxide technology as the most cost-effective commercial solution for refrigeration gas, and announced that 100% of the cooling and vending machines placed in official venues of the Beijing 2008 Olympic Games—approximately 6,350 units—will be HFC-free.

The company also increased the use of its proprietary Energy Management System, EMS-55, which reduces energy consumption of the system's refrigeration equipment by up to 35%. By the end of 2006, approximately 200,000 EMS-55 units were in place, saving up to 250 million kilowatt-hours, with a corresponding greenhouse gas reduction of over 100,000 metric tons.

New Bottle Designs Reduce Plastic Content

In 2006, the Coca-Cola system advanced its sustainable design efforts, known as e3, by improving the efficiency, life-cycle effectiveness, and eco-innovation of its packaging. These efforts led to a reduction in weight of Coke's iconic glass contour bottle, saving 89,000 metric tons of glass in 2006, the CO_2 equivalent of planting more than 13,000 acres of trees. In 2007, Coca-Cola redesigned its curvy plastic 20-ounce bottle, which was first introduced in 1993. The new 20-ounce bottle is completely recyclable and uses 5% less PET than its predecessor. While the company does not project the amount of plastic it will save, it notes that in 2005 it reduced glass use by 52,000 tons globally and plastic use by over 10,000 tons (equivalent to nearly 400 million 20-ounce Coca-Cola bottles).

One of the ways Coca-Cola is improving its water-use efficiency in its plants is through ionized air rinsers, which do not use water.

Vital Statistics

Main site: Atlanta, Georgia	
Main product: More than 2,800 beverages, including Coca-Cola, Diet Coke, Sprite, and Fanta	
Number of employees: 93,400 corporate employees	
Green partners: WWF • USAID • CARE • Global Water Challenge • UNEP	
Success: Aligning global system around ambitious goals in the environmental space • Global water stewardship • Sustainable packaging • Climate protection and energy management	
Challenge: Developing qualitative and quantitative measurements to enable progress reports toward goals	
Awards: National Recycling Coalition's Recycling Works award 2008 finalist • Water Stewardship Initiatives, Coca-Cola China, Secretary of State's 2007 Award for Corporate Excellence • Bhagidari Award, Coca-Cola India water conservation and environmental management, Delhi government	

The Answer to Green Energy Is Blowing in the Wind

FPL Group is taking the lead among U.S. energy-services companies in combating climate change, through both its operations and its advocacy.

The company, with annual revenues of more than $15 billion and a growing presence in 27 states, is nationally recognized as one of the country's cleanest energy companies, in terms of low greenhouse gas emissions. FPL Group's two principal subsidiaries are Florida Power & Light Company and FPL Energy, LLC.

FPL Energy, which provides energy to 4.5 million customers, generates more than 90% of its electricity using clean fuels with minimal greenhouse gas (GHG) emissions. Its fuel sources include wind and solar—it is the U.S. leader in both—as well as emissions-free nuclear and hydroelectric power. FPL Energy owns the largest wind farm in the world, the 735-megawatt Horse Hollow Wind Energy Center in Texas, and operates the largest solar fields in the world—with combined generating capability of 310 megawatts—in California's Mojave Desert. Until recently, the growth of wind-generated power was hampered by economic hurdles, resulting in less than 1% of total U.S. electricity coming from wind. However, a number of factors have converged to make wind increasingly attractive—from environmental, economic, and energy-security perspectives—making wind power the fastest-growing renewable energy resource worldwide.

The biggest environmental benefit of wind power is the absence of greenhouse gas emissions associated with harvesting it. In 2006, FPL Energy's 53 wind farms in 16 states displaced nearly 6.4 million tons of carbon dioxide (CO_2), more than 14,000 tons of sulfur dioxide (SO_2), and over 9,000 tons of nitrogen oxide (NO) emissions that otherwise would have been released into the atmosphere. In Texas alone, FPL Energy's 11 wind farms generated 3.6 million megawatt hours of electricity in 2006, an amount that would have required 17,000 rail cars full of coal, stretching about the 117 miles from Houston to San Antonio.

Another advantage of wind power is low operating costs. While it costs about twice as much to construct a wind farm as it does to build a natural-gas-fired power plant (per megawatt of capacity), the ongoing costs of wind are minimal, as turbines generally only require rou-

OPPOSITE: FPL Energy, a subsidiary of FPL Group, is the nation's largest producer of wind energy and plans to triple its 4,900-megawatt wind portfolio by 2012.

tine maintenance on a quarterly basis. Furthermore, wind is a homegrown resource that does not need to be imported, and so promotes energy independence.

These are among the reasons why, in July 2007, FPL Energy announced a $20 billion plan to increase its industry-leading wind generation capacity to 14,000 megawatts by 2012. "With demand for energy continuing to increase, we believe wind power can have a positive impact on diversifying our energy supply and improving our environment," said Mitchell Davidson, president of FPL Energy, in the announcement. "We need more economic, reliable, and domestic sources of electricity to operate our homes and businesses and wind energy is an important and growing part of our energy supply. As the largest owner and operator of wind and solar power in the nation, the goal we announced today is part of our ongoing commitment to clean energy generation."

Two months later, in September 2007, FPL announced a three-part, $2.4 billion investment in solar power at the Clinton Global Initiative in New York City. About $1.5 billion of this will go toward new solar thermal generating facilities over the next 7 years, starting with a 300-megawatt solar facility in Florida that will avoid an estimated 11 million tons of CO_2 emissions over a 20-year period. FPL will also invest about $500 million to create a smart network providing its 4.5 million customers with the ability to monitor their energy consumption—which encourages conservation that leads to GHG emissions reductions.

The third part consists of a consumer education program enabling consumers nationwide to purchase renewable energy credits (RECs) created by FPL Group's renewable energy facilities to help offset their own carbon footprints. FPL projects program revenues to run about $400 million in the first half decade—all of which will be pumped back into developing new renewable energy capacity.

FPL Energy's existing 310 megawatts of solar capacity consists of 7 facilities covering over 2,000 acres of the Mojave Desert with more than 900,000 mirrors capturing and concentrating sunlight that is transformed into electricity—representing about 1% of FPL Energy's total output. That capacity will double by 2011 when its projected large-scale solar thermal power plant—one of the largest such plants in the world—begins producing

power. While most people associate solar energy with photovoltaics that convert sunlight directly into electricity, FPL Energy relies on solar electric generating systems (SEGS) that heat a synthetic oil, called therminol, which in turn heats water, creating steam that turns a turbine to produce electricity.

About nine-tenths of FPL's Turkey Point Nuclear Plant property remains in its natural state of mangroves and freshwater wetlands.

FPL Group is also a large and growing player in the emissions-free nuclear power business. The company owns and operates five nuclear power plants—two in Florida (which provide 20% of the electricity for its customers there) and one each in Iowa, Wisconsin, and New Hampshire. Nuclear power supports the company's commitment to addressing climate change, as this clean fuel source generates virtually no GHG emissions.

Though some environmentalists still oppose nuclear power, others, such as scientist James Lovelock—who proposed the broadly accepted Gaia hypothesis that the earth is a single living organism—and Greenpeace co-founder, Patrick Moore, have shifted from opposing nuclear power to considering it a necessary and essential solution to the climate crisis, given our current energy needs and systems. And climate scientists such as Harvard University's John Holdren do not discount the potential value of nuclear power as a climate solution, though Holdren points out that economic, safety, radioactive waste, and proliferation obstacles still need to be solved.

In June 2007, the company's chairman and CEO, Lew Hay, testified before the Senate Committee on Environment and Public Works in favor of placing a direct price on carbon emissions, a strategy also endorsed by economist William Pizer, who in 1999 found that price mechanisms are five times more effective than the most efficient quota systems at economically reducing carbon emissions. "The physics of the problem suggests a preference for prices," Pizer said. Joining Pizer in endorsing a price-based solution are former vice president Al Gore, former Federal Reserve chairman Alan Greenspan, and editorial writers at the *Economist*, the *Los Angeles Times*, and the *Washington Post*.

FPL Group has always demonstrated that strong environmental and economic performance can go hand in hand. And others agree. The company has been ranked the top-rated company in the electric utility sector five straight times by Innovest Strategic Value Advisors, a research firm that analyzes corporate financial and environmental sustainability performance. And in 2007 *Fortune* magazine named FPL Group as the most admired company in the electric and gas sector.

Sunshine Energy

The physics of electricity dictates that a specific quantity or type of electricity, having been added to the power grid, cannot be directed to a particular home. So renewable energy cannot be solicited specifically by consumers, it can only be added to the grid to offset the amount of electricity generated by nonrenewable energy. Because consumers cannot easily buy renewable energy directly, they can, however, support the growth of renewable energy financially through innovative programs such as FPL's Sunshine Energy program.

The 250-kilowatt solar array installed by FPL at Rothenbach Park in Sarasota, Florida

Some 34,000 Florida Power & Light customers pay a small premium each month to support the development of renewable energy through the Sunshine Energy program, recognizing that renewable energy sources cost a little more than other forms of power generation financially, but the environmental payback is invaluable. Since 2004, these customers' contributions have helped to avoid 249,000 tons of carbon dioxide emissions—the equivalent of removing 44,000 cars from the road for a year. Each individual in the program is having the same impact as avoiding 12,000 miles of driving.

Vital Statistics

Main site: Juno Beach, Florida
Main product: Energy-related products and services
Number of employees: 14,600
Success: Generating more than 90% of its electricity using clean fuels
Challenge: Reliable, affordable power while minimizing environmental impact
Awards: Global 100 Most Sustainable Corporations in the World—Corporate Knights and Innovest • KLD Global Climate 100 Index (GC100) • #1 among electric and gas utilities on *Fortune* magazine's list of America's Most Admired Companies in 2007 for being most ethical

GE's Ecomagination Strategy: Seizing the Green in Green

As they say at General Electric, green is green. Environmentally sound business is profitable. Imagine, then build, innovative products that will help the environment and position GE as a corporate leader. Ecomagination, the marketing umbrella for GE's green business strategy that started in 2005, has been driven from the start by chairman and CEO Jeffrey Immelt.

Shortly after Immelt took over as chairman and CEO of General Electric in 2001, he agreed with the U.S. EPA to develop a plan to clean up polychlorinated biphenyls (PCBs) from the Hudson River. The PCBs were a legacy of GE from the 1960s and 1970s, and a longtime point of contention with environmentalists. A year later, a group of investors filed a shareholder resolution with GE asking the company to measure and disclose its greenhouse gas emissions. The resolution garnered a surprising 20% of the votes cast at the company's annual meeting, according to the *Wall Street Journal.* The following year, Immelt pledged to disclose GE's emissions. "We are much better as a company getting ahead of [climate change policy] than we are pretending like it doesn't exist," he said.

But GE—a $172 billion conglomerate that produces everything from lightbulbs and aircraft engines to television shows—took a while to hit its stride. When GE first measured its GHG emissions from industrial operations in 2004 (11 million metric tons), it didn't include emissions from power plants in which GE Energy Financial Services had made equity investments. Immelt met that year with utility company executives who were clients, most of whom were opposed to carbon-reducing regu-

OPPOSITE: The GEnx engine achieves dramatic gains in fuel efficiency and performance with significantly lower emissions than other engines in its class, and the GEnx is the quietest large commercial engine GE has ever produced.

lations. Immelt suggested that the government would someday impose carbon limits, and they'd be better off getting ahead of the problem—as GE was trying to do.

A year later, in 2005, GE launched its Ecomagination initiative, which included a variety of green investments and products—now numbering close to 50. While many of the initiatives, such as more fuel-efficient aircraft engines, were already under way, Immelt was putting a stake in the ground and asking to be held accountable. Under the Ecomagination umbrella, GE pledged to invest $1.5 billion by 2010 in research and development of new technologies, to "develop and drive the technologies of the future that will protect and clean our environment." The R&D projects include advanced gasification techniques, fuel efficiency, hybrid systems, lighting, water purification, wind turbines, solar panels, and low-emission locomotives.

GE Energy Financial Services, the energy financing group, has about $14 billion in total energy investments and invests $5 billion a year in energy and water projects, much of that in coal, oil, and gas. But investments in renewable energy increased from $630 million in 2004 to $2 billion in 2006—and will double to $4 billion by 2010. Much of this investment is in large, capital-intensive wind, solar, hydro, and geothermal projects, but it also includes venture capital investments in start-up technologies. For example, GE has made equity investments in A123 Systems, a start-up company developing next-generation lithium-ion battery technology for hybrid and plug-in vehicles. GE is also backing at least three different wind-energy companies.

By 2006, revenues from GE's Ecomagination portfolio of green products and services had eclipsed $12 billion, and reached $14 billion in 2007; the fruits of this new research are expected to push revenues to $20 billion by 2010. "These extraordinary revenues and orders are the initial payoff from directly aligning our product portfolio with our customers' needs and evolving trends, while 'doubling down' on investments in leading edge technology and innovation," said Immelt in announcing the gains. "When I was looking at the growth potential of our businesses three years ago, I saw an emphasis on clean energy and energy efficiency, on scarcity and the rise of regulatory pressure. And I thought—we've got something here. Ecomagination is growing beyond our

GE's most popular wind turbine, the 1.5MW turbine, can produce enough electricity for about 400 homes each year.

expectations, evolving into a sales initiative unlike any other I've seen in 25 years at GE."

In addition to products that help others save energy and reduce emissions, GE is practicing what it preaches. Between 2004 and 2006, GE reduced its GHG emissions from industrial operations by 4%, even with a 21% growth in revenues. It has since committed to reducing its GHG emissions by 1% by 2012, a seemingly insignificant number, but the company says emissions would increase 40% due to project growth if business were to continue as usual. Over that same period, GE looks to increase its own manufacturing efficiency by 30%. But these numbers don't count the power plants, and GE is still heavily invested in high-emitting coal-based utilities, which critics such as Rainforest Action Network argue negates GE's other gains.

After its initial pass on GHG reporting, GE has since reported that emissions from its partially owned power plants resulted in about 11 million metric tons of carbon emissions—about the same as the GE industrial footprint. That figure doesn't include plants in which GE owns a stake but which are leased to utilities. If included, the emissions total would be twice as high.

To offset this grim news, GE Energy Financial Services and AES Corporation, a global electricity generation and distribution company, have partnered to reduce emissions of methane (a more harmful greenhouse gas than CO_2) by 10 million metric tons by 2010. The joint venture, GE AES Greenhouse Gas Services, will produce GHG credits primarily by capturing methane emissions from agricultural waste, landfills, coal mines, and wastewater and turning them into clean power. GE AES will then market these GHG credits to companies looking to offset their GHG emissions. For example, GE AES will sell offsets from projects such as the Scholl Canyon Landfill methane-gas-to-energy project in Glendale, California. Right now, any such purchase of credits is voluntary, but GE AES expects that government mandates will soon force companies to buy offset credits. Immelt, in fact, who credits a 2001 National Academy of Sciences report with persuading him that global warming was a reality, wants the U.S. government to pass legislation limiting carbon emissions. The position doesn't endear him to utility companies that buy GE equipment for their power plants. At the same time, Immelt doesn't want "to say no to coal," and the company has also lobbied against California's effort to ban energy-sapping incandescent lightbulbs, once the bread and butter of the company. Immelt may be a green visionary, but it's not easy to change a company's practices overnight.

Bringing Green Jobs: GE's Hybrid Locomotive

GE has developed the world's first hybrid heavy-haul-freight locomotive. The Evolution Series Hybrid Locomotive reduces fuel costs and cuts down on noise and emissions. GE does not explicitly state the fuel efficiency gains, but says its new Evolution engine will use 170,000 gallons less fuel over its lifetime than its predecessors. On average, nitrous oxide and other emissions from the Evolution Series engines are 40% lower than those from the previous generation of GE locomotives.

The Evolution line uses a 12-cylinder engine that produces as much power as the previous 16-cylinder engine. With the hybrid, the engine horsepower is supplemented by capturing thermal energy in batteries (the amount used to brake a 207-ton locomotive and the train it's pulling) then using the power to drive the engine. By the end of 2007, GE had manufactured more than 2,300 Evolution locomotives for countries such as Brazil, China, and Kazakhstan.

The popular train engines are a key reason GE's transportation business is among the company's best-performing divisions and why GE's 2008 annual meeting was held in Erie, Pennsylvania, where the engines are made. "What we are doing in Erie is really a play on globalization," says transportation president Johnn Dineen, who likes to joke that Erie is one of the few places in the United States to have a trade surplus with China. "The Evolutions Series fleet has fewer failures per locomotive per year than the rest of our GE fleet," says Rich Regan, vice president—mechanical at CSX. GE is also selling Evolution locomotives to Kazakhstan, where it has set up factories to assemble parts shipped from the United States. A 16-cylinder version for the Chinese market is designed to pull heavier cargo loads but still reduces emissions by 28%.

Vital Statistics

Main site: Fairfield, Connecticut	
Main products: Energy • Health care • Commercial and consumer finance • Media and broadcasting • Water, aviation, and rail applications	
Number of employees: 325,000	
Success: $14 billion in green revenues in 2006 • $100 million in annual energy savings from applying advanced GE technology to inefficient processes	
Challenge: Communicating with 325,000 employees in 100 countries • Rapid commercialization of products	

Making Money the New-Fashioned Way

When Goldman Sachs unveiled its blueprint for sustainability in 2005, businesses around the world took notice. The investment bank's legendary financial success underscores the careful reasoning behind every move it makes, and the business-oriented Environmental Policy Framework makes clear that valuing the environment goes hand in hand with creating wealth. Each of the company's major business areas has incorporated the framework into its operations. "Companies that are environmentally sensitive will be one way to generate good returns to their shareholders," said Goldman Sachs managing director Abby Joseph Cohen in a February 2007 interview.

In the area of principal investments, Goldman Sachs is identifying new opportunities and creating new markets for renewable energy. To date, it has made significant investment in slowing climate change by directing more than $2 billion of its own capital to various alternative energy ventures in the United States, Europe, and Asia, including cellulosic ethanol, waste recycling, wind farm development, and thin-film solar panel manufacturing.

Among its alternative energy investments: SunEdison, one of the largest solar photovoltaic installers in the United States; Nordex and Nordic Windpower, leaders in multimegawatt wind turbine technologies; Iogen, which built and operates a plant that converts agricultural materials such as corn, corn stalks, and switchgrass to bio-based cellulosic ethanol; and Beijing Goldenway Biotech, which builds and operates recycling stations that turn biowaste into protein-rich feed and fertilizer additives.

Goldman Sachs is also positioning itself to profit from growing carbon emissions trading markets, which emerged as a result of the 2005 Kyoto Protocol. In major markets such as the European Union Emissions Trading Scheme, carbon emissions credits are now being bought and sold depending on whether a company is emitting more or less carbon dioxide than it is allowed. Europe's carbon emissions trading market was valued at about $30 billion in 2006, and the global carbon trading market is expected to far exceed that in the coming years. Although the United States has yet to enact mandatory

OPPOSITE: Across the Hudson from New York City, the LEED-certified Goldman Sachs tower in Jersey City, New Jersey, is the tallest building in New Jersey.

limits on carbon emissions, Goldman Sachs acquired an investment stake in 2006 in Climate Exchange, which owns the U.S. and European trading platforms Chicago Climate Exchange and European Climate Exchange, as well as the newly created California Climate Exchange. "Innovative trading in these new markets can be a source of meaningful action to address global climate change," said CEO and chairman Lloyd C. Blankfein in the company's 2006 annual report.

Goldman Sachs is laying the groundwork for other market-based solutions through its Center for Environmental Markets, which was established in 2005 to undertake independent research through partnerships with both academic partners and nongovernmental organizations. One such project, with the Woods Hole Research Center in Massachusetts, is examining how to value forest ecosystems and analyze economic alternatives to cutting valuable rain forests.

Goldman Sachs is also committed to incorporating environmental, social, and governance (ESG) factors into its investment research. Through its GS Sustain research, it combines analysis of the sustainability of corporate performance with traditional fundamental analysis. It uses a proprietary framework for analyzing competitive advantages in mature industries and identifying winners in emerging industries, including alternative energy, environmental technology, and biotechnology. The result is a set of objective metrics on ESG issues that can be integrated with overall measures of corporate performance, industry themes, and returns-based valuation methodologies to highlight long-term investment ideas for investors.

Goldman Sachs hasn't forgotten about its own carbon footprint. In 2006, it developed a reporting system and collected the data to develop a baseline for the year 2005. It set its target to reduce carbon emissions by 7% by 2012. A reporting system was also established for Cogentrix, a power plant operator owned by Goldman Sachs.

An early leader in developing green buildings, Goldman Sachs in 2000 constructed a new office building in Jersey City, New Jersey, which at the time was the largest commercial facility in the world to achieve Leadership in Energy and Environmental Design (LEED) certification. In 2006, the investment bank started requiring that all new construction meet LEED Gold certification or other green building standards. Its new headquarters in New York City is scheduled for completion in 2009. The 43-story tower will house 9,000 employees in 2.1 million gross square feet of office space and is designed to capture Gold certification, with its green roof, sustainable water system, and ice storage and chilled-water system.

Shovels broke ground in 2005 for the forthcoming Goldman Sachs World Headquarters building in lower Manhattan, which is anticipated to receive LEED Gold certification.

The End of the Earth

Tierra del Fuego, an archipelago at the southernmost point of South America and often called the end of the earth, is an out-of-the-way place even for the globe-trotting executives at Goldman Sachs. But when the firm acquired defaulted debt in 2002 that was collateralized by 640,000 acres of ecologically important forest land there, it saw an opportunity to create a different kind of value than its usual investment banking operations produce. It approached the Wildlife Conservation Society (WCS), an international conservation organization, for help in creating a huge world-class nature preserve to benefit the people of Chile. Goldman Sachs transferred the land to WCS in 2004, and by 2006, the two orga-

A view of the 750,000-acre nature preserve in Tierra del Fuego

nizations had committed almost $19 million to the preserve. In 2007, the nature preserve was expanded to more than 735,000 acres through a transaction that provided WCS with title to a tract of land joining the two separate parcels of the original reserve, thereby allowing for more effective management to protect the ecological viability of key species in the region.

Since then, park rangers there have been trained in firefighting, controlling illegal hunting, and performing basic research. Scientists are conducting more sophisticated research projects, including analyzing guanaco migration patterns and their effect on forest regeneration. A public use plan opened the area to the public for trekking, fishing, biking, camping, and kayaking. For the company's efforts in Tierra del Fuego, Goldman Sachs received the U.S. Secretary of State's 2006 Award for Corporate Excellence.

Vital Statistics

Main site: New York, New York
Main product: Financial services
Number of employees: 30,000
Green partners: Woods Hole Research Center • Wildlife Conservation Society
Success: Invested more than $2 billion of capital in alternative energy ventures
Awards: U.S. Secretary of State's 2006 Award for Corporate Excellence

Mapping a Course Toward Carbon Neutrality

Google™

Google, one of the world's most popular search engines, is on track to become carbon-neutral for 2008 and beyond. It's doing this largely by purchasing renewable energy for server farms and other facilities, as well as carbon offsets to help reduce global warming pollution in other parts of the world.

Google's first step toward carbon neutrality was to partner with the Environmental Resources Trust to audit its carbon footprint. The audit measured greenhouse gas emissions from Google's purchased electricity, employee commuting, business travel, construction, and server manufacturing. The results of the audit are not public, however, because Google considers the information to be proprietary.

Google has taken several specific steps to reduce its energy use and carbon emissions and to promote sustainability, steps that have justifiably burnished its image as an environmentally responsible company. For example, employees who purchase fuel-efficient vehicles receive a subsidy from the company, and daily shuttles that run on biodiesel carry thousands of employees on their daily commutes around the Bay Area. Many materials in the buildings at Google's headquarters are recycled, made with wood from sustainable forests, or painted with organic compounds. Recycled blue jeans are used for soundproofing. The company's ergonomic Steelcase chairs are made of 92% recycled material, and Café 150, one of several campus cafeterias, serves only food from farms within 150 miles of Mountain View to reduce transport costs and emissions.

To help meet its energy needs, Google has installed one of the world's largest solar-panel installations, a 1.6-megawatt system with more than 9,000 panels that cover several buildings at Google's headquarters. Since solar output is greatest during peak afternoon hours, when electricity costs are highest, the panels generate roughly 30% of the power needed for the buildings. Google,

OPPOSITE: Google's solar panels generate roughly 30% of the power needed for the buildings at Google's headquarters.

Google has installed a 1.6-megawatt solar-panel system covering several buildings at its headquarters. The system includes more than 9,000 panels.

which developed its solar energy system with about $4.5 million in utility subsidies and tax incentives, expects the system to pay for itself within 7.5 years.

Despite these strides to make its corporate headquarters energy-efficient, Google's server farms, the facilities that power Google's online functionality, are likely the most energy-intensive part of its operations. *TechWorld* magazine estimates that Google operates more than 500,000 servers and 100,000 electric-powered disk drives—more than any other IT company in the world. And the company is in the process of building new server farms. Its new data center in The Dalles, Oregon, will initially cover 34,000 square feet with possible expansion to follow. More are being built in North Carolina and Oklahoma.

From Google's perspective, the virtues of multiple data centers are proximity to users and high-bandwidth connections to local Internet service providers (ISPs). Given its rapid growth and increasing demands for electricity to power its technology, Google will need to expand and broaden its commitment to energy-saving programs. Tackling energy efficiency across multiple centers and in multiple states will prove an especially key challenge for the company.

Google is partnering with other IT companies to reduce greenhouse gas emissions beyond those coming from its own operations. For example, together with another technology giant, Intel, Google created the Climate Savers Computing Initiative (CSCI), a nonprofit organization that promotes smart new technologies to reduce computer power consumption.

"A typical desktop PC wastes over half the power delivered to it—even when not in use," according to Google's green czar, Bill Weihl. "Through some very simple measures, there is an opportunity to save 70%–80% of the power currently consumed by desktop computers." Consumers can turn off their computers when not working on them, but Google is also exploring ways to make the computer more energy-efficient as it works.

Google's efforts to address the major cause of climate change has earned high praise. Carter Roberts, president of the World Wildlife Fund-U.S., is among the company's admirers. "Google…innovates to address an issue that affects almost every person, place, and animal on the planet," says Roberts. "The company committed to buying 50 megawatts of renewable energy and worked with WWF, Intel, and other industry leaders to develop and launch the CSCI to move carbon reductions broadly through its sector."

Employees who puchase fuel-efficient vehicles receive a subsidy from the company.

Google and its philanthropic arm, Google.org, have also announced a new strategic initiative to develop electricity from renewable-energy sources that will cost less than electricity produced from coal. The newly created initiative, known as RE<C, will initially focus on advanced solar-thermal power, wind-power technologies, enhanced geothermal systems, and other potential breakthrough technologies.

Google recognizes that it can do more. It knows that its carbon offsets, though an important part of any strategy to reduce global warming, are not as effective as direct reductions in greenhouse gas emissions. To ensure that the carbon offset component of its carbon neutrality policy is effective, however, Google needs to monitor more closely the carbon offsets it is paying for, be they a forest project in the Amazon or a clean energy project in Russia, to ensure they are achieving real reductions. Google could also take a more visible role as an advocate for state and federal policies to encourage renewable-energy projects. Finally, Google could better leverage its global reach through its information portals to raise public awareness about climate change and related issues. Google's strides have been impressive, but opportunities abound for the company to further extend its leadership as a model of environmental responsibility.

Car of the Future?

Google.org, the company's philanthropic arm funded by 1% of the firm's equity and profits, has chosen climate change as a principal focus. A key initiative of the company, RechargeIT, researches plug-in vehicles. Google.org joined with California utility PG&E in 2007 to demonstrate an innovative vehicle-to-grid (V2G) hybrid car and announced a $10 million request for proposals from companies and technologies that can help accelerate production and commercialization of plug-in vehicles. It also funded $1 million in grants to organizations that are leading the plug-in revolution. The project has developed a small car-share fleet of plug-in hybrids, which Google employees can reserve and use at no cost and that have an extended driving range for longer trips. Tests show that plug-ins can achieve at least 30 miles per gallon more than traditional hybrids. For the majority of Americans, who drive 35 miles or fewer per day, such plug-in hybrids could be a great alternative. Already, you can use Google Maps to locate hybrid plug-in centers across the United States. And you can certainly expect the car to include GPS tracking.

RechargeIT is a Google.org initiative that aims to reduce CO_2 emissions, cut oil use, and stabilize the electrical grid by accelerating the adoption of plug-in hybrid vehicles and vehicle-to-grid technology.

Vital Statistics

Main site: Mountain View, California
Main products: Search engine • Online advertising network
Number of employees: 16,000 worldwide
Green partner: EI Solutions
Success: Incorporating renewable energy sources into business operations
Challenge: Powering new business with renewable energies at scale

They Live Up to Their Name

If ever there was a company whose core values reflect the vision of its founder, it's Green Mountain Coffee Roasters, Inc., under the aegis of its founder and chairman, Robert Stiller. The Vermont company built its reputation on its specialty coffees, of which it sells more than 100 varieties, and today it is recognized as a leader in organic and fair trade coffee as well as social and environmental responsibility. Each year the company donates at least 5% of its pretax profits to socially responsible initiatives in communities where it does business.

For the past two years, GMCR has received the top ranking in *CRO* (Corporate Responsibility Officer) magazine's list of 100 Best Corporate Citizens. Company profits and sales soared in 2007 as well. Green Mountain Coffee Roasters coffee is sold in all 50 states and in 25 countries—the equivalent of more than three million cups of coffee a day.

Stiller takes great pride in the tight bond between his employees and growers who work side by side to produce organic, fair trade coffee using the best sustainable agriculture practices. The company's growers are in Mexico, Guatemala, Peru, Sumatra, and other corners of the world.

"When [our employees] go out to our countries of origin and see things firsthand and experience the relationship that we have with these farmers, they come back and their lives are changed," says Stiller. "They are really so much more motivated to do well with the fair trade and organic coffees. It's also meaningful to the farmers that somebody cares about them and that they are connected to a community supplying coffee to consumers."

In 1990, when Green Mountain Coffee Roasters began offering organic coffee, the market was small and the company was considered a pioneer. Its ongoing commitment to sustainable coffee has transformed it into one of the country's largest providers of double-certified fair trade organic coffee. In places such as Huatusco, Mexico, Green Mountain Coffee Roasters has helped to finance coffee cooperatives in their efforts to go organic, leading to the production of organic bananas, flowers, and macadamia nuts as well as coffee. The interplanting of these crops improved soil quality and brought higher profits for farmers. The company's investment in Huatusco helped to create a state-of-the-art wet mill, as well

OPPOSITE: Numerous Green Mountain employees have been flown to Central America for coffee-source trips.

Green Mountain employees have participated in coffee-source trips for more than a decade.

as to support a nonprofit organization called Coffee Kids that encourages coffee growers to establish personal savings accounts by granting small loans to help them launch their own small businesses. Green Mountain Coffee Roasters has also funded coffee-washing stations, drying patios, and nurseries in Mexico.

In Aceh, Sumatra, Green Mountain Coffee Roasters helped establish a coffee cooperative that now has 2,000 members. The cooperative is currently the largest producer and seller of fair trade organic coffees in Sumatra.

Along with its efforts to produce organic coffee, the company is striving to increase production of Fair Trade Certified coffee. Fair trade products allow farmers to count on fair prices for their harvest, affordable access to credit, direct access to markets, and support for community development of schools and better roads. To qualify for Fair Trade Certification, farmers must form or join a cooperative in which power and profits are shared, and as awareness of the practice grows and small farms continue to struggle, many are looking to do so.

Finding new buyers and markets for organic and fair trade coffee is integral to the company's strategy. In 2006, sales of Fair Trade Certified organic coffee grew 69% from the previous year. That number is expected to continue to grow alongside consumer awareness. The company began sourcing and roasting Fair Trade Certi-

fied organic coffee for Newman's Own Organics in 2002, and today it is being sold in more than 600 McDonald's retail outlets across the northeast United States. Although 28% of the company's coffee is currently Fair Trade Certified or Fair Trade Certified Organic (up from 25% in 2006), the company is always looking for ways to increase that number. Green Mountain Coffee Roasters is also focused on greening its operational environmental footprint and its packaging.

In 2003, Green Mountain Coffee Roasters started offsetting greenhouse gas emissions with the purchase of renewable energy credits that help finance wind and other climate-friendly energy projects. Further developments include the composting of burlap bags and coffee chaff and the conversion of all vehicles at its Waterbury, Vermont, headquarters to use B20 biodiesel.

The company's cutting-edge "ecotainers," introduced in 2006, eliminate the company's use of 250,000 pounds of oil-based polyethylene in the 130 million cups the company sells each year. The cups were created in partnership with the International Paper Company and feature a waterproof membrane made from corn instead of the more typical plastic. After use, and under the proper conditions, the cup will break down into water, carbon dioxide, and organic matter. "It's a way to promote more socially responsible materials and to get away from fossil fuels," explained Don Holly, Green Mountain Coffee Roaster's director of corporate quality.

The company hopes to use more sustainable packaging in the years to come. This is a big challenge for Green Mountain Coffee Roasters, and company representatives concede that due to stringent freshness demands "nearly all of our packaging relies on nonrenewable materials that are nonrecyclable, nonreusable, nonbiodegradable, and made from petroleum-based products." The eco-friendly cup was a step in the right direction, and the company recently announced that its 10- and 12-ounce bags now incorporate 19.4% PLA polymer made from corn, a renewable resource.

In an attempt to hold itself accountable, Green Mountain Coffee Roasters released its first corporate social responsibility report in 2006. "Producing our first external corporate social responsibility report helped us understand ourselves better and inspired us to take new challenges," says Stiller. Given the vision and values with which Stiller started Green Mountain Coffee Roasters, it is clear that finding new ways to meet the company's commitment to environmental sustainability and corporate social responsibility will always be on the agenda.

Growing Coffee and Protecting Chimps in Africa

One of the six new single-origin coffees Green Mountain Coffee Roasters introduced in 2007 has an unusual partner. Tanzanian Gombe Reserve coffee was the result of a collaboration between Green Mountain Coffee Roasters and the Jane Goodall Institute. "We were working with some farms in the area [where primatologist Jane Goodall does chimpanzee research] for a couple years, developing a better coffee for them so they could market it and make more money," Stiller recalled. "Jane Goodall [was] out doing some promotions to protect the environment around the habitat and partnered with us to produce and name a coffee to bring more knowledge and awareness to the issues."

The land around the Gombe National Park in Tanzania suffered from severe deforestation. The Kalinzi Cooperative, a group of 2,700 farmers who live near the park, was formed and the farmers began growing coffee beans under the forest canopy. Because the trees were permitted to remain, the habitat of the chimps was not disturbed, providing them with a safe home and the farmers with increased economic viability. "Our effort to involve local citizens in restoring the forests and practicing sustainable agriculture is the most important work we can do to ensure a future for the Gombe chimpanzees and the people of Africa," said Dr. Goodall of the collaboration.

Lindsey Bolger, director of coffee sourcing and relationships at Green Mountain, Jane Goodall, and members of the Kalinzi Cooperative.

Vital Statistics
Main site: Waterbury, Vermont
Main product: Specialty coffee
Number of employees: 1,030
Green partners: Coffee Kids • The Kalinzi Cooperative • Ceres
Success: Increasing production and sales of Fair Trade Certified organic coffee.
Challenge: Environmental packaging
Awards: Vermont Governor's Award for Environmental Excellence and Pollution Prevention • #1 Best Corporate Citizens–*CRO* magazine • Co-winner, Best First Time Sustainability Report from Ceres-ACCA North American Awards for Sustainability Reporting • 2007 SB20: World's Top Sustainable Stocks • *Forbes* 200 Best Small Companies

Designed for Sustainability

⬤HermanMiller

Michigan-based Herman Miller, Inc., is renowned for creating great places to work through the design, manufacture, and distribution of furnishings, interior products, and related services. The company counts well-known modern designs, which include the Eames and Aeron chairs, among its many accomplishments. Herman Miller, Inc., began as Star Furniture in 1905 and in the 1950s, D. J. DePree mandated that his company "will be good stewards of the environment." DePree simply believed taking care of the environment was the right thing to do, and so the corporate strategy of Herman Miller has always been to design products with an emphasis on product durability, innovation, and quality.

DePree's objective was evidenced from the start by his internal company rules that, in retrospect, were remarkably responsible and enlightened. Among the company's founding requirements: windows must be in all Herman Miller buildings, including manufacturing sites, so that employees benefit from natural light. Today we call this "harvesting natural daylight," but to DePree it was common sense. He also mandated that 50% of any Herman Miller corporate site be designated as green space. These rules, still in effect today, illustrate the company's dedication to social and environmental responsibility, and several decades later, CEO Brian Walker echoed DePree's founding words. "Environmental advocacy is part of our heritage and a responsibility we gladly bear for future generations."

While environmental and social responsibility has always been a cornerstone in Herman Miller's success, it was a group of employees who started the Environmental Quality Action Team (EQAT) in 1989 to address the many issues that this international company, with multiple manufacturing plants and office sites, encounters while trying to establish environmental standards. EQAT coordinates all environmental work at Herman Miller through its nine sub-teams: Communications, Design for the Environment, Environmental Affairs, Green Buildings, ISO 14001 (which is focused on the continuous improvement of its environmental management system in pursuit

OPPOSITE: The Leaf personal light uses energy-efficient LED technology to bring the human touch to lighting.

of its goals for the year 2020), Environmental Low Impact Processing group, Indoor Air, Energy Reducing, and Packaging/Transportation (which finds ways to reduce the amount of packaging needed for both incoming and outgoing products). As a result, its first formal environmental policy established zero landfill use as its first-ever environmental goal in 1991. Today, more than 400 employees dedicate part of their time at work to participating on one of the nine EQAT sub-teams.

In Chippenham, England, the company's VillageGreen office complex achieves the highest rating of Excellent under BREEAM (Building Research Establishment's Environmental Assessment Method), which is used to assess the environmental performance of both new and existing buildings.

While maintaining its high-quality standards, Herman Miller is constantly incorporating more environmentally sustainable materials, features, and manufacturing processes into new product designs. The Design for the Environment (DfE) team, which is responsible for these environmentally sensitive design standards, incorporated a protocol to do just that. Influenced by product and industrial process design firm McDonough Braungart Design Chemistry (MBDC), Herman Miller adopted the MBDC Cradle to Cradle Design Protocol, enabling it to venture beyond regulatory compliance to evaluate new design products in order to incorporate an all-encompassing, holistic approach to product design and manufacturing.

Since 1999, all new Herman Miller products have been evaluated within the rigors of the MBDC Protocol, which requires that products be designed for recyclability at the end of their useful lives. During the product design process, the DfE team meets with designers and engineers to review material chemistry to ensure that they are the specific materials needed and of the highest safety standards available; disassembly of the product so that, at the end of its life, its material can be recycled; and the potential for a product's recyclability. Part of this initiative also requires that suppliers meet this protocol as well. The Mirra chair, introduced in 2003, was the first Herman Miller product designed completely using the DfE Cradle to Cradle Protocol. The development of the Mirra chair includes the following examples using the Cradle to Cradle criteria: metal is 100% recyclable steel and aluminum and has a high percentage of recycled content; the tilt structure is built to ease removal of plastic components for disassembly; and all of the electricity that runs the Mirra assembly lines comes from Green-e Certified power—50% wind power and 50% biomass. Leading environmental designer and thinker William McDonough commented, "Herman Miller has been a pioneer in the environmental movement for decades. With their adoption of MBDC's Cradle to Cradle Design Protocols, they have taken that commitment to a new and immensely more powerful level, moving beyond eco-efficient to true sustainability."

In 1993, Herman Miller helped fund the start-up of the United States Green Building Council (USGBC), a nonprofit organization dedicated to understanding and promoting sound environmental building practices. This organization embraced the company's mission for new and future building projects set out by its founder and enabled Herman Miller's Facilities Group to learn from industry experts. In 1995, Herman Miller's GreenHouse, a manufacturing facility designed by William McDonough & Partners, was selected as a pilot for the development of USGBC's Leadership in Energy and Environmental Design (LEED) certification process. Chosen as a model of what is possible, it was awarded Pioneer status and stands as proof that green design can be aesthetically pleasing, environmentally sound, and financially beneficial.

Continually working toward greater sustainability is a priority for the company, and in 2004, Herman Miller announced Perfect Vision, its most comprehensive environmental initiative, by setting sustainability goals for the year 2020. Aggressive goals include zero landfill use, zero hazardous waste generation, zero volatile organic compound (VOC) emissions, zero process water emissions from manufacturing, 100% green electrical energy use, 100% of sales from DfE-approved products, and company buildings constructed to a minimum LEED Silver certification.

Herman Miller has garnered its share of well-deserved accolades. In 2007, Herman Miller was chosen for the Sustainable Business 20 list for the fifth time as one of the world's top sustainability stocks, which includes companies with strong environmental initiatives and solid financial performance. *Working Mother* magazine ranked Herman Miller among its 20 Best Green Companies for America's Children in November 2007.

GreenHouse Bees

In the summer of 2000, more than 600,000 honeybees took up residence in 12 hives at Herman Miller's GreenHouse facility in Holland, Michigan. Initially brought in to pollinate the GreenHouse's plants and help the wildflowers thrive, the honeybees also helped to curtail a larger problem at the GreenHouse. A population explosion of paper wasps resulted in wasp nests in the eaves, the windowsills, and even the air-conditioning equipment. The company's policy of no pesticides meant employing a more creative solution—one that ultimately helped its natural environment. The new honeybee tenants would take over the wasps' food source, ensuring that the wasps would have to find somewhere else to go. The sweet by-product—the honey—is put into four-ounce bottles, labeled (featuring shots of the GreenHouse wildflowers taken by company employees), and given to customers and visitors to the facility with the story attached. The other by-product, beeswax, is environmentally friendly and has hundreds of uses. So Herman Miller, naturally, started making candles.

Vital Statistics

Main site: Zeeland, Michigan

Main product: Office furniture and services

Number of employees: 6,900

Success: 11 LEED-certified building projects (6 Gold, 2 Silver, 2 Certified, 1 Pioneer) • First ergonomic task chair and first office-furniture system designed and developed according to Cradle to Cradle Protocol

Challenge: To achieve measurable corporate sustainability targets by 2020: zero landfill, zero hazardous waste generation, zero air and water emissions from manufacturing • Company buildings constructed to a minimum LEED Silver certification • Use of 100% green energy to meet power needs

Awards: "Most Admired" company in *Fortune* magazine 19 of the past 21 years • Dow Jones Sustainability World Index • The 100 Best Corporate Citizens in America—*CRO* magazine • EPA WasteWise Gold Achievement Award for reduction in packaging

Inventing the Way to Green

When *Fortune* magazine named its Ten Green Giants in April 2007, HP made the list as having done the most to remedy the increasing environmental impact of information technology (IT) companies—particularly through its electronic waste (e-waste) recycling efforts. "HP owns massive e-waste recycling plants, where enormous shredders and granulators reduce 4 million pounds of computer detritus each month to bite-sized chunks—the first step in reclaiming not just steel and plastic but also toxic chemicals like mercury and even some precious metals," wrote Oliver Ryan in *Fortune*.

HP's electronic products recycling program, which began in 1987, had recycled a total of 1 billion pounds of e-waste by mid-2007. It took in over 250 million pounds globally in 2007, an increase of 50% over 2006. The continued proliferation of computers and digital gadgets means that the need to reduce waste going to landfills will continue to increase. The company goal is to reach 2 billion pounds of electronics recycling by 2010, effectively doubling this annual recovery rate.

HP's own machines are 100% recyclable, but HP will take any brand of equipment, though there is a small charge of $35 or less. It will also offer money toward an HP trade-in, give a cash rebate for certain equipment, or facilitate a donation. HP has recycling programs in 50 countries, regions, and territories worldwide, including a recently expanded program in China and a pilot program in Africa. One of its own computers, the Long Lifecycle Business Desktop PC, is made with 95% recycled materials.

Recycling is one of HP's strategies for improving the sustainability of its products; another is improving the energy efficiency of its new offerings. "We've reached the tipping point where the price and performance of IT are no longer compromised by being green, but are now enhanced by it," said Mark Hurd, HP chairman and chief executive officer. "Environmental responsibility is good business.... [It's the] hidden component in HP products, embedded in our design and engineering, including accessibility, energy efficiency, and recycling."

Designing computers with the end of their life in mind also positioned HP favorably to comply with the

OPPOSITE: These envelopes from HP's ink cartridges are recycled along with the cartridges' external plastic casings.

RoHS (Restriction of Hazardous Substances) Directive, which bans specific substances (lead, mercury, cadmium, hexavalent chromium, and the flame retardants PBB and PBDE) in products at the design phase. HP had already restricted use of lead, mercury, cadmium, and hexavalent chromium prior to 1999, and by 2007 it had completely eliminated them except where exempted under RoHS due to lack of technically feasible alternatives. HP has also eliminated brominated flame retardants (BFRs) in the external plastic parts of all new HP-brand product models introduced since 2007. The company maintains an ongoing goal of eliminating the remaining uses of BFRs and PVCs in HP-brand products as it identifies acceptable alternatives that will lower product environmental and health impacts without compromising product performance.

HP began addressing energy efficiency in the design phase of products in 1992 with its Design for Environment (DfE) program. HP DeskJet printers were redesigned to reduce their off-mode power consumption, and the power supplies on several brands of personal computers are now 15% more energy-efficient than their predecessors.

In 1996, it established a Power and Cooling Team to address the two largest areas of energy usage by data servers. HP customers can reduce the cost of cooling, which represents up to 70% of the total power needed by a data center, with an array of products. The Dynamic Smart Cooling service, introduced in 2006, reduces cooling energy costs by 20 to 45% by regulating the airflow and temperature of computer room air-conditioning.

With more than 172,000 employees in 170 countries, HP operations facilities consume considerable amounts of energy. Electricity accounts for 97% of HP's GHG emissions, so the company is focusing on consolidating operations into core sites. It launched its HP Workplace Transformation initiative in 2006 to improve space utilization and install more energy-efficient equipment. The goal is to reduce energy consumption by 15% from 2006 to 2010 from HP-owned and leased facilities worldwide.

The company plans to accomplish its goal both by reducing floor space and by upgrading building infrastructure. The company announced plans to consolidate 85 data centers in 29 countries into 6 data centers in 3 U.S. locations. The data centers will incorporate HP's Smart Cooling technology to reduce data-center energy usage by air conditioners, fans, and vents. Other savings will come from replacing cathode ray tube monitors with more energy-efficient flat-panel display monitors. Networked printers, which reduce the need for deskside models and reduce paper consumption by 10%, will be installed. "Energy efficiency is an integral part of the environmental program HP has had in place for decades and is a key component in making HP a leader in sustainability," said Pat Tiernan, HP's vice president of corporate, social and environmental responsibility. "Sustainability should span the entire business, from product reuse and recycling to a socially and environmentally responsible supply chain and energy efficiency in products and internal operations—it's the whole package... Switching to renewable energy sources such as solar and wind power makes both environmental and business sense."

The company is expanding its use of renewable energy, both by purchasing green energy and by installing solar panels. HP hired Airtricity to deliver 90% of the energy used in its facility in Ireland in 2008. The energy will be generated through wind farms located both on- and offshore.

Under a power purchase agreement with SunPower Corporation, HP will install its first-ever, large-scale solar power installation at its facility in San Diego. SunPower will sell the solar power to HP at a reduced, locked-in rate. The solar electric system will be financed and owned

Technicians wipe data from hard drives of PCs.

by a third party, allowing HP to take advantage of the savings in cost and emissions with no up-front expenditure. The project is expected to save HP approximately $750,000 in energy costs over the next 15 years, and reduce carbon dioxide emissions by more than 1 million pounds a year.

Savings will be extended to HP employees by giving them rebates if they install a SunPower solar system in their homes. Employees in the United States will receive a rebate from SunPower of up to $2,000, and HP will match that rebate with its own $2,000 rebate.

In addition to reducing its carbon footprint, HP is gaining recognition for its transparency on its GHG emissions. The company earned a perfect 100 score to garner best-in-class honors for GHG emissions and climate strategies disclosure in the 2007 Carbon Disclosure Project (CDP) report. Conducted by Innovest Strategic Value Advisors, the report compiles a Climate Leaders Disclosure Index spotlighting 68 *Financial Times* 500 companies for best practice on carbon disclosure.

Focusing on Suppliers

The wide range and number of products made by HP requires the company to pay $50 billion annually to suppliers to procure materials, components, and manufacturing and distribution services for its products. Each of the 600 suppliers at over 1,000 sites worldwide is expected to meet social and environmental responsibility (SER) standards that HP was an industry leader in developing in 2002.

Audits are used to analyze whether suppliers are conforming to the standards. Suppliers unable to meet the standards receive training and management support from HP, and they must submit an improvement plan with a completion schedule. HP readily admits that the challenge in training and monitoring so many suppliers is considerable. A third-party auditing firm hired to review the supply chain SER program in 2006 found that only 40% of nonconforming suppliers were making significant and timely progress on their action plans. The third-party audit recommended several action items, among them establishing accountability at a higher level of HP management, and ensuring that SER goals are incorporated into contracts and purchase orders.

Because HP shares its suppliers with others in the technology industry, the issues it faces in ensuring that suppliers meet environmental compliance rules are not unique. HP encourages other electronics companies, as well as customers, shareowners, and governments, to share their concerns and successes in developing sustainable solutions for extended supply chains. Its goals pertaining to its supply chain are posted on its website.

Vital Statistics

Main site: Palo Alto, California
Main Products: Printing • Personal computing • Software • Services • IT infrastructure
Number of employees: 172,000
Green partners: Airtricity • Sun Power Corporation
Success: Recycling a billion pounds of e-waste
Challenge: Eliminating remaining hazardous substances from HP products
Awards: Dow Jones Sustainability World Index • FTSE4Good Index lists—U.S., Global, U.K., and Europe • Number 10 globally and number 1 in United States in environment, social impact ratings by the *Economist* • Global 100 Most Sustainable Corporations in the World—Corporate Knights and Innovest

A Unique Culture of R&D

HONDA

Honda Motor Company has a lofty vision: to be recognized as "a company that society wants to exist." This vision is most apparent in the company's commitment to the environment. Honda's multilevel approach to combating global climate change and energy sustainability focuses on three areas: product and technology innovation, green manufacturing, and waste minimization. With more than 1.75 million cars and light trucks sold in North America in 2007, Honda's ongoing success in these endeavors will have lasting impact.

Already established as a leader for its fuel-efficient, low-emission, high-performance gasoline-powered engines, Honda, American Honda Motor Co., Inc., in particular, has also been ahead of the curve in advancing hybrid, clean diesel, and other alternative fuel technologies. The company's history of milestones includes mass-producing the first 4-cylinder car to break the 50-mpg fuel economy mark in 1986; being the first to voluntarily introduce low-emission vehicle technology, in the mass-produced Honda Civic in 1997; introducing the first gas-electric hybrid in North America in 1999; and pioneering the first production hydrogen-powered fuel cell vehicle in 2002. Honda's 2005 fleet of vehicles had the highest average fuel economy of all major auto manufacturers, and its passenger car economies are 20% above the standards established by the federal government.

These and other accomplishments led the Union of Concerned Scientists to name Honda the Greenest Automaker for the fourth consecutive time in 2007. The award is given to the manufacturer with the lowest overall production of smog-forming emissions and global warming emissions in its U.S. automobile fleet. "The winners are using clean technology across their entire fleets. The losers are installing it piecemeal, or not at all," said report author Don MacKenzie, highlighting the wide performance gap between top scorers Honda and Toyota versus other automakers.

A strong sense of environmental responsibility has characterized Honda's corporate culture since the 1960s and is the result of an emphasis on independent research and development. Honda R&D Co., established in 1960 as a separate company and funded with 5% of annual

OPPOSITE: The Acura Design Studio was engineered to include energy-saving attributes such as an Energy Star reflective roof to reduce heat gain and lower air-conditioning requirements in the Southern California building.

revenues from parent company Honda Motor Co., Ltd., is virtually free from restrictions regarding how to use that funding in the development of advanced technology. The one limitation imposed on research is that it ultimately produce a customer benefit. Based on the philosophy of company founder Soichiro Honda, engineers are taught that "success is 99% failure," and they are given plenty of freedom to pursue their own ideas.

Every CEO of Honda Motor Company was formerly a president of Honda R&D. Current CEO Takeo Fukui was part of the group of engineers at Honda in the late 1960s who became convinced that cleaner mobility was necessary to protect the world for future generations. The group's rallying cry, "Blue skies for our children," was the vision that continues to drive Honda's research efforts to this day.

Honda is striving to improve the environmental performance of its products with a three-pronged strategy: making the internal combustion engine cleaner and more efficient, developing better hybrid and clean diesel technologies, and developing alternative fuel technologies. These strategies are being pursued within the company simultaneously, in a spirit of friendly competition, with the understanding that there isn't just one winner. Multiple technologies reach the marketplace, serving the customer by enhancing performance as well as reducing costs. The new technologies are evaluated in a real-world environment, and are then used as building blocks for future advancements.

Honda continues to focus on making cleaner and more fuel-efficient internal combustion engines because

The Acura Design Studio, which broke ground in 2006, was built with the goal of receiving LEED Gold certification from the U.S. Green Building Council. The studio uses reclaimed water for landscaping and an intelligent lighting system that makes greater use of natural light.

currently that is the single most significant means of reducing tailpipe and CO_2 emissions. All Honda and Acura vehicles use electronically controlled variable valve timing. Further, Honda's advanced Variable Cylinder Management (VCM) technology saves fuel by operating on three, four, or six cylinders depending on driving conditions, which increases fuel efficiency. Honda was a leader in developing low-emission vehicle (LEV) technology and voluntarily offered vehicles with that technology in all 50 states, not just the states that required it by law.

Unlike most other car manufacturers, which can meet the U.S. EPA's stringent emissions standards only by averaging across their fleets, every Honda and Acura vehicle sold in North America in 2007 met or exceeded those standards. The natural-gas-powered Civic GX earned the highest possible green score for model year 2007 from the American Council for Energy Efficient Economy (ACEEE), using a rating system that incorporates tailpipe emissions and greenhouse gas emissions over the full product life cycle. Four other Honda cars also made it into the ACEEE's top 12 list.

Honda is continuing to develop better hybrid and clean diesel technologies. Honda built the EV Plus electric vehicle, which provided critical experience that advanced the company's hybrid and fuel cell programs. Real-world experience with the EV Plus was the foundation for creating a total systems approach to meet the many and often mutually exclusive needs of the marketplace, including efficiency, range, performance, reliability, comfort, and crash safety. Honda created a clean diesel engine and, learning from experience marketing it in Europe, advanced the technology to meet U.S. Clean Air Act requirements. Honda's next-generation diesel engine has a unique reduction catalyst that turns nitrogen oxide in fuel into harmless nitrogen, reducing normal greenhouse gas emissions by up to 50%.

To promote energy sustainability, Honda is developing alternatives including fuel cell, bioethanol, and compressed natural gas (CNG) technologies. The Civic GX, a dedicated CNG-powered passenger car, is now available for sale in both California and New York. In addition to reducing CO_2 emissions by 25% and having near-zero tailpipe emissions, natural gas is readily available because more than 50% of American homeowners use it for heating. Although public CNG refueling stations are relatively scarce, Civic GX owners who buy home refueling appliances could save as much as 50% over the price of gasoline.

In addition to improving the environmental performance of its products, Honda is working to make its factories and offices green by increasing energy efficiency, reducing waste, and enhancing recycling. Three of its North American production facilities reduced the energy required to manufacture a car by 6% from 2006 to 2007, earning the company the Environmental Protection Agency's Energy Star label for the most energy-efficient automobile production facility in America.

Three of the company's plants in America are zero-waste plants, and Honda reduced overall waste going to landfills by 66% between 2001 and 2007, a reduction achieved by increasing both recycling and waste-to-energy conversion for items that are nonrecyclable.

There have been some bumps on the company's R&D road, however. Honda introduced the EV Plus, the first battery-powered electric vehicle for retail consumers, in 1997. The car was discontinued after only 330 were produced, when it became evident that the technology didn't support customer demands for range, performance, and reliability. Even now, 10 years later, no major car manufacturers have been successful in developing a plug-in battery that is durable enough to last the lifetime of a car, typically 100,000 to 150,000 miles. Hybrid cars on the market today use small electric motors with rechargeable batteries only to power the car at low speeds for short distances. The goal of creating a battery strong enough and durable enough to be the sole source of power for 40 to 50 miles, the average daily commute, remains elusive.

Fuel Cell Car

Believing that hydrogen power represents one of the best potential alternatives to gasoline, Honda has led the industry in developing fuel cell technology. It introduced the world's first production fuel cell car, the Honda FCX, in the United States and Japan in 2002. In addition to hydrogen's efficiency and lack of harmful exhaust emissions, hydrogen power can be produced using a variety of sources, including natural gas, biofuels, and solar and wind energy. The biggest challenge to fuel cell technology is developing refueling options. One approach is Honda's Home Energy Station concept, a home-based product that uses natural gas to produce heat and electricity for the home while producing hydrogen fuel for a vehicle. Another option is solar energy. Honda established its own solar-powered hydrogen refueling station in 2001 at its Torrance, California, campus. The next-generation fuel cell vehicle, the FCX Clarity, will be marketed to fleet and retail customers in the United States and Japan in 2008. It will have a maximum speed of 100 mph and a range of about 270 miles.

Vital Statistics

Main site: Torrance, California
Main products: Automobiles • Light trucks • Motorcycles • Business jets • Jet engines • Other mobility products
Number of employees: 27,000 in the United States
Success: First LEVs and SULEVs • First hybrid • First natural gas vehicle with home refueling • Environmental leadership on fuel economy • First and only NHTSA/EPA-certified fuel cell vehicle available for lease to consumers
Challenge: Expanding production of fuel cell vehicles and home refueling infrastructure
Awards: Union of Concerned Scientists Greenest Automaker

Tackling the Invisible Enemy

HSBC Group, one of the largest banking and financial institutions in the world, made headlines when it announced in 2004 that the entire organization would be carbon-neutral by 2006. And it made even more headlines when it achieved its promise three months ahead of schedule. Now the bank has expanded its environmental goals beyond its own walls and put sustainability at the heart of its strategic business plan. HSBC received the highest score among 40 global banks in Ceres's Corporate Governance and Climate Change: The Banking Sector report released in 2008.

"Climate change represents the largest single environmental challenge we face this century," said Stephen Green, group chairman of HSBC Holdings PLC. "It is all the more dangerous because it is such a slow and hard-to-track phenomenon; it is truly the invisible enemy."

Given the impact climate change will have on modern life, HSBC has determined that the business must be grown both commercially and sustainably. The bank indirectly impacts climate change through its lending and investment decisions. Since the bank recognizes that climate change has the potential to limit future growth in demand for its services, it makes good business sense for HSBC to inform and empower its customers to understand and curb the factors leading to climate change. To that end, the bank has launched a Carbon Finance Strategy to help clients respond to the challenges of creating a low-carbon economy.

HSBC requires an assessment to be made of existing and potential economic, environmental, and social factors when it decides whether or not to finance a particular project. The company has developed corporate-wide sector guidelines and policies using internationally accepted standards approved by the International Finance Corporation and the Equator Principles. The sectors covered by these guidelines are forest land and forest products, freshwater infrastructure, the chemicals industry, the energy sector, and the mining and metals sector. These guidelines aim to ensure that HSBC does not finance companies involved in environmentally or socially damaging activities. HSBC recognizes that some of its clients do operate in high-risk industries that negatively

OPPOSITE: Paul's Hill wind farm in Scotland was financed by HSBC and is an example of the projects it will support under its Carbon Finance Strategy.

impact the environment; however, it believes that by engaging with clients to support them as they work to improve the environmental and social performance of their businesses, the company can make a bigger contribution to sustainable development. Where HSBC believes clients do not meet its standards, it will exit relationships—and indeed has done so.

Recognizing that the growth of concern over climate change and the need for urgent action creates opportunities, HSBC created a Climate Change Fund, which provides a timely, comprehensive, and practical outlet for investors seeking to participate in this global theme. The fund invests in a portfolio of companies best placed to benefit from the challenges presented by climate change.

HSBC has been an outspoken worldwide leader in advocating the need to reduce the impact of climate change. It was a founding member in 2004 of the Climate Group, an independent nonprofit organization dedicated to advancing business and government leadership on climate change. In May 2007, the bank committed $100 million to the HSBC Climate Partnership, whose goal is to inspire action by individuals, businesses, and governments to combat climate change. The partnership, which includes the Climate Group, Earthwatch Institute, the Smithsonian Tropical Research Institute, and the World Wildlife Fund, has a range of aspirations, which include the protection of major rivers and implementing greener practices in cities such as Hong Kong, London, Mumbai, New York, and Shanghai. As part of this partnership, HSBC and the Smithsonian Tropical Research Institute announced that they will begin the largest-ever field research project to determine the long-term effects of climate change and how the world's forests can help regulate climate over the coming decades.

HSBC's own carbon footprint is another area of focus. The bank has committed to reduce the energy consumption of its employees over time and to ensure that the bank's operations remain carbon-neutral. When the bank decided in 2004 that it would become carbon-neutral—not an easy task for an organization with 10,000 offices in 83 countries and a growing business—it was not a decision taken lightly. With no how-to guide to follow at the time, HSBC could have outsourced the entire operation to a third party, but instead it built the expertise in-house. Its Carbon Management Plan is a blueprint for

HSBC employees release turtles into the ocean at Sandspit Beach in Karachi, Pakistan.

how HSBC achieves carbon neutrality. Three methods are used. The first is to reduce energy consumption and improve energy efficiency in its buildings, including the use of low-energy lighting, variable-speed drives in air conditioners, and more efficient heat management systems. The second method is to reduce fossil fuel consumption by buying "green electricity" produced from clean or renewable energy sources that do not emit carbon dioxide, such as wind, solar, and hydropower. The third step taken by HSBC to achieve carbon neutrality is to reduce emissions by buying carbon offset credits. To remain carbon-neutral in 2006 and 2007, HSBC bought carbon offsets from several projects in Asia, including energy efficiency in steelmaking in Thailand and China and hydroelectric projects in China.

HSBC's commitment to reducing the carbon footprint of its operations is evident in the 2007 launch of the Global Environmental Efficiency Programme, a five-year plan with $90 million worth of funding behind it. Examples of projects already completed under this program include installing solar photovoltaic panels at a facility in the United Kingdom and construction of the bank's first "carbon-zero" branch in Greece, New York. The building is equipped with solar panels, rainwater harvesting, and ground source heat pumps that use the earth's constant temperature to provide heating and cooling.

Climate Confidence Survey

To better understand public perceptions on climate change, HSBC undertook a survey of consumer attitudes toward climate change in nine of the world's major markets. The survey, called the HSBC Global Climate Confidence Index, based on research conducted with 9,000 consumers in April 2007, showed that people in developing economies were more concerned, committed, and optimistic regarding the problem of climate change than those living in developed economies. People from India and China were most optimistic, while citizens of France, Germany, and the United Kingdom were most pessimistic in the belief that we can stop climate change. Respondents from the United States, however, were far more hopeful about the possibility of change than citizens from other developed economies. Regardless of their level of optimism, respondents were unified in their belief that governments should take the lead in tackling the problem. Across all age groups and nationalities, 68% felt that government should drive environmental change, although only 33% said they feel that governments play that role today.

Vital Statistics

Main site: London, England

Main product: Banking and financial services

Number of employees: 330,000

Green partners: Climate Group • Earthwatch Institute • Smithsonian Tropical Research Institute • World Wildlife Fund

Success: Becoming carbon-neutral in 2005 • Launch of the HSBC Climate Partnership in 2007 • Launch of the Global Environmental Efficiency Programme in 2007 • Creation of the Climate Change Fund in 2007 • Creation of the Climate Change Centre of Excellence in 2007 • Appointment of Lord Nicholas Stern as special advisor to the chairman on economic development and climate change

Challenge: To strike a balance between environmental, social, and economic factors while satisfying internal and external stakeholders

Awards: Sustainable Bank of the Year—*Financial Times* • EPA Climate Protection Award • Top-ranking bank in Ceres report on governance and climate change • Member of the Carbon Disclosure Leadership Index • Dow Jones Sustainability World Index

Big Blue Is Green

IBM's commitment to environmental protection began more than 35 years ago, at a time well before global warming and climate change were worldwide concerns. IBM's visionary founding family, father and son T. J. Watson Sr. and Jr., believed their company had a responsibility to be a good corporate citizen, and in 1971, CEO Tom Watson Jr. formalized a corporate policy on responsibility to the environment. IBM has sustained its commitment to environmentalism for decades—whether governments and the public have been focused on the issue or not. Over the years, the policy has been updated numerous times, and it is supported by a comprehensive global environmental management system (EMS) that is almost as old as the corporate policy itself.

On the strength of its EMS, in 1997 IBM became the world's first multinational to earn a single global registration to the ISO 14001 EMS Standard, an internationally accepted standard that identifies the elements of an EMS needed for an organization to effectively manage its impact on the environment and to measure, track, and obtain third-party audits of its system. IBM achieved this because its EMS governs operations to the same standards and requirements worldwide—no mean feat for such a large enterprise. These corporate directives include pollution prevention, chemical and waste management, energy

management, environmental evaluation of suppliers, product stewardship, and incident prevention and reporting. Every employee is expected to follow the policy and report any concerns to managers, who are expected to take action quickly.

IBM's charter memberships and leadership roles in pioneering climate protection programs attest to its commitment over the years. It contributed its expertise to help the U.S. EPA develop the Energy Star program for computers in 1992, one of the first initiatives designed to reduce power consumption by personal computers. IBM executives are on the steering committee for the Electronics Industry Code of Conduct, a standardized set of best practices to improve environmental and social outcomes for electronics industry suppliers. IBM was also a charter member of the World Wildlife Fund's Climate Savers program in 2000, a participant in the first year and all subsequent years of the Carbon Disclosure Project in 2002, a charter member of the Chicago Climate Exchange in 2003, and a founding member of the Green Grid in 2007.

Through its Project Big Green initiative, IBM is devoting $1 billion per year across its businesses to provide energy-smart innovations and solutions to dramatically increase the energy efficiency of data centers.

How does this long-standing commitment to environmentalism manifest itself internally? Energy conservation is a major component of IBM's climate protection program because the greatest potential impact it can have is through reducing the energy used to power its own facilities. It established an energy conservation program in 1974, and it is the cornerstone of the company's climate protection program. From 1990 to 2006, IBM's energy conservation actions saved 4.5 billion kilowatt-hours of electricity, avoided nearly 3 million metric tons of CO_2 emissions (equal to 44% of the company's 1990 global CO_2 emissions), and saved over $290 million in energy costs. To extend this significant achievement, IBM set a new global climate goal in 2006: to reduce CO_2 emissions associated with its energy use 12% between 2005 and 2012 through energy conservation, the use of renewable energy, and/or funding an equivalent CO_2 emissions reduction by the purchasing of renewable energy certificates or comparable instruments. This revision continues IBM's focus on energy conservation but also places an increased focus on the use of renewable energy.

IBM has already increased its renewable energy purchases from 2.7% of its worldwide electrical usage in 2005 to 7.3% in 2006, an increase of 180%. IBM was one of the top 20 renewable energy purchasers on the 2006 U.S. EPA Green Power Partners list.

Emissions reductions are also achieved by two programs that encourage employees to work from home. The work-at-home program allows employees' "work" office to be in their home, and the mobile employees program allows employees to work from home a designated number of days each week. More than a third of IBM's global workforce of over 100,000 participates in one of the programs. In addition to the approximately 8 million gallons of fuel saved by U.S. employees in the programs in 2006, 3,600 metric tons of carbon dioxide emissions were avoided when employees carpooled or used mass transit to get to work.

The company has also targeted carbon dioxide emissions produced from transporting parts and products. In 2006, the company joined the U.S. EPA's SmartWay Transport Partnership, a voluntary collaboration between freight carriers and shippers and the U.S. EPA to improve fuel efficiency and reduce GHG emissions. IBM increased the percentage of freight it shipped with SmartWay carriers in North America from 55% to 68%. It is extending its SmartWay commitment globally by initiating new policies including reduced idling time and the requirement for certain fuel-efficient technologies.

IBM was an early leader in product design for the environment, establishing a formal product stewardship program in 1991 that focused on developing more energy-efficient products. The company set goals based either on Energy Star criteria, where they applied, or on achieving improvements over previous generations.

But as companies grow more dependent on computing to conduct business, expanding needs for data centers are causing huge growth in their energy use. In 2007, the company announced it would invest $1 billion per year in Project Big Green, a new service designed to help clients build and redesign corporate IT infrastructures to be more energy-efficient and cost-effective. The service will diagnose a customer's existing data center and include an energy assessment. Using a recently introduced IBM product, consultants will measure temperatures in data centers, including hot spots, air leakages, and other inefficiencies. An improvement plan will use the latest IBM technologies for cooling, power management, and server optimization. The company has assembled a team of 1,000 experts worldwide to offer the service.

With over 8 million square feet of data-center space, IBM runs the world's largest and most sophisticated data-center operations, so the company is well positioned to be its own best Project Big Green customer. By using the same solutions it is offering clients, it expects to double the computing capacity of its own data centers by 2010 without increasing the use of power. It is consolidating 3,900 of its own computer servers onto new mainframes using the Linux operating system. (IBM plans to recycle the servers through its own Global Asset Recovery Services program.) The new server environment is expected to use about 80% less energy than the previous systems. Since 1997, the company has consolidated its own worldwide data centers from 155 to 7.

Bigger *and* Better

IBM is using its state-of-the-art technology to build a green data center that will help both it and its clients reduce energy consumption. The company announced in 2007 that it is investing $86 million to expand its Boulder Data Center by 80,000 square feet. The new data center will incorporate many of the features and technologies the company announced as part of its Project Big Green.

High-density IBM computing systems will use virtualization technology, the ability of a single mainframe to behave as if it were hundreds or even thousands of servers. Virtualization, which IBM pioneered 40 years ago and has been perfecting ever since, parcels out a system's resources, including processing, networking, storage, and memory, to many "virtual" servers. Each virtual server functions as a real machine. Additionally, IBM will use its Cool Blue Portfolio of energy-efficient power and cooling technologies for data centers. The overall design of the building is also expected to significantly reduce power consumption over other similarly sized facilities.

Vital Statistics

Main site: Armonk, New York
Main product: Information technologies, solutions, and services
Number of employees: 355,766
Success: Renewable energy purchases • Project Big Green
Challenge: Technological challenge of continual advancement
Awards: EPA Climate Protection Award • EPA/DOE's Green Power Leadership Award • EPA SmartWay Excellence Award • Low Carbon Leaders Award—the Climate Group

Home Is Our Planet

IKEA's basic business foundation, to offer well-designed and functional home furnishings at low prices, lends itself to the idea of conservation. After all, being cost-conscious requires the economical use of resources, just as sustainability does. IKEA takes resource conservation a step further, though, by setting high environmental standards throughout its business processes. From the raw materials used in its furniture production to the lightbulbs stocked on its shelves, the company exhibits a respect for nature embodied in its often-repeated motto, "IKEA strives to offer low prices, but not at any price."

The company's Swedish heritage is reflected in the extensive use of wood in its furnishings—in fact, 50% of the raw materials in its products are wood or wood fibers.

Because wood is renewable, recyclable, and biodegradable, IKEA considers it an environmentally sound raw material, provided it doesn't come from virgin or biodiverse forests. IKEA has a four-step model with increasingly rigorous environmental standards that its wood suppliers must meet. By 2009, IKEA wants all of its wood suppliers to meet the most basic minimum requirements and at least 30% to comply at the highest, or fourth, level of this sustainable model.

The minimum requirements include not using wood sourced from protected or threatened areas. Mahogany is never used, for example. Suppliers must declare where the trees are grown, and the wood must be produced in compliance with local forest regulations. IKEA has worked with the nonprofit organization Global Forest Watch to map intact natural forests so they can avoid buying timber logged in those areas.

Fourth-level standards, the highest, add many other criteria. Most important is the requirement that the supplier achieve certification from the Forest Stewardship Council, an organization that has created a system for ensuring sustainably managed forests. IKEA forestry specialists educate and work with suppliers to help them meet the criteria. They also conduct audits of the wood supply chain to ensure compliance.

IKEA's long-term goal is to source all of its wood from suppliers meeting the most stringent standards, but there

OPPOSITE: IKEA's Lack side tables are made from recycled wood waste.

are hurdles. IKEA requires its suppliers to provide documentation to show that the wood has been properly and legally harvested, but even with audits, not every piece of wood can be individually tracked. IKEA is working with the World Wildlife Fund, which has an extensive network of local contacts and knowledge in forest-rich countries such as Russia and China, to find long-term solutions to the problem.

IKEA applies another set of criteria to its more than 1,350 suppliers in Europe, Asia, and North America that manufacture its products. Called IWAY, short for the IKEA Way of Purchasing Home Furnishing Products, the criteria relate to both environmental and social goals, including ground contamination, waste, water and air pollution, child labor laws, and worker safety. Potential IKEA suppliers are audited first to ensure they meet IWAY standards. The audits include facility tours, employee interviews, and document reviews. The rules applying to transport companies, for example, include standards about the age of vehicles, type of fuels used, and requirements that drivers receive training in fuel-efficient driving techniques. Suppliers are audited at least every two years.

IKEA's internal operations are also evaluated regularly for their energy efficiency and environmental impact. For IKEA, smart packaging is one of the most effective ways to reduce the environmental impact of transporting products long distances. IKEA distributes most of its furniture in flat packs (that's why you often have to assemble it yourself) so that more goods fit on the truck or ship. But not all IKEA products can be disassembled. Conventional watering cans, for example, with their large hollow cores and long spouts, are bulky and uneconomical to transport. So IKEA designed a can that is stackable, reducing fuel usage and lowering greenhouse gas emissions and carbon dioxide emissions. IKEA employees are always on the lookout for potential energy savings. One observant employee noticed that the packing box for IKEA's largest sofa was three centimeters wider than the sofa itself. By reducing the box size by just one centimeter, IKEA is able to fit four extra sofas on each trailer.

Efficient use of resources is one of IKEA's guiding principles. Its Eden table uses heartwood, the innermost part of the tree trunk, which is usually discarded. Its Ivar chair comes unpainted, both to offer flexibility to the customer and to ensure that any wood left over in production can be used for other pieces of furniture. IKEA's Lack coffee table has legs made from recycled wood waste. In 2006, IKEA recycled or reclaimed 86% of the waste in its distribution centers; for 2009 the goal is 90%.

The IKEA PS Gulholmen rocking chair, designed by Maria Vinka, is made from woven banana leaves, a natural material once considered a waste product. It's stackable to save space, both in transport and in the home.

Even IKEA customers are encouraged to think about how their behavior affects the environment. Less than 1% of polyethylene plastic bags used in the United States are recycled nationally; these bags can take decades to decompose in a landfill. Though the company sells reusable, recyclable blue bags, IKEA customers in the United States were taking home over 70 million plastic bags annually. So in 2007, IKEA started charging five cents for each plastic bag dispensed in its 29 American stores. The company projects that this will reduce the number of plastic bags used by its customers by at least 50% in the first year. In the United Kingdom, where the program was started in 2006, plastic bag usage was reduced 95%. Proceeds from the campaign, up to $1.25 million, go to American Forests, a nonprofit conservation organization, to plant trees to offset carbon dioxide emissions.

IKEA has been stocking compact fluorescent lightbulbs (CFLs), which use 80% less energy than standard incandescent bulbs, for over 10 years, although initially they were not popular because of the quality of the light they shed. In recent years, technical improvements have made the light warmer and softer. Not only do the bulbs use less energy, they last up to ten times longer. Though the bulbs cost slightly more than incandescent bulbs, the CFL's longer life span and reduced energy usage translate into a $30 savings over the bulb's lifetime as well as a reduced environmental impact. Because the bulbs contain trace amounts of mercury, Ikea began a recycling program for them in 2001 in all of its stores. After the mercury is separated, it is reused. IKEA stores also offer recycling bins for CFLs, batteries, and other waste.

Boiled in Oil

Rattan furniture is a popular mainstay in the IKEA product line, but customers occasionally complained that items stored inside rattan chests came out smelling like diesel. Warehouse workers also noticed the smell when they opened packing containers of rattan furniture. When IKEA employees investigated, they learned that rattan is boiled in diesel oil to make it more pliable and easy to weave. All rattan factories used this technique, including IKEA's supplier in Vietnam. IKEA worked with the supplier to try new, more environmentally appropriate solutions, including salt and water and coconut oil, among others. Eventually, someone suggested palm oil. At a strength of three parts water to one part palm oil, the method worked. Malaysian suppliers produce the palm oil from trees harvested from old plantations, so production of the oil doesn't endanger tropical forests. The result is a more eco-friendly manufacturing process, happier factory workers who no longer have to endure the smell of diesel fumes, and more natural-smelling furniture.

Vital Statistics

Main site: Delft, Sweden
Main product: Home furnishings and accessories
Number of employees: 110,000
Green partner: World Wildlife Fund
Success: Tremendous growth globally: 19.8 billion euros in 2007 from 5.4 billion in 1997 • Supports initiatives to benefit children and the environment, including UNICEF, Save the Children, and American Forests
Challenge: Keeping prices affordable
Awards: *BusinessWeek*'s list of the Best Global Brands • *Fast Company*'s Fast 50 • *Fortune* magazine's 100 Best Companies to Work For • Foreign Policy Association Award for Global Corporate Social Responsibility

Sustainability Through Innovation

Intel's co-founder Gordon Moore likes to work with clear, scientifically measurable goals. Moore's foundation, the Gordon and Betty Moore Foundation, has chosen saving Northwest salmon as one of its major causes. Salmon can be counted as they migrate to and from their breeding and feeding grounds, and when you can count something, you can measure its progress.

For four decades the company has used "relentless innovation" to invent computer chips that are faster, smaller, more energy-efficient, and more environmentally friendly. Since the company's early days (it was founded in 1968), Moore's standards-based approach and environmental values have been applied to the company's manufacturing processes. For instance, environmental engineers work together with the engineers who are planning how to manufacture new products, in the earliest stages of product development, to make sure performance goals for water, waste, energy use, and chemical emissions are built into the manufacturing process.

More recently, the company has focused on the "big footprint" implications (water, waste, and energy) of the products themselves. Intel's primary products are ones that most people never see: the silicon-based microprocessor chips that are the brains of the computer, store high-resolution photos in the digital camera, and tell the online vendor what items are to be purchased.

Zoom in on an Intel chip and you are looking at etched pathways, just nanometers thick, that guide electrons along their paths. Each dual-core chip contains millions of transistors—about 400 million, to be exact—that control the flow of electrons on their way. As electrons move through the chip they leak a tiny bit of energy; multiply that by hundreds of millions and you're talking about a huge amount of energy from a chip about the size of a dime. Their movement also generates heat, which keeps the chips from performing at their best. When chips get too hot, the electrons dance around and can't do their jobs efficiently, like young children who can't focus on their homework.

Energy efficiency—keeping the electrons cool, calm, and on task—is important for performance as well as for the environment. Intel scientists' and engineers' focus on efficiency has resulted in the company's newest generation of chips, designed to incorporate many energy-saving ideas, including what Moore calls the biggest breakthrough in chip manufacturing in 40 years, the Hi-k silicon technology.

OPPOSITE: This multimillion-dollar evaporator system is capable of treating more than 200,000 gallons of water a day for reuse and recycling. The company now reclaims more than 3 billion gallons of wastewater each year.

The Hi-k technology stops those hundreds of millions of transistors on each chip from leaking power. Transistors can then be placed closer together, paving the way for smaller, more powerful and energy-efficient chips. The focus on energy has resulted in many other energy-saving innovations. One example is "power gating"— circuits that power off when they are not needed. Another innovation limits how many pixels get updated when a displayed page refreshes; only pixels that have changed need to be refreshed. Yet another involves the threshold of transistors: new materials need less voltage to turn on each transistor.

Taken together, these advances in chip design, though invisible to the naked eye, produce huge energy savings—about 40% over earlier models. Intel's success means quieter desktop computers that can run several programs at once and play fast-paced video games with thrillingly detailed graphics, all while saving energy and fitting on denser, tinier circuitry. "Moore's Law is alive and well in the 21st century," the company says, referring to the trend, observed in 1965 by Gordon Moore, that because of relentless innovation, the number of transistors that can fit on a chip will double every 18 months.

Intel says that a devotion to environmental sustainability was built into the company's foundation by Moore. However, environmental initiatives have been ratcheted up in recent years. The company's new chip fabrication plant in Arizona, nicknamed Fab 32, is an example of what can be accomplished. The plant is producing the first generation of chips that are completely free of two environmental toxins, lead and halogenated flame retardants. Removing these toxic materials from the manufacturing process took ten long years of engineering work.

Fab 32 also uses new water conservation and water recycling ideas that allow about 70% of water discharged in the plant to be reused—important in drought-prone Arizona. Through water conservation practices, the company claims to have saved over 9 billion gallons of fresh water. More than 70% of chemical and solid waste is currently recycled as well, and the company is working on improving those numbers. The Fab 32 plant also produces 15% less greenhouse gas emissions per chip compared with older facilities. And though it may not have direct economic benefit, Intel will seek LEED certification for the facility.

In the past, Intel plants have not always been so light on the environment. In New Mexico, water activists accused the company of "pumping the reservoir dry" with a facility that uses 1.5 billion gallons of water each year. So for the past several years, Intel has facilitated the Community Environmental Working Group, led by a local environmental activist and made up of community members who have been involved in environmental improvements at the factory. The group has also worked to create a Xeriscape nature walk along the eastern slope of the Intel site in Rio Rancho, including a 2,300-foot meandering path that offers panoramic views of the Sandia Mountains and the Rio Grande River Valley. In 2006, the company dedicated $2 million to improved water management at facilities in several cities.

Thousands of Intel employees at Intel sites around the world perform volunteer work in more than 40 company-sponsored events each April in conjunction with Earth Day.

In recent years, the company has attacked waste and chiseled away at its carbon footprint in all corners of its manufacturing facilities, carrying out scores of projects to save energy. For instance, Intel has many processes that need both heating and cooling. These used to be done separately—heating by gas boilers and cooling by water evaporation. To increase efficiency, Intel has installed heat-capture systems: absorption chillers take heat out of air that needs to be cooled but then save that heat and use it where heating is needed. Not only does this innovation save energy, but also, since cooling is no longer done with evaporation, it saves precious water as well.

Intel has recently taken an increasingly public role in developing climate change solutions. Intel is a founding member, along with Google, of the Climate Savers

Computing Initiative, advocating for computer makers to set a highly efficient standard for computer power supplies. Intel conducts its own research on improving performance per watt in data centers and works with utilities such as Pacific Gas & Electric to encourage companies to use energy-efficient solutions. This has little to do with microprocessors but a lot to do with energy efficiency. In 2006, the company joined several organizations looking to hold down carbon use in order to fight climate change: the Chicago Climate Exchange, the Environmental Protection Agency's Climate Leaders, and the technology industry's Green Grid consortium, all organizations looking for solutions to the climate change challenge.

In February 2008, the EPA announced that Intel had become the largest purchaser of certified renewable energy credits (RECs) in the United States. Intel selected Sterling Planet, a leading supplier of renewable energy, to provide it with power from solar, wind, hydroelectric, landfill-gas-to-energy technologies, and biomass projects. Intel's purchase of 1.3 billion kilowatt-hours annually is the estimated equivalent of removing 185,000 cars from the road per year.

Waste Not, Want Not

One of Intel's ideas was to examine its waste. How many chemicals escaped its plants? How much water was lost? How much solid waste got thrown away? One part of the waste stream that Intel examined was its product packaging. New handling equipment eliminated the need for 4,000 wooden pallets each year, plus the bulk and fuel needed to ship those pallets. A more compact packaging design saved thousands of pounds of cardboard and plastic. For products that needed to be cushioned, Intel changed from nonrecyclable polyurethane foam to a recyclable type of foam. No detail is too small: Intel's packaging team reduced the thickness of the protective plastic wrap that covers new products for shipping by 1/10 of a millimeter, and saved 18,000 pounds of plastic a year.

Intel hosts a recycling event in New York City's Union Square.

Vital Statistics

Main site: Santa Clara, California
Main product: Microprocessors
Number of employees: 85,000
Success: Recycling more than 70% of waste materials worldwide • Reusing billions of gallons of water at chip facility in Arizona
Challenge: Driving for smaller footprint in spite of manufacturing growth
Awards: #5 on Best Corporate Citizen list—*Business Ethics* and *CRO* magazine • Dow Jones Sustainability World Index • 100 Global Most Sustainable Corporations in the World—Corporate Knights and Innovest • EPA's Best Workplaces for Commuters from the Fortune 500 Companies • Prime Minister's Hibiscus Award for Environmental Performance (Intel Malaysia)

Taking Sustainability Higher Than Everest

Interface®

Interface Corporation, the world's largest producer of modular carpet products, was a typical energy- and resource-intensive manufacturing business in the decades after Ray C. Anderson founded it in 1973. Then in 1994 Anderson had what he calls "an epiphany," an event that ultimately led him to become a fierce champion of sustainability. Asked by an internal task force to present his environmental vision for Interface, Anderson found inspiration in a book he happened upon, Paul Hawken's *The Ecology of Commerce.* Anderson admits that before reading the book, he hadn't given much thought to his company's relationship with the natural ecosystem. But as he read, he became convinced that he must transform not only Interface but the larger industrial world as well.

"We pass this way only once," says Ray Anderson. "We can leave the earth better off or worse by our individual or collective actions. It's that simple. We can help or we can hurt the earth and future generations. Which will it be?"

Today Anderson is a highly recognized and influential leader in sustainability, and his Georgia-based company, with over $1 billion in sales in 2006, has achieved an impressive record of environmental success. His involvement spurred a collective effort from many Interface associates who are themselves recognized experts in sustainability. In 1997, Interface was the first company in the world to publish a corporate sustainability report, something an estimated 70% of Fortune 500 companies now do. The EPA gave Interface its Climate Protection Award in 2004 for its efforts that include an innovative program called Trees for Travel, which has offset the equivalent of 93 million air travel miles by planting over 62,000 trees. Since 1996, Interface has reduced its greenhouse gas emissions by 60% through improved efficiencies and the use of renewable energy. The company's environmental awards are too numerous to list.

Executives at Interface attribute their accomplish-

OPPOSITE: Ray C. Anderson, visionary founder of Interface, Inc.

ments to a systems-based approach to building a sustainable business. Given the global company's diversification and growth (the business has manufacturing sites on 4 continents and sales locations in over 100 countries), a corporate-wide strategic plan is necessary to reach its goal of Mission Zero, a promise to eliminate any negative impact on the earth by 2020. This translates to a tangible objective, which is to have 100% renewable energy and fuel by 2020 regardless of whether the renewables come from on-site or off-site sources. Ultimately, Interface wants to become not only the world's first sustainable corporation but also to be a "restorative enterprise," meaning that the company will have a positive impact on the rest of the industrial world through its example and influence. As a way to share the benefits of its discoveries and improvements, Interface has launched Interface-RAISE (www.interfaceraise.com), a consulting arm that helps other businesses develop sustainable business strategies.

The company is aware of its own ambitiousness, and it likens the challenge of achieving its goal to a journey up what it calls Mount Sustainability, a mountain that is "higher than Mount Everest." Interface has a seven-part framework (the seven faces of Mount Sustainability): (1) eliminating waste, (2) benign emissions, (3) renewable energy, (4) closing the loop, (5) resource-efficient transportation, (6) sensitizing shareholders, and (7) redesigning commerce.

Some of the seven fronts are similar to sustainability efforts at other companies, including eliminating waste and toxic emissions, using renewable energy, and transporting employees and products more efficiently. What sets Interface's efforts apart is its focus on monitoring and measuring its performance. For example, in 1997 Interface inventoried every smokestack and wastewater discharge point from each of its 37 facilities worldwide. Employees collected data on emissions stack by stack and pipe by pipe, and then set about making sure the emissions were lower than the most stringent pollution regulations. By 2006 Interface had reduced the overall air emissions from stacks by 42% and wastewater discharges by 68%, and employees are still working toward further improvements.

A less common approach to becoming sustainable is Interface's goal of "closing the loop." Typically, industrial systems are linear, take-make-waste systems that deplete natural resources and allow waste to accumulate in the environment. Interface wants to "close the loop" so that manufacturing uses fewer resources and becomes a cyclical material flow where waste from one process or product is "food" for another. One Interface strategy is to redesign production processes so less material is necessary; since 1994, the average weight of raw materials used to produce a square yard of carpet is down 7%.

Another "close the loop" strategy is to use more recycled material. Interface has gone from less than 0.5% recycled or bio-based material in 1995 to 20% in 2006. Its carpet recycling program, ReEntry, allows clients to recycle their used carpets at no charge. Since the program's beginning in 1994, Interface has diverted more than 66 million pounds of carpet from landfills. Interface uses the recycled material in a variety of ways, including to manufacture new carpet backing and to make postconsumer recycled nylon 66, both industry firsts. From the carpet reclaimed in 2004, 60% was recycled and 37% was used for energy capture and conversion. This means the carpet unsuitable for recycling or repurposing was incinerated at a facility that creates steam for

Interface has helped fund the construction of a wind turbine in Karnataka in Southern India.

other manufacturing groups. The remaining 3% was re-purposed, meaning it was reinstalled, usually in the form of a donation to a nonprofit organization.

Another innovative approach is Interface's commitment to "redesign commerce" so that the company focuses on the delivery of service and value instead of material, a tall order for a manufacturing company. One step to meet that goal was the launch of the Evergreen Service Contract, the industry's first-ever carpet leasing program. Commercial clients with an Evergreen contract receive periodic changes of the carpet tile in high-traffic areas or in areas needing rejuvenation for other reasons. When possible, a combination of new and reused carpet can be used to reconfigure the space, which is both less costly and more environmentally sound than using all new carpet tiles. Another advantage is that Interface owns the carpet for its useful life, ensuring that it can be reused or recycled instead of ending up in a landfill.

Like every company, Interface must weigh the need to make capital investments in developing new sustainable technologies against shareholder expectations for financial performance. Although on-site renewable energy is not an option for all of Interface's facilities, the company has invested in on-site renewable energy at three of its sites: Bentley Prince Street; Interface FLOR in LaGrange, Georgia; and the Scherpenzeel facility in the Netherlands. When on-site renewable energy is cost-prohibitive, Interface purchases off-site renewable energy. Seven of its facilities are powered entirely by renewable energy.

Energizing People

The origins of Interface's stellar environmental track record can be traced to its visionary founder and chairman, Ray C. Anderson. But how does one man imbue a staff of 5,000 with that same zeal? He encouraged everyone to see change as a challenge and to let go of established behaviors. One effort to eliminate waste is an initiative, QUEST, which stands for Quality Utilizing Employee Suggestions and Teamwork. QUEST teams were established throughout the world to identify, measure, and eliminate waste streams. Team progress is communicated to all participants every month, which stimulates competition and spurs new ideas. One team at the company's Guilford, Maine, facility realized that they could reduce water consumption with the purchase of a simple brass nozzle. The nozzle, which cost $8.50, saved an estimated 2 million gallons of water each year. Another initiative is called the Global Sustainability Council and applies a cross-functional approach to solve sustainability challenges. This council is composed of employees from around the world in each of the basic units of the company—for example, sales, operations, human resources, and information technology. Meeting via videoconferencing or audio conferencing, this council sets priorities, makes strategic decisions, and shares best practices and learning company-wide.

Vital Statistics

Main site: Atlanta, Georgia
Main products: Modular carpet • Broadloom carpet
Number of employees: 4,873
Success: Market leader in attractive modular carpet segment
Challenge: Maximizing impact of company • Educating and empowering employees • Getting enough carpet back to the Cool Blue line for recycling • Feasibility of renewable energy for on-site projects • Driving the solar energy market to make solar energy more available and more affordable
Awards: *Business Ethics* 100 Best Corporate Citizens • EPA's Climate Protection Award

Green Jeans

The world has never been quite the same since Levi Strauss created the first pair of blue jeans in 1873. The San Francisco–based entrepreneur patented the idea of putting rivets on the pockets and at the base of the fly to make the jeans stronger for workingmen, and by 1890, when the pants became known as 501 jeans, an American icon had been born. Today, Strauss's descendants, who run the privately held company, take as much pride in its environmental stewardship as in its financial success.

Since 1991, when it created global sourcing and operating guidelines that included environmental provisions, Levi Strauss & Co. has taken many steps toward sustainability. But not until 2006 could it boast of offering an entirely sustainable blue jean.

Levi's Eco jean, sold in Europe, is made from 100% organic cotton. The buttons are crafted using coconut shells. The hanging price tag is made from postconsumer material. The rivets that made the 501 jeans famous have been replaced by reinforced stitching. And the jeans are finished using only natural compounds, including indigo, Marseille soap, potato starch, and mimosa flower. Eco jeans are sourced and manufactured in locations relatively close to one another, so the emissions caused by shipping are minimized. The cotton is from Turkey, most of the other components are sourced in Europe, and the jeans are manufactured in Hungary.

In the Hungarian factory, which produces a variety of Levi's products, a separate "factory within a factory" was created so that the Eco jean manufacturing process is as environmentally sound as the materials are. Equipment was thoroughly cleaned so the organic cotton wouldn't be tainted by conventionally grown cotton, and employees were trained on the importance of controlling the production areas to make sure less sustainable products and processes are kept out. As a result of all these efforts, the Levi's Eco jean was awarded the EKO Sustainable Textile certification from Control Union Certifications, a worldwide inspection organization for organic products.

Though not certified Sustainable like the European Eco jeans, other Levi's jeans made with organic cotton are available in the Americas and throughout Asia. The company continues to experiment with fits and finishes

OPPOSITE: The European Eco jean is made entirely of certified sustainable materials.

using organic cotton, and it is also expanding to include new fibers and blends made with recycled materials.

Levi Strauss & Co. is focusing on the manufacturing process as a key area for improvement. Dyeing, rinsing, bleaching, and cleaning fabric produces large volumes of wastewater. With factories and suppliers in Asia, Europe, and North America, company executives knew it was important to create a single set of wastewater guidelines that applied to all contractors. In 1995, Levi Strauss was the first in the apparel business to apply wastewater quality guidelines that its suppliers must meet in order to do business with the company. The Global Effluent Guidelines (GEG) are targeted primarily at laundries and finishing facilities that discharge wastewater directly into a natural body of water, although there are also rules for factories sending water to wastewater treatment facilities.

Wastewater must meet the stricter of either local antipollution requirements or GEG requirements. Suppliers are required to conduct tests to confirm compliance with the requirements using a lab that they may choose. Sampling and analysis procedures vary widely, however, so in 2006, Levi Strauss & Co. performed its own validation study on 113 laundries and 9 fabric mills that discharge wastewater directly into the environment. More than half were in full compliance, but results from the others indicated that improvement was necessary. In 2007, the company dispatched teams to work directly on-site with suppliers who needed help to satisfy the GEG. In addition to helping the company target specific contractors, the validation study provided a consistent data set that is being used to set baseline standards against which future improvements can be measured.

Contractors doing business with Levi Strauss & Co. are also required to abstain from using materials listed on the company's restricted-substance list. Certain dyes, flame retardants, and metals are among the substances banned. The list, compiled with the help of experts in toxicology, dermatology, chemistry, regulatory research, and law, is one of the few science-based and peer-reviewed lists that exist for apparel manufacturers. Levi Strauss & Co. shares it with other multinational clothing and footwear brands so that best practices can be exchanged and improved.

In 2007, company employees began compiling data on the environmental impact of certain best-selling items. A particular type of jeans, for example, would be assessed from the cotton field to the emissions and waste caused by the production and transportation of the pants, consumer use and care, and finally disposal. Armed with the data, executives can target improvements where they will yield the greatest environmental benefit. When a product life cycle assessment was completed for the stonewashed 501 jeans, for example, executives learned that the most significant energy savings to be gained was from educating consumers about caring for their jeans. Company calculations show that warm-water washing and machine drying uses 16 times more energy than cold-water washing and line drying. New care labels on the jeans will instruct customers to use the more sustainable laundering methods.

Also in 2007, the company turned its attention to measuring greenhouse gas emissions. Although apparel manufacturing isn't as energy intensive as other industries, company executives recognized that with more than 10,000 employees and a business presence in over 110 countries, there was room for improvement. A greenhouse gas emissions inventory was performed for all facilities in North and South America, including head-

Levi Strauss & Co. employees plant trees with Friends of the Urban Forest in San Francisco.

quarters, distribution centers, retail stores, and sales offices. The data was independently verified and will be used to set a baseline against which future emissions reduction goals and progress can be measured. The same process is planned for other parts of the world. When the research is completed in 2008, Levi Strauss & Co. will develop a comprehensive environmental strategy with clearly stated targets for improvement.

Partnerships with outside organizations will help the company learn from other businesses. Levi's is working with Business for Social Responsibility to share its GEG experience with other apparel companies, and it recently joined the Green Power Market Development Group of the World Resources Institute, a collaboration of 12 corporations interested in building markets for renewable energy sources.

Every Little Bit Counts

When John Anderson became chief executive officer at Levi Strauss & Co. in 2006, he brought his own management style to the executive suite at headquarters in San Francisco, including replacing bottled water with pitchers of filtered water. The company veteran, who has been with the business since 1979, wanted to reduce the negative environmental impacts caused by manufacturing, transporting, and disposing of plastic water bottles.

The company's Community Involvement Team responded to their new boss by launching a campaign to reduce the usage of plastic water bottles at its headquarters. They talked with employees in the facilities department, who worked to ensure that the building's water filtering system was large enough to offer filtered drinking water to all employees at headquarters. Facilities personnel also negotiated with the vending machine supplier to remove bottled water from on-site machines. The cafeteria phased it out as well, and within a few weeks bottled water was not available anywhere in the headquarters. Working together, employees had eliminated the waste caused by the annual consumption of over 2,500 cases of bottled water.

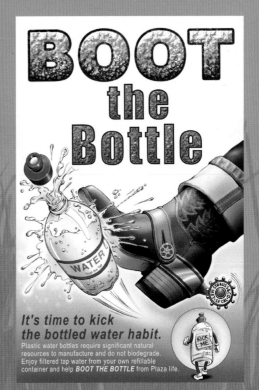

It's time to kick the bottled water habit.
Plastic water bottles require significant natural resources to manufacture and do not biodegrade. Enjoy filtered tap water from your own refillable container and help *BOOT THE BOTTLE* from Plaza life.

Vital Statistics

Main site: San Francisco, California
Main products: Jeans and casual sportswear • Levi's, Dockers, and Levi Strauss Signature brands
Number of employees: 11,000
Green partners: Business for Social Responsibility • Green Power Market Development Group of the World Resources Institute
Success: Developing wastewater guidelines for all contractors
Challenge: Building on the Eco jean to produce a wider range of ecologically sustainable fabrics

The Makers of Big Mac
Try to Make More with Less

European consumers have historically rejected genetically modified foods, so fast-food giant McDonald's turned to naturally grown soy to feed chickens that would eventually become McNuggets in its European stores. The soy was grown for Cargill, a McDonald's supplier, in the interior of the Amazon rain forest after massive clear-cutting by farmers. When Greenpeace saw satellite maps in 2003 that showed the scale of Amazon deforestation, they staged protests at McDonald's outlets in Europe, posted an article titled "McAmazon" ("Whatever the fast food giant wants you to believe the golden arches stand for, McDonald's today stands for rain-forest destruction"), and blocked Cargill's port city of San-tarem, Brazil. The surprising end result: Greenpeace and McDonald's are now partners in enforcing a moratorium on soy farming in the Amazon.

"We listened to what Greenpeace was saying about soy from the rain forest, and I think we surprised them by saying, 'You're right. We have a problem here,' " said Bob Langert, McDonald's vice president for corporate social responsibility, who has worked at McDonald's since 1983. "We have a firm policy against using beef—or any other products—that come from the rain forest. So when we learned that some of our soy was coming from there, we got involved."

John Sauven, head of Greenpeace's rain-forest initiative, was pleasantly surprised: "We didn't start out with the idea of focusing on McDonald's or partnering with them, and someday we may well go after them again on other issues. But on this one, they played a highly positive role." On July 25, 2006, four months after its "McAmazon" campaign, Greenpeace published "McVictory" on its website with a picture of Ronald McDonald hugging a tree, declaring, "McDonald's is now the leading company in the campaign for a moratorium on the expansion of soya farming in the Amazon."

OPPOSITE: McDonald's works with its suppliers to develop and implement programs in keeping with its social, environmental, and animal welfare guidelines.

In 2001, McDonald's worked with Conservation International to develop an evaluation tool that rates fisheries for sustainability. Since implementing the program, one-third of annual purchases have been shifted to more sustainable sources.

McDonald's, with revenues of $21.5 billion and net income of $3.5 billion in 2006, already had a no-rainforest-production policy for beef, which is one reason it was able to react so quickly on the soy issue.

McDonald's is no stranger to this sort of odd bedfellow partnerships. As far back as 1989, McDonald's and Environmental Defense entered a landmark alliance. That year, McDonald's printed its annual report on paper recycled from its own products. The partnership began with a six-month joint review of McDonald's practices. Within three months, McDonald's stopped packaging its sandwiches in polystyrene boxes. McDonald's was one of the first Fortune 500 companies to study the issue of sustainability and to set goals that it has continued to meet.

"The cooperative approach pioneered by the Environmental Defense Fund and McDonald's laid the foundation for an entirely new approach to solving environmental problems," said Richard Vietor, professor of environmental management at Harvard Business School, on the occasion of the 10th anniversary of the partnership in 1999. "[They] showed both business and environmental activists that sometimes they can share the path toward a more sustainable society."

Most of the environmental gains made by McDonald's have been in the areas of packaging, waste reduction, and recycling. Some 83% of McDonald's 330 unique packaging designs are now made from paper or wood fiber material, with only 17% from less environmentally desirable thermoplastics.

McDonald's is also working to eliminate unnecessary packaging (it reduced the amount used in its U.S. french fry boxes by 1,100 tons in 2005 and in 2007 light-weighted its 32-ounce polypropylene cup, saving 650 tons of resin per year), increase the content of recycled paper and compostable products, and support sustainable forests. It is a member of the Paper Working Group, one of 11 major companies working to increase the availability and affordability of environmentally preferable paper products. The company is still working to increase the amount of postconsumer recycled paper—recycled paper with the highest environmental benefit—in its packaging, beyond the 33% level it reached in 2006.

To reduce its greenhouse gas emissions McDonald's recently embarked on a long-term plan to reduce its carbon footprint through aggressive energy efficiency programs. Electricity in company-owned restaurants accounts for 98% of McDonald's direct GHG emissions (with hydrofluorocarbons from refrigerants making up the remaining 2%). One priority is more efficient HVAC systems, which account for 30%–40% of energy consumption. Another is remodeling restaurants to conserve energy, with more insulation in roofs to prevent heat loss, awnings over dining areas to reduce direct sun and, subsequently, the need for air-conditioning, and exploring the possibility of building all of its new restaurants to Leadership in Energy and Environmental Design (LEED)–certification standards. The company took a first step in this direction in 2006 by building a LEED-certified restaurant in Savannah, Georgia.

Another daunting challenge for McDonald's is incorporating sustainability throughout its massive global supply chain. Many of its vendors are small, while some are large multinational corporations in their own right; some are dependent on McDonald's, and others serve multiple clients. As a result, the company's leverage to force change in the way suppliers use water, energy, and packaging varies. But McDonald's is starting at the top with the largest suppliers, such as its principal packaging supplier, Perseco, with whom it has developed environmental guidelines for consumer packaging.

On another supply chain front, McDonald's has made measurable progress in supporting sustainable fisheries. In 2000, McDonald's learned from suppliers of its Filet-O-

Fish sandwich that catches were declining and not sustainable. Government quotas were becoming stricter and illegal markets were growing. Overfishing was a threat to fish stocks and fishers' livelihoods, as well as a threat to McDonald's supply chain. In 2001, McDonald's worked with Conservation International (CI) to develop an evaluation tool to rate fisheries for sustainability. Since implementing the program, 18,000 metric tons representing one-third of annual purchases have been shifted to more sustainable sources.

CI also helped McDonald's develop an Environmental Scorecard with key suppliers of potatoes, poultry, pork, beef, and buns to measure water use, energy consumption, solid waste production, and greenhouse gas emissions. In the first year of the pilot program, measuring 2004 against 2003 indicators, suppliers reported the most dramatic gains in reduced water use—56% for beef production, 30% for bun production, and 18% for pork production. In an attempt to formalize procedures and replicate this success in other arenas, McDonald's formed an internal Sustainable Supply Chain Working Group (SSCWG) in January 2007. Says CI's John Buchanan: "McDonald's is clearly ahead of the pack in the restaurant category, and in the broader area of food and agriculture, they are one of the leaders." Nonetheless, while the company is moving in the right direction, it is well aware that to achieve sustainability across its supply chain and in all its restaurants more work needs to be done.

Cooking Oil: As Good as Petroleum?

The cooking oil McDonald's uses in its U.K. restaurants is being recycled as fuel for its fleet of 155 trucks. The move will put more than 6 million liters of waste oil to use and cut McDonald's U.K. carbon emissions by 75% (1,675 tons), the equivalent of taking 2,400 cars off the road per year. The fuel is composed of 85% waste cooking oil and 15% pure rapeseed oil. McDonald's has already switched its fleet in Austria to biodiesel made from waste cooking oil. If McDonald's can't use all its waste oil, surely someone else can—perhaps a commodity in search of a market?

Vital Statistics

Main site: Oak Brook, Illinois	
Main product: Global quick service restaurants	
Number of employees: 390,000 (2007)	
Green partners: Enivronmental Defense • Greenpeace • Conservational International	
Success: No-rainforest-production policies for soy and beef • Building sustainable fisheries	
Challenge: Incorporating sustainablility throughout its giant global supply chain	

Paper Made with Wind: A Leading Industrial Purchaser of Wind Power

MOHAWK
manufactured with windpower

With green power driving the mills, and the purchase of carbon emission reduction credits to offset thermal energy, Mohawk's next hurdle is to buy all its pulp from sustainable forests certified by the Forest Stewardship Council. Historically, paper mills have been the single largest industrial consumer of water and among the largest emitters of greenhouse gases. That convinced Mohawk Fine Papers, a New York–based, independent paper manufacturer–makers of Strathmore, Beckett, and Mohawk brand papers–to green its business. But it has also been pressured by consumers and environmental organizations.

According to George Milner, senior vice president of energy, environmental and governmental affairs, "These are issues of paramount importance to our customers.

Many are asking themselves, What will it mean to do business in a carbon-constrained world that is undergoing rapid climate change? They want assurances that their suppliers are acting in a responsible manner. In our case, they want to know the sources of our fiber, the size of our carbon footprint, and other significant environmental aspects, such as the quantity of water we consume, the quality of our wastewater discharges, and our waste-disposal practices."

In response, Mohawk can say it is one of the nation's largest industrial consumers of wind energy, buying 100 million kilowatt-hours annually (equivalent to taking more than 11,000 cars off the road each year), which is more than enough to power operations at its three mills. The mills themselves are not directly powered by wind, but Mohawk buys wind-generated power from the electricity grid. The wind-generated power Mohawk buys is sent to the grid, displacing an equivalent amount of power that otherwise would be generated with fossil fuel. The purchases put Mohawk in a league with companies and organizations such as PepsiCo, Whole Foods Market, the World Bank, and the U.S. Air Force. In 2007, the EPA presented Mohawk with a 2007 Green Power Leadership Award for helping to advance the development of the nation's green power market.

In addition to buying renewable energy credits (monitored through the Kyoto Protocol), Mohawk buys verified

OPPOSITE: At Mohawk's Beckett Mill, bales of paper are stacked and ready to be recycled back into the paper-making process.

emissions reduction credits (monitored by the Environmental Resources Trust) to offset the emissions resulting from its consumption of thermal energy, such as the natural gas fired in its boilers for paper manufacturing. The use of these offsets qualifies premium papers such as Strathmore and Beckett lines as carbon-neutral. Currently, 7 of Mohawk's 18 product lines are carbon neutral. Thermal energy is direct energy created during the manufacturing process, as opposed to the indirect energy used to fire the boilers. All paper materials promoting the 2007 Emmy Awards were printed on a mix of Mohawk's carbon-neutral papers.

Between 2001 and 2006, Mohawk reduced its electricity consumption per ton by 14%. It should see more gains due to a switch from steam to natural-gas-fired boilers, which reduces both energy consumption and emissions. The company, however, unlike many public companies, does not publicly set benchmarks for future environmental goals.

Mohawk's recycled papers made from postconsumer waste are process-chlorine-free, either unbleached or bleached without chlorine. Recycled paper has multiple benefits, such as saving trees and reducing waste, although the virgin fiber may have originally been processed with chlorine compounds. To date, Mohawk does not produce any papers that are totally chlorine-free (TCF), which is FSC's highest processing standard.

Mohawk has also taken steps to support sustainable forestry. The Forest Stewardship Council, which works to recognize acceptable sources of wood products worldwide, certifies papers according to their source and manufacturing process. To earn FSC certification, a product made with pulp or paper must pass through a complete "chain of custody" from an FSC-certified forest to an FSC-certified paper maker. FSC has three basic labels: FSC Pure (100% virgin fiber from FSC-certified forests); FSC Mixed Sources (fiber from FSC-certified forests along with other fiber); and FSC Recycled (100% of fiber from postconsumer waste). Several Mohawk papers earn either FSC's Mixed Sources or Recycled labels, but none earns the top label of FSC Pure.

Another challenge for Mohawk is using pulps that are totally chlorine-free. Traditionally in paper making,

The Concept paper from Mohawk is luxurious and is also made carbon-neutral within production processes.

elemental chlorine is used in the manufacture of pulp to whiten and brighten the fiber. TCF pulps are not readily available nor is there a sufficient supply of FSC-certified fiber to meet all of the company's needs. However, Mohawk does not source fibers that are bleached with elemental chlorine, the least desirable form of bleaching, nor does it use non-FSC-certified fibers that come from controversial sources as defined by FSC policy. This is accomplished through extensive supplier surveys. The postconsumer recovered fiber used in recycled grades is processed without the use of chlorine compounds, thereby making their 100% postconsumer grades process chlorine-free (PCF).

Clearly, Mohawk has made great strides over the past two decades. It was the first paper company to introduce a postconsumer recycled coated paper in 1991, and the first paper company to use wind power for manufacturing. In 2007, Mohawk's fleet of five trucks was converted to a biodiesel fuel mix, which reduces emissions, and it offsets corporate fleet mileage (company trucks plus rental and lease cars) through NativeEnergy's Wind-Builder program.

"We continually seek ways to expand our sustainable practices," says Tom O'Connor, chairman and CEO. "We're acutely aware that, as a paper manufacturer, we are part of an industry that depends heavily on energy, water, and other natural resources in the production of ephemeral, nondurable goods. Because of this, over two decades ago we embraced the concept of extended stewardship, meaning that we continually examine every aspect of our business with the objective of making our environmental footprint as small as possible. By investing in wind energy we are aiding the growth of this emission-free energy alternative."

Calculating the Benefits of Recycled Paper Made by Wind

Mohawk provides an environmental calculator on its website that shows how much waste and energy are saved by using selected recycled papers. Conversions are provided by Environmental Defense and/or the EPA. Using the calculator, the company claims that 100,000 copies of a typical 10-K company report printed on Mohawk Options Smooth, 100% postconsumer waste cream white paper (101,000 sheets or 14,140 pounds)—rather than an equivalent grade made from virgin fiber and produced with nonrenewable energy—generates environmental benefits equivalent to:

- Not driving 7,070 miles in an average vehicle
- 12,562 pounds net greenhouse gases prevented
- 96,152,000 BTUs of energy not consumed
- 6,830 pounds of solid waste not generated
- 135.74 trees preserved
- 57,661 gallons wastewater flow saved
- 391.97 pounds of waterborne waste not generated

Mohawk buys 100 million kilowatt-hours of wind power each year.

Vital Statistics

Main site: Cohoes, New York	
Main product: Premium printing, writing, and digital papers	
Number of employees: 750	
Green partners: Green Seal • Green-e • FSC • Clean Air–Cool Planet • EPA Climate Leaders • EPA Green Power Partnership • EPA Climate Track	
Success: Reduced electric consumption per ton of paper produced by 14% • Reduced thermal energy consumption per ton of paper produced by 8%	
Challenge: Securing adequate supplies of environmentally preferable raw materials, such as FSC-certified fiber and high-quality postconsumer waste fiber	
Awards: EPA Performance Track • EPA Climate Leaders program • EPA Green Power Partner of the Year	

A Reluctant Start Yields to a Central Role for Climate Change

national**grid**

National Grid's environmental programs have grown over the past few years like kudzu. The international electricity transmission and gas company's green efforts now range from managing the landscape and ecosystems that transmission lines run through to limiting its own carbon footprint and encouraging customers to use energy efficiently, saving them hundreds of millions of dollars on their energy bills.

Yet when first developing its corporate policy on climate change just a few years ago, National Grid seemed hesitant to admit the connection between humans and global warming. The company's policy statements minced words about how "the climate of our planet is constantly changing," even while admitting that the "rate of change" was being affected by "a rise in the concentration of certain gases...released as a result of human activity." Still, however cautious it may have been, once the company put its toe in the river of environmental responsibility, it got swept away and is now a leading corporate voice for strong climate policies to curb global warming pollution.

"The energy industry has a vital role to play in climate change....It is therefore crucial that governments make an early start on the legal framework we need to make effective investment decisions," said National Grid chief executive, Steve Holliday, at the Bali Climate Change Conference treaty talks in December 2007 in urging governments to establish a strong regulatory regime to tackle climate change.

National Grid customers, numbering more than 3.4 million in the northeastern United States, can now get rebates for purchasing energy-efficient thermostats and hot-water heaters; the company will send a technician to customers' homes and businesses to test for leaks and conduct energy audits that identify where energy is escaping. Customers are flooded with information about energy-saving opportunities such as replacing incandescent lights with compact fluorescents, turning off computers, and unplugging chargers that are not in use. Such practices are paying big dividends. In Rhode Island alone, in 2006, energy conservation programs saved more than $53 million, reduced CO_2 emissions by over 3 million tons over the past 20 years, and eliminated the need to build two new power plants.

GreenUp, the company's renewable energy program, was ranked as one of the Department of Energy's National Renewable Energy Laboratory's top 10 renewable

OPPOSITE: National Grid linesmen working on restringing (replacing conductors) the company's electricity transmission network in the northeastern United States.

National Grid's electricity converter in Sellindge, Kent (Southeast England), which forms part of the undersea interconnection with France.

energy programs in the country, both by sales and by volume of participants (24,000 customers as of December 2006). GreenUp allows National Grid customers who are concerned about global warming pollution to choose to pay a small premium each month to receive electricity that comes from renewable sources such as wind, which is still more expensive to produce than electricity from coal-fired power plants. The GreenUp program, while helping to develop markets for renewable energy, also meshes well with legal requirements for utilities; the New England states in which National Grid operates, like more than 20 other states across the country, have adopted Renewable Portfolio Standards requiring that a portion of the electricity supplied by utilities come from renewable energy sources. The standards range from 3% (rising to 4%) in Massachusetts to a goal of 25% by 2013 in New York State, whose energy is already supplied by 19% renewable energy, mostly hydropower.

In January 2008, National Grid took a major step by dropping its objection in Rhode Island to signing long-term contracts with suppliers of renewable energy, a decision that advocates of wind farms say could unleash a flood of new wind proposals in the Ocean State. "I think it's an incredibly great development," said Cynthia Giles, director of the Conservation Law Foundation's Rhode Island Advocacy Center. "This is a big deal in encouraging private developers to come into the state." Environmentalists are looking for similar commitments from National Grid in other northeastern states.

National Grid has also been participating in the Regional Greenhouse Gas Initiative, a plan by the northeastern states to start a cap-and-trade system to reduce CO_2 emissions from the region's power plants. When the states first posted the rules for the cap-and-trade system in August 2007, National Grid's vice president for the environment, Joe Kwasnik, said, "We strongly support the transparent and equitable process of auctioning CO_2 allowances to fossil power generators, which will also provide needed revenues for investment in no- or low-carbon technology."

Deciding how to spend environmental resources in a $15 billion company is no small challenge: National Grid chose to adopt ISO 14001, an internationally accepted set of standards for companies seeking to minimize their environmental impact. The company set a goal of 60% greenhouse gas (GHG) emission reductions by 2050, in line with targets set by the British government (National Grid U.S. is a subsidiary of a British parent company). In 2007, National Grid announced that it had already achieved a 35% reduction in greenhouse gas emissions. The company announced that it was set to achieve the 60% emissions reduction well ahead of the target date.

The first level of GHG savings was attained largely by reducing methane leaks from gas pipelines through replacement. Methane is a greenhouse gas that is roughly 21 times more potent than CO_2. Plugging leaks in natural gas transmission lines is one of the strategies promoted by the EPA's energy-saving Gas STAR Program. Transmission lines cover more than a million miles in the United States alone, and lose more than 5 million metric tons of gas each year. At National Grid, pipeline gas leaks accounted for 57% of its direct emissions in 2006.

The company concedes that it expects to have a more difficult time controlling losses on transmission lines carrying electricity across long distances. Nationally, and partly due to laws of physics, long-distance transmission of electricity results in losses of more than 7% of the electricity transmitted. New "smart grid" technologies, which are information systems designed to keep better track of supply and demand so that power can be sent on the shortest routes from source to load, will help to raise efficiency. Innovative technology such as remote control thermostats also makes a difference in energy conservation.

Another near-term challenge for National Grid is to integrate Keyspan, a regional utility, whose $7.3 billion acquisition was completed in August 2007. The Keyspan acquisition is National Grid's fifth merger since it came into the U.S. market in 2000, and it means that National Grid now owns generating plants, which creates additional challenges for the company. As National Grid grows it will be increasingly difficult to maintain energy efficiency throughout its huge service territory while maintaining customer approval and support.

In 2007, National Grid issued its first U.S.-specific corporate responsibility report and declared that "respect and care for the environment are central to how we operate." Proclaiming climate change the most pressing challenge for the company and the world, National Grid pledged to deliver energy in a way that minimizes its impact on the environment; to increase its ability to supply clean, renewable energy; and to try and influence customers to make responsible energy choices. National Grid was a sponsor of a 2007 McKinsey Global Institute report, which concluded that energy efficiency has the potential to reduce U.S. energy-demand growth by the equivalent of 11 million barrels of oil a day and greenhouse gas emissions by 1.3 billion tons a year.

In 2007, the company received the Arbor Day Foundation's Tree Line USA award for the eighth year in a row. Its programs for trimming and maintaining trees along 12,200 circuit miles of electricity distribution lines, training workers to preserve and prune trees, and sponsoring public tree plantings are considered exemplary.

Innovation to Meet Energy Needs

National Grid took a big step toward its goal of obtaining all of its own energy from carbon-free renewable sources when it agreed to form a joint venture with U.K.-based 2OC (that's the formula for carbon dioxide backward), a start-up "geopressure" energy firm. The joint venture will use National Grid's pipelines to test the feasibility of generating energy by installing turbines at pressure reduction stations. Natural gas travels through long-distance pipelines at high pressure, which must be reduced before the gas can be delivered to customers. 2OC plans to install turbines at eight pilot sites, and start by generating up to 45 megawatts of electricity—enough to meet all the internal electricity needs at National Grid—using the energy created as the pressure is reduced. Steve Holliday, who plans to invest over $100 million in the project, said, "It's clear that for society to tackle climate change—and for us as a company to reduce our carbon footprint—we need to start thinking of new ways to meet our energy needs."

Vital Statistics

Main site: London, England
Main product: Electricity and natural gas delivery in the United States and United Kingdom
Number of employees: 18,000 in the United States (28,000 worldwide)
Green partner: 2OC
Success: GreenUp Renewable Energy Program
Challenge: Delivering high service standards to customers while addressing climate change
Awards: A+ rating—Roberts Environmental Center's Pacific Sustainability Index • Dow Jones Sustainability World Index • STOXX Index • Top performer in the 2007 Corporate Responsibility Index run by Business in the Community (U.K.)

The Sports Gear Giant Redesigns for Zero Waste

Chemicals, toxins, plastics, adhesives, gases, and glues are out. Hemp, organic cotton, recycled rubber, cork, and vegetable dyes are in. It's all part of Nike Considered design, an ethos embedded in all new products.

After years of controversy over sweatshop manufacturing and sulfur hexafluoride (SF_6), a noxious greenhouse gas that was the "air" in its Nike Air shoes, the Oregon-based company has assumed a leadership role in responsible environmental practices. In 2006, Nike ranked thirteenth on *Business Ethics* magazine's Best Corporate Citizens list, and first for its environmental programs, specifically its Nike Considered sustainable design platform.

Nike has given its footwear designers principal responsibility for integrating sustainability principles into its operations, but the Nike Considered team also includes chemists, biologists, and material specialists. For example, John R. Hoke III, Nike's vice president of footwear design, pushes his colleagues to use less energy and chemical content, and no glues, adhesives, or plastics. These parameters led to development of an innovative interlocking snap-fit system held together with organic cotton stitching. With Nike Considered design, the company looks to develop sustainable products from the ground up, using as many nontoxic and recyclable elements as possible, and producing as little waste as possible.

The first product from the Nike Considered shoe line was the Considered Boot in 2005, which uses hemp laces and molds to the owner's foot. The Soaker water shoe, introduced in 2007, uses snap-fit construction that requires less adhesive and uses recycled rubber in its sidewall and 100% recycled polyester laces. The Nike "long ball" lace shoes are made without any glues or chemicals, and the rubber has been replaced with cork, making the shoes completely biodegradable and 100% recyclable. In 2007, Considered design moved into Nike's All Conditions Gear line, and Nike has shared its plans to embed the Considered approach in all of its branded footwear by 2011.

The company is working to integrate sustainability through its design ethos from the conceptual stage: designing out problems and designing in solutions from the start. Sometimes this focus on sustainability can provide true business innovation. Nike's air-bag technology is a good example. Nike cut from its design SF_6 after learning of its impact on the climate and dedicated years of work to ensure athletic performance was not compromised. At its peak in 1997, Nike shoes containing air bags emitted

OPPOSITE: The Nike Considered line utilizes materials found primarily within 200 miles of the Nike factory, which reduces the energy used for transportation, diminishing the resulting climate change impact.

more than 6 million metric tons of carbon dioxide, a primary global warming pollutant. After 14 years of research, a team of designers and scientists were finally able to eliminate all fluorinated gases by pressing together 65 wafer-thin layers of plastic film and applying a new thermoforming manufacturing technique, melting the plastic into the right shape. The resultant seal was so tight and strong that it could be applied across the whole sole of the shoe rather than just the air pocket. The development led to the Nike Air Max 360, which the company calls the "ultimate expression of Nike Air technology" and the "most significant innovation since we began incorporating pressurized cushioning to shoes in 1978."

"We wanted to do the right thing for the environment and the athlete, but we wondered if the two could ever be harmonious," says Tom Hartge, Nike's global running brand director, who was product manager for running shoes as the company navigated new F-gas-free designs.

While incorporating fewer and greener materials into design is critical to its sustainability strategy, Nike also believes its Considered ethos will appeal to retailers and consumers alike. About 70% of the materials currently used in Nike footwear are considered environmentally preferable to traditional materials. By 2011, the company

hopes to increase that amount to 84%. As part of this effort, Nike expects to increase its use of environmentally preferred rubber, which contains 96% fewer toxins by weight than traditional rubber, from 50% to 60%. Indeed, by the end of 2006, the use of environmentally preferred rubber had eliminated 3,000 metric tons of toxic materials in Nike products. Nike has also started to use recycled polyester derived from plastic bottles and consumer textile products.

Nike also is taking a leadership role by responsibly sourcing materials for its products. Through fiscal year 2006, more than half of Nike's cotton-containing garments incorporated organically grown content. The company is one of the world's largest buyers of organic cotton and aims to use a minimum of 5% organic cotton in all cotton garments by 2010.

In addition to a focus on environmentally preferred materials, Nike is sourcing materials produced within 200 miles of its factories where possible, thus reducing the energy used for transportation and associated greenhouse gas emissions. A goal of Nike's is also requiring that leather tanneries within its supply chain recycle wastewater to keep toxins out of the environment, and to color the leather with environmentally friendly vegetable-based dyes.

The Nike Soaker has a recycled rubber sole, uses less solvent-based adhesives, and creates a bare minimum of waste during the build process.

Despite Nike's significant committment to improve, the company still faces challenges on its path toward sustainability. The company announced its goal to reduce waste by 17% over its 2007 baseline by 2011. One particular challenge is eliminating polyvinyl chloride (PVC) for ink systems in apparel manufacturing factories. Reducing PVC usage is cost-prohibitive in some applications, and in others no reasonable alternative has been presented, according to the company. However, most Nike products are now PVC-free.

Reincarnated Sole
Puts Kids on the Court

Nike started its Reuse-a-Shoe program in 1993 to help promote healthier lifestyles for kids through physical activity. Nike grinds up used rubber, foam, and fabric along with defective and counterfeit shoes and waste material into reusable material called Nike Grind. The rubber is primarily used to create playing fields, the foam for synthetic basketball courts, and the uppers for padding underneath hardwood basketball floors. In most cases, Nike Grind constitutes 10%–20% of the total material used. Some of these Nike Grind products are also being used in the Nike Considered line of footwear. Since the program began, Nike has recycled more than 20 million pairs of shoes and the materials have been used to create more than 250 basketball courts and other playing surfaces in communities that wouldn't otherwise be able to afford them.

Nike's Air Zoom Affinity was produced with 38% less waste and 40% less solvents and uses 33% recycled materials.

Vital Statistics

Main site: Near Beaverton, Oregon	
Main product: Athletic footwear and apparel	
Number of employees: 30,200	
Green partners: World Wildlife Fund Climate Savers Program • Climate Group • Carbon Disclosure Project • Ceres • Natural Step	
Success: Addressing sustainability through design • Embedding sustainability approach • Achieved 18% reduction in CO_2 footprint from 1998 to 2005	
Challenge: Managing efforts through supply chain	
Awards: National Design Award • EPA's Top Workplace for Commuters • LEED-EB Gold Award • Best Corporate Citizens—*Business Ethics* magazine	

Triple Bottom Line: Performance Pays Off

More than 1,800 employees at Novo Nordisk voluntarily gave up a Sunday morning in November 2006 to talk about climate change. The employees crowded into a movie theater lobby in Copenhagen filled with exhibits on global warming, and later in the auditorium they saw the documentary film *An Inconvenient Truth.* Several months after that, former U.S. vice president and 2007 Nobel Peace Prize winner Al Gore, the film's producer, gave a motivational speech about climate change to 300 Novo Nordisk employees. These events served as the backdrop for an internal awareness-raising effort in support of the proactive climate strategy put into place by the Danish pharmaceutical company, which had already proven itself a leader in sustainability.

Since 1994, Novo Nordisk has been implementing strategies to meet the goals of its own Triple Bottom Line, a philosophy that environmental, social, and economic dimensions are intertwined and must be considered in every business decision. This is reflected in the company's formally stated objectives—to conduct its activities in a way that is financially, environmentally, and socially responsible—and underpins the company's market approach.

The company produces a single annual report that outlines not only financial results but the ways the company minimizes its environmental and social impacts. The company's primary products, diabetes care products and biopharmaceuticals, are energy-intensive to manufacture, so it has always been critical that the company reduce use of energy from a cost perspective.

OPPOSITE: At Novo Nordisk's production facility in Kalundborg, Denmark, cooling towers erected in 2003 have provided Novo Nordisk with more effective, resource-saving cooling.

For years, the company's global environmental management program focused on improving its Eco-Productivity Indices (EPIs), measurements of how products were being produced using fewer resources, including energy and water. There were no short-term paybacks for achieving these goals, which required substantial investments for technological and facilities improvements—yet the annual targets were more ambitious each year.

The ongoing cLEAN program, an adapted LEAN manufacturing program to increase productivity, has been integral to the company's climate strategy. In addition to meeting productivity goals, managers are held accountable—and rewarded financially—through an organizational tool called the Balanced Scorecard, which measures performance against specific targets for environmental compliance, pollution prevention, and energy efficiency.

Novo Nordisk first recognized that global warming required its attention in 2003. As a first move, it began working with the World Wildlife Fund (WWF) to determine ways to reduce its carbon footprint. By engaging in a partnership with the WWF under the auspices of the organization's Climate Savers program, Novo Nordisk designed an ambitious strategy to achieve an absolute reduction of greenhouse gas emissions by 10% by 2014 compared with 2004 levels. The ambitious reduction goal is to be accomplished despite projected annual double-digit sales growth over the same period. The reductions will be accomplished by increased energy efficiency and use of renewable energy; purchases of carbon offset credits are not part of Novo Nordisk's climate strategy. Progress toward meeting the goal is verified each year by an independent auditor and the results are submitted to WWF.

As it began to implement this goal, the company scrutinized its entire production process. Over three years, it conducted energy screenings to identify opportunities for savings at all of its 13 global production facilities, the majority of which are in Denmark. An energy steward was appointed for each site and internal incentives were established, encouraging local sites to conduct feasibility studies. By setting an internal price on carbon, the local management was incentivized to cut carbon emissions. These measures were implemented despite the fact that Novo Nordisk didn't yet have the data necessary to make the business case that the projects were financially viable.

The screenings revealed a surprising number of energy reduction measures with short payback periods. In Denmark, where 87% of the company's CO_2 emissions occur, significant savings were achieved at one factory from improvements in the ventilation system, which accounts for nearly 50% of the energy use there. Eight projects were named at a plant in North Carolina, ranging from more efficient use of boilers to minimizing energy losses in the steam system. Most of the improvements paid for themselves within 18 months. Overall, between 2004 and 2007, Novo Nordisk implemented energy-saving projects that resulted in carbon dioxide reductions of an estimated 12,000 tons.

In May 2007, Novo Nordisk announced an innovative agreement with its leading energy supplier in Denmark, DONG Energy, which will work with Novo Nordisk to identify energy-saving options at its production sites. In return, Novo Nordisk pledges until 2020 to convert the energy savings from its Danish factories into purchases

Vibeke Burchard and Jens Frederik Studstrup are charged with driving the implementation of Novo Nordisk's climate strategy. Their first mission was to identify potential for energy savings that can help reduce CO_2 emissions.

of green electricity. The energy will come from a new wind farm that DONG Energy is building. The agreement will help DONG finance the new wind farm, thus providing an opportunity for other Danish firms to convert more of their power to wind. Novo Nordisk expects to have converted electricity supplies for all its Danish factories to renewable energy by 2014.

Thinking ahead, Novo Nordisk has joined two international climate groups looking to build momentum for the UN Climate Summit in 2009. The company joined the Copenhagen Climate Council, a group of global business leaders working to achieve an effective global climate treaty to reduce greenhouse gas emissions.

The company's diverse initiatives earned Novo Nordisk the 2007 Dow Jones Sustainability World Index award as best in class in the health care industry. "This honor provides us further encouragement for operating our business according to the Triple Bottom Line philosophy," said Jerzy Gruhn, president of Novo Nordisk in the United States. "A company...can be economically vital, as well as socially and environmentally responsible."

Measuring Progress

A new performance measure was put in place by Novo Nordisk in 2006—the Eco Intensity Ratio (EIR). It replaced its long-standing Eco-Productivity Index (EPI), a measurement with a similar purpose but without the additional features of the EIR. Both measure energy and water consumption. The purpose of the change was to be able to measure both the individual steps and the total performance of a product, production facility, or business group.

The EIR, defined as resource consumption per unit, can stand alone, or individual EIRs can be added from each process step or intermediary product in the process flow, from chemical interactions to packaging and transporting. EIR targets are defined both annually and on a long-term basis. The long-term EIR target for 2010 is a 10% reduction in water and energy consumption compared to 2005.

Vital Statistics

Main site: Headquarters in Bagsværd, Denmark.

Main product: Diabetes-care products and biopharmaceuticals

Number of employees: 26,000 in 79 countries

Green partners: WWF Climate Savers Programme • DONG Energy

Success: 12,000 tons of CO_2 emissions are estimated to have been eliminated by energy-screening programs from 2005 to 2007

Challenge: Expanding the scope of reduction activities beyond production

Awards: 2007 number 14 on CNBC *European Business* magazine's list of the world's top low-carbon pioneers • Short-listed for FT (*Financial Times*)/Citi Private Bank Environmental Award for the Greatest Improvement in Carbon Efficiency Achieved by a Large Enterprise, Europe, for Novo Nordisk's Partnership with DONG Energy • Two prizes from the World Business in association with INSEAD for Best Management and Sourcing of Energy and Best Sustainable Green Business • Supersector leader in healthcare in the 2007/2008 Dow Jones Sustainability Indexes

Leading the Examined Life

Patagonia, Inc., the Ventura, California–based outdoor clothing company, is unusually blunt with consumers about the role it plays in destroying the environment. According to the company website, all businesses pollute, and Patagonia is no exception. What sets Patagonia apart is its belief that business can be the driving force to inspire solutions to environmental threats. Since 1985, Patagonia has made annual contributions of 1% of total sales to grassroots environmental groups focused on saving the planet. So far, more than 1,000 organizations, whose activities include alternative energy, social activism, and reduction of the growth of resource extraction, have received a total of over $29 million.

In 2002, Yvon Chouinard, founder of Patagonia, persuaded other businesses to do the same, and co-formed an alliance of companies called 1% for the Planet, with the members donating 1% of their sales to the environmental cause. So far, over 10,000 businesses have joined 1% for the Planet.

Yvon Chouinard has always put the environment first. An avid climber and outdoorsman, he went into business in the 1960s making pitons, small pieces of hardware that rock climbers hammered into cliffs to tie their ropes to. Although his company's hard steel pitons were technically superior to other products on the market at the time and generated 70% of his income, Chouinard became aware that they caused permanent damage by cracking the rock. In 1971 he introduced new aluminum spring-loaded camming devices that could be inserted into cracks in the rock, where they would expand. Unlike pitons, however, they could be removed by pulling on a trigger that caused the device to contract. By 1972, Chouinard had committed his company, then called Chouinard Equipment, to the advocacy of the new hard-

OPPOSITE: In 1993, Patagonia became the first company to produce clothing made from recycled plastic soda bottles.

ware and to so-called clean climbing, which left the rock unscarred. The concept not only revolutionized the sport, it was the cornerstone of success for his company. Today Patagonia is known for its high-end outdoor gear and clothing for a wide variety of sports, including rock and mountain climbing, surfing, skiing, boarding, hiking, and fishing—sports connecting individuals with nature. Patagonia's corporate culture emphasizes quality of life and its employees tend to be avid outdoor enthusiasts with an appreciation for nature and a commitment to preserving it. The company celebrates employees' endeavors, including one man's 100-mile endurance run in Pasadena, California, and another's 270-mile hike on Vermont's Long Trail. As the website says, "For us at Patagonia, a love of wild and beautiful places demands participation in the fight to save them."

Yvon Chouinard forging a piton at the original forge behind the Patagonia headquarters.

Patagonia began spending time and money on saving the environment in the early 1970s, when employees at company headquarters lobbied to defeat development around the nearby Ventura River. That successful effort, which was started by a lone but committed 25-year-old biology student, led the company to decide to focus its grant-making on small grassroots groups working to save or restore habitats. Patagonia hosts representatives of these groups at an all-expenses-paid conference led by professionals to teach strategy, marketing, and publicity skills. Patagonia works at the national level as well, by annually adopting an environmental cause that has global impact. Patagonia's 2007 campaign was to protect the Arctic National Wildlife Refuge by lobbying for legislation that will permanently designate it as wilderness. Patagonia's web-

site provides links to state representatives so voters can communicate easily and directly with lawmakers.

To minimize its own impact on the environment, in 1991, Patagonia undertook an internal assessment to examine the environmental impact caused by manufacturing its products. The results were alarming to executives, who immediately began making important changes. Not surprisingly, the oil-based polyester and nylon fabrics used in many products were large energy consumers and sources of pollution. In 1993, the company became the first to produce clothing using fleece made from recycled plastic soda bottles instead of from virgin fleece, which is made by combining petroleum-based products at high temperatures. Recycled bottles are emptied onto a moving belt where they are sorted by color, sterilized, and then crushed into tiny chips. When the chips are dry, they are heated in a vat, forced through spinnerets, and extruded into fibers. Since the program's inception, more than 86 million soda bottles have been recycled for Patagonia products. The technology has expanded to include the ability to use second-quality fabrics and worn-out garments as additional sources for recycled polyester, and Patagonia now uses it in a wide variety of garments including Capilene underwear, shell jackets, and board shorts. Since 2005, customers have been encouraged to return worn-out Capilene and Patagonia fleece garments for recycling, as well as fleece made by other manufacturers, such as Polartec, through Patagonia's Common Threads Garment Recycling program. Today, over 50% of the company's products are recyclable through this program.

Surprisingly, Patagonia's 1991 environmental assessment revealed that cotton was an even larger polluter than oil-based polyester or nylon because of the toxic pesticides used in its cultivation. Conventional methods used to raise cotton involve massive amounts of chemicals, and research shows that synthetic fertilizers and other substances have permanent effects on soil, water, air, and many organisms. Organically grown cotton costs more, but the methods used improve soil quality, use less water, and support diverse ecosystems. At first, the company made only T-shirts with organic cotton. But by 1996, Patagonia had converted its entire line of 66 sportswear items to organically grown cotton, despite the limited availability of the fabric at the time.

The company's willingness to publicly examine its own practices and habits is revealed most tellingly through the recent launch on its website of the Footprint Chronicles. A self-described project of "learning out loud," the aim is to expose the social and environmental impact of the company's products from genesis to reincarnation. So far, Patagonia has picked five of its top-selling products and plans on adding five more every season. Each product's pros and cons are discussed, reader input is invited, and metrics are given for carbon dioxide emissions, waste, energy consumption, and miles traveled. For example, the Synchilla vest gets overall high marks for being made from 100% recycled materials and because the North American supply chain keeps travel distances short (many other products travel around the world during the production cycle).

Surprisingly, though, since the vest is moved using trucks, which have higher emissions than other forms of transportation, emissions are higher for the vest than for other products coming longer distances by boat. The Footprint Chronicles concludes that though a geographically close supply chain may intuitively appear better, further examination that includes all environmental impacts may prove otherwise.

Patagonia has established the ambitious goal of making its entire product line recyclable by 2010, but executives are well aware of the challenges in doing so. One key hurdle is finding a substitute for PFOA, a synthetic chemical necessary to manufacture the water-repellent finish for high-performance fabrics suitable for extreme weather conditions. Recycling a higher proportion of waste, such as the small plastic bags required by international law to cover garments, is another goal. Patagonia is also researching ways to reduce the amount of transportation necessary to manufacture its garments.

Paper Trail

Patagonia is a mail-order company that produces several million catalogues every year, requiring vast amounts of paper. Its paper procurement policies are among the most environmentally sensitive in the industry, but Patagonia is working for continued improvement. Most of the company's catalogue paper stock is made with 45-pound stock containing 40%–45% recycled paper fiber. The virgin fiber used in creating the stock is certified as coming from nonendangered forests and is produced within 200 miles of the printing facility, reducing carbon emissions associated with transport. Patagonia is also reducing the weight of paper used. By switching from 50-pound stock to 45-pound stock in 2002, the company estimates it has saved more than 12,782 trees. Employees are urged to communicate electronically whenever possible, both internally and with customers. Catalogue print quantities are reduced by targeting appropriate audiences, and trim sizes are selected that make the most efficient use of paper on the press and at the mill. Patagonia also favors paper suppliers with sustainable production processes.

Vital Statistics

Main site: Ventura, California
Main product: Outdoor apparel
Number of employees: 1,300
Green partner: 1% for the Planet
Success: Using only 100% organic cotton since 1996 • Implementing the world's first garment recycling program, where even competitors' garments are accepted • First company in California to use 100% renewable power
Challenge: Having entire product line either recycled or recyclable by 2010
Awards: The Coolest Company on the Planet—*Fortune* magazine

Embracing Change

Pacific Gas and Electric Company®

Pacific Gas and Electric Company, a California-based utility that delivers more than half of its electricity from carbon-free energy sources, has been able to provide its customers with among the cleanest energy in the nation, while aggressively pursuing energy efficiency to an extent not seen elsewhere in the industry. One of PG&E's newest initiatives is investing an additional $1 billion to install 10 million "smart meters" that will allow its customers to better monitor and conserve their energy use, especially during peak demand hours.

California is America's most environmentally conscious state, so it might seem like a relatively easy place for a utility to go green. Yet this was not at all obvious just a few years ago when Peter Darbee was named PG&E's CEO. At that time, the company was a traditional electric power company, its stock in the doldrums, just pulling out of bankruptcy after California's three-year experiment with deregulation, a reviled company for which many employees didn't like to admit they worked.

In just a couple of years the company transformed itself into a model of the good that can happen when a company embraces environmental leadership. Customer approval ratings nearly doubled, and PG&E's stock price is up by 50% since Darbee took over. "Educating and engaging our customers in the fight against climate change" is the watchword of the new, award-winning, green Pacific Gas and Electric Company.

The turnaround began when Darbee invited experts, including scientists, in to discuss global warming. Based on what he heard, even as the nation's leadership dithered, PG&E announced that it believed the link between greenhouse gas emissions and the earth's warming climate was real, and that urgent action was needed to curb humans' contributions to global warming.

Since power companies emit about 40% of the nation's global-warming-related pollution, Darbee reasoned that utilities had a role to play in controlling those emissions. This rationale also meshed well with California's Renewables Portfolio Standard, which mandated that utilities find fossil-fuel-free sources for 20% of their electricity by 2010.

Before Darbee, PG&E's basic stance toward state regulation had been to fight it with battalions of law-

OPPOSITE: As an official Plug-In Partner, PG&E pledged to automakers that the company would buy plug-in hybrid electric vehicles to make its vehicle fleet even cleaner.

yers, some fresh off the Erin Brockovich case in which the company agreed to pay $333 million to settle a class-action suit claiming the utility had poisoned 1,250 people by allowing chromium 6 to leak into the drinking water near one of its pumping stations (the case was made into a 2000 movie starring Julia Roberts). Now, in the words of a Stanford University climate change expert, PG&E could "stop trying to derail the train and try to drive it."

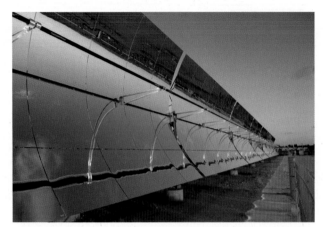

PG&E entered into a renewable energy agreement with Solel-MSP-1 to purchase renewable energy from the Mojave Solar Park, to be constructed in California's Mojave Desert.

Reducing greenhouse gas emissions became part of company policy, but Darbee didn't rest there. He made global warming a central theme. Setting the pace for other utilities, Darbee jumped on a soapbox and publicly supported increased state regulation of carbon emissions. PG&E was a key supporter of California's 2006 efforts to legislate limits on CO_2 emissions (the law says that the state's carbon emissions in 2020 must be cut to 1990 levels, a 25% decrease).

To be fair to other utilities, PG&E had a bit of a jump on greening even before its environmental awakening, since more than half of its energy came from carbon-free sources. California state regulators classify only 12% of PG&E's electric supply as renewable, but more than half of its electricity comes from sources that produce no greenhouse gases: the Diablo Canyon nuclear power plant produces about 24% of PG&E's power supply. Another 20% comes from large hydroelectric plants, which do not qualify as renewable under the state's Renewables Portfolio Standard. The geothermal fields near

Yosemite National Park provide clean power as well. Less than 1% of PG&E's electricity comes from coal-fired plants. PG&E sold most of its generation to raise money during its bankruptcy. In spite of its public efforts to help California companies reduce their greenhouse gas emissions, PG&E has not set a specific GHG reduction target for itself.

Still, PG&E under Darbee was aggressive about soliciting bids for renewable energy supplies and signing power purchase agreements. Some of the technologies PG&E signed up are rather cutting-edge: more than 500 megawatts of energy from solar thermal, a technology that uses huge mirrored lenses to focus the sun's rays and heat steam to turn a turbine. Though a few solar thermal plants had been built in the 1980s, new plants became too expensive when tax credits expired, and no new plants had been built in 20 years. California's Mojave Desert is one of the sunniest locations in the country, ideal for solar thermal power.

Before any new solar thermal plants had even started generating electricity, PG&E doubled its commitment, promising to purchase 1,000 megawatts. Darbee announced the new, expanded commitment at the 2007 Clinton Global Initiative. Power purchase agreements were pivotal for companies looking for financing to build multimillion-dollar solar plants in the California desert using advanced technology. These companies needed investors, and having a guaranteed long-term customer and an agreement in writing helped.

Bob Cart, CEO of GreenVolts, the tiny start-up providing the solar technology for the Mojave Desert project, scored the power purchase agreement with PG&E on the strength of a prototype but no pilot plant of any kind.

PG&E is researching other new energy technologies even less developed than solar thermal, such as wave energy—electricity generated by buoys positioned off the coastline—and tidal energy from turbines set in the powerful currents flowing under the Golden Gate Bridge.

PG&E was the first utility to join the Green Grid consortium, a group of information technology companies pledged to improve that industry's notoriously large climate change footprint. PG&E collaborated with IBM to reduce the energy used at its own data centers by more than 80%. California state regulators had the foresight in the 1980s to decouple utility rates from the amount of electricity sold, which has helped spur creativity. That way, PG&E does not profit from the amount of energy it sells, but by energy efficiency investments and helping its consumers to conserve.

To address pollution created by ships at ports, which traditionally burn vast amounts of dirty diesel, PG&E formed a program to test mobile liquid-natural-gas generators to help clean up the ports without having to build a lot of new infrastructure.

Vehicle emissions are out of utilities' normal purview, but Darbee even figured out how to contribute to reducing carbon footprints in that sphere. PG&E is testing hybrid electric bucket trucks for its own fleet: each could save $4,500 to $5,500 in gasoline each year, which, of course, is accompanied by carbon savings. The company is a major advocate of a new idea called "vehicle-to-grid" (V2G). The idea here is that plug-in electric hybrids—which several companies say they plan to introduce in the next few years—can help utilities regulate electric power demand via special two-way sockets in parking garages. At peak hours, if enough cars were plugged in, utilities could draw out some power to ease pressure on the grid. The cars' main time to recharge would be at night when electric demand is reduced, less expensive, and more renewable energy, such as wind, is available.

Lighting the Way

Recognizing that efficiency—doing the same work with less energy—is the cheapest way of generating new energy, PG&E runs a wide range of efficiency programs, include free energy audits, rebates for customers who buy efficient appliances, and cash incentives for farmers who retrofit agricultural pumps. In one promotion, the utility gave away a million compact fluorescent lightbulbs in one month, saying that if all the bulbs were used, they could save 400,000 megawatt-hours over the lifetime of the bulbs. PG&E says its energy efficiency programs over the past three decades have helped customers save enough energy to power more than 33 million homes, while preventing more than 125 million tons of carbon from being emitted into the atmosphere, and helped avoid the need for California to build two dozen large power plants.

Vital Statistics

Main site: San Francisco, California

Main product: Delivery of natural gas and electricity to 15 million Californians

Number of employees: 20,000

Green partners: Green Grid • IBM

Success: Providing customers with among the cleanest energy in the nation • Over 50% of power (on average) from carbon-free sources • Leading energy efficiency programs helped customers save more than $22 billion

Challenge: Competitive energy pricing market • Cultivating renewable technologies

Awards: Recognized by California Integrated Waste Management Board for commitment to waste reduction and environmental stewardship • Environmental Business of the Year—California Planning and Conservation League • Recognized by Natural Resources Defense Council for environmental leadership

Mining for the Future

RIO
TINTO

It is a known fact that mining and exploration disturb the environment. But for Rio Tinto, a world leader in mineral resources, respect for the environment is at the heart of the company's approach to sustainable development. In addition to implementing practical programs for managing biodiversity, water, waste, and air quality, it is also developing technological innovations that will change the very nature of mining. The Mine of the Future is Rio Tinto's project for transforming how the industry will operate in the 21st century. Recently introduced improvements include mining without large surface excavations and a new iron-making process that reduces greenhouse gas emissions.

The company is laying the technological and conceptual foundations for the Mine of the Future by using a mining method called block caving in which minerals are extracted through a relatively narrow opening, avoiding the need for open pits that destroy large sections of land. The rock is deliberately cut so that it will fracture and cave in; then it is hoisted up through a shaft. From the isolation of a control room, operators use viewing monitors and joysticks to operate loaders, rock breakers, and conveyor belts. In addition to being more environmentally sound, the remote-controlled operation is safer and more cost-effective than conventional mining techniques. The company has been gaining block caving experience at its mines in Northparkes, Australia, and Palabora, South Africa, and it believes that block caving is likely to be the method used for its copper mines being developed in Mongolia and Alaska.

After 20 years of research, Rio Tinto is operating the first commercial iron-making plant using a new, more energy-efficient, less polluting technology. The centuries-old process of reducing iron ore in a blast furnace released large amounts of carbon dioxide. Rio Tinto's new HIsmelt technology eliminates some of those steps and produces high-quality pig iron straight from ore mixed with coal. Now in use at its facility in Perth, Australia, the process reduces air pollution and greenhouse gas emissions.

OPPOSITE: Parker Point loading facility, Pilbara Iron, Australia

Another example of the company's emphasis on technological innovation is its effort to capture and store carbon emissions. The aim is to take the carbon dioxide released from burning coal and store it underground in permanent geological structures. Rio Tinto has invested in 13 projects in the United States and Australia to develop and commercialize this technology.

An operator for Palabora Mining Company looks in on the action and checks to see if the draw bell has been cleared of obstructions in Limpopo Province, South Africa.

Not all of the company's environmental footprint improvements are technology-based. Rio Tinto has also reduced emissions by financing a unique, first-ever program to pay farmers for not burning vegetation on their land. Rio Tinto Aluminium in Australia is a major partner in the program, known as Minding the Carbon Store, which was launched in November 2006 by the Carbon Pool, a carbon trading company. Rio Tinto paid farmers in Queensland not to burn their trees, a process that releases carbon. Under the plan, Rio Tinto Alcan owns the rights to the carbon contained in the intact vegetation, which it can then use to offset its greenhouse gas emissions. So far, the program has stopped about a million tons of greenhouse gases from being released—the equivalent of a year's emissions from 250,000 cars. The project also saved 13,000 hectares of woodland and preserved wildlife and stopped soil erosion.

In total, the company manages 35,000 square kilometers of land, with operations in ecologically important regions such as Madagascar, Brazil, and Guinea. About 5% of the company's land was used for mining in 2006, and by the end of the year, more than a quarter of that land had been rehabilitated. The company's biodiversity strategy calls for making a "net positive impact," meaning that it pledges to leave as much, if not more, natural variety in place after its operations have closed than existed before. A new diagnostic tool developed in 2006 helps managers to define all the risks and opportunities of a project and to prioritize actions. The first trial of the tool was completed with the Pilbara Iron Expansion Projects in Australia.

The diagnostic tool is also being used in Madagascar, where the first net positive impact project is being piloted. For 20 years, the company has been evaluating several sites along the coast for mining mineral sands. Detailed biodiversity research and conservation projects include biological inventory studies, seed biology, and conservation projects. Logging for charcoal fuel production is a major conservation issue, and the company's mine rehabilitation plan calls for replanting fast-growing tree species. Now, with the new diagnostic tool and a commitment to the net positive impact strategy, Rio Tinto is taking an even more rigorous approach. Working groups of both internal and external experts are developing performance indicators and defining specific offsets to compensate for unavoidable impacts. The framework developed in Madagascar will then be implemented in several different environments, including sites in Australia and the United States, where it will be further refined.

Mining and mineral processing are energy-intensive activities that rely on fossil fuels. Rio Tinto's goal is to reduce energy usage per ton of product by 5% by 2008 compared to a 2003 baseline. It was halfway there by 2006 with a 2.6% improvement since 2003. Energy audits have been completed at sites that account for 80% of the company's energy usage, and savings measures have been implemented.

The company also set a target to reduce greenhouse gas emissions by 4% from 2003 to 2008, but it has accomplished only a fraction of the reductions so far. Despite that lack of progress, the company ranked highest in the metals sector in the U.K.'s Carbon Disclosure Project, with a score of 100 out of 100 on its Climate Disclosure Leadership Index.

Rio Tinto's operations require water, which is often in short supply, particularly in the arid and semiarid regions where it does business. The company's water standard calls for minimizing the amount of water it removes, reusing it whenever possible, and restoring it to a state as clean as possible when it is discharged. By 2006, it reduced the amount of fresh water used per ton of product by over 11% compared to 2003 levels.

The company's new iron-making plant utilizing the HIsmelt technology in Australia makes no extra demands on the local water supply, despite the fact that water is required for cooling. Instead of drawing on underground aquifers, Rio Tinto negotiated an agreement with the State Water Corporation to use treated wastewater. At the time the HIsmelt facility was being constructed, State Water was considering the feasibility of building an effluent treatment plant near the site. Rio Tinto's offer to buy the treated water ensured enough demand to make the treatment plant financially viable.

Acid Rocks

One of the most serious environmental risks for the mining industry is acid rock drainage (ARD) from mineral waste. When sulfide-containing rocks are disturbed and exposed to air and water, their acid-generating potential increases, and over time the acidic minerals may leach out of the rocks, potentially threatening water quality.

Rio Tinto has conducted more than 21 reviews of its operations assessed as being at medium to high risk for ARD. Its reviews are highly regarded as being the industry benchmark, and it plays a leading role in the International Network for Acid Prevention.

A tool developed in 2006 is now being used by operations personnel at three sites to improve their management of acid-generating mineral waste from initial exploration drilling through mining and processing and site closure.

Vital Statistics

Main site: London, England, and Melbourne, Australia

Main products: Aluminum • Copper • Diamonds • Energy products • Gold • Industrial minerals (borates, titanium dioxide, salt, and talc) • Iron ore

Number of employees: 65,000

Green partners: Earthwatch Institute • United Nations Environment Programme—World Conservation Monitoring Centre • WWF

Success: Land rehabilitation • Reporting and disclosure

Challenge: Meeting demand • Attracting talent • Finding global solutions to climate change

Awards: FTSE4Good Index • Business in the Community's Corporate Responsibility, Environment, and Community Indices • Carbon Disclosure Leadership Index • Dow Jones Sustainability World Index

Better Living Through Green Chemistry

You can't say the company is organic, but one by one SC Johnson is replacing toxic chemicals with lower-risk and in some cases, more biodegradable agents. And it's leading the charge toward renewable energy—without offsets. More than 30 years ago, SC Johnson (formerly the S. C. Johnson Wax Co.), the family-owned maker of household cleaners and chemicals such as Windex, Pledge, Raid, Shine, Shout, and Johnson Wax, took the bold step of removing chlorofluorocarbons from its products, three years ahead of the 1978 U.S. mandate. The decision forced SC Johnson to put aerosols on hold in other countries where a suitable substitute didn't yet exist. "The decision was not easy and many industry executives accused us of trying to wreck the chemical business," says Scott Johnson, former vice president for global environmental and safety action.

But the move was in keeping with the company's history, as the 122-year-old, $7.5 billion (2006) business had pioneered water-based aerosols in the 1950s, and was a stepping-stone to its current efforts to rid its products of potentially dangerous toxins and gases. In 2001, SC Johnson started rating ingredients and raw materials according to their impact on the environment. In 2002, again ahead of regulatory requirements, SC Johnson stopped using chlorine-based paperboard packaging worldwide and eliminated polyvinyl chloride from packaging because it's not biodegradable and has been linked to health problems.

Using its patented Greenlist process, SC Johnson rates more than 95% of the raw materials it uses, including solvents, propellants, insecticides, and surfactants. The last mentioned are agents used in detergents; they lower the surface tension of a liquid, making it more spreadable. The goal was to go beyond legal and regulatory requirements and increase year on year the percent of raw materials that have the least impact on the environment and human health.

OPPOSITE: SC Johnson's twin cogeneration turbines reduce the company's reliance on coal-fired electricity and remove 52,000 tons of greenhouse gases annually.

The company rates materials as acceptable, better, best—or unacceptable unless a viable alternative cannot be found (0 rating). In 2001, the company rated 17% of its materials as 0s; that number was down to 1.5% in 2006. The organophosphate insecticide DDVP was eliminated in 2004, and the insecticide propoxur was eliminated from the company's Raid ant powder in 2006 because of toxicity and its persistence in the environment. In 1993, before the company's Greenlist process began, paradichlorobenzene was eliminated from toilet products because of its effect on ozone in the upper atmosphere. Over that same period, the use of "better" materials improved from 8% to 18.2% and of "best" materials from 4% to 16.1%. In its best-selling Windex window cleaner, volatile organic compounds now comprise less than 4% of the solution's formula.

Assuming the mantle of an environmental best practices leader, SC Johnson now licenses the Greenlist management system royalty-free to other companies through third-party administrator Five Winds International. "By approaching their operations with green chemistry in mind, companies have successfully stopped using, literally, billions of pounds of hazardous substances," says Paul Anastas, director of the Center for Green Chemistry and Green Engineering at Yale. "That's amazing, but it's only a fraction of what is possible," says Jim Fava, managing director at Five Winds International: "From our perspective, Greenlist is one of the most exciting breakthroughs in corporate sustainability over the last few years. It's a good fit with what we call 'value without burden.'" SC Johnson won the Presidential Green Chemistry Award and the Ron Brown Award for Corporate Leadership in 2006 for its Greenlist program. Since devising the Greenlist process in 2001, SC Johnson's reformulations have removed more than 61 million pounds of volatile organic compounds (VOCs) from the environmental footprint of the company's products.

But SC Johnson hasn't been able to eliminate everything on its list yet. It spent $1 million attempting to replace the 0-rated ingredient ethylenediaminetetraacetic acid (used in bathroom-care products) because of its poor biodegradability and is currently working on sample formulas with new ingredients. Through its research, SC Johnson found a preferable ingredient, but the cost of the new product was too high and therefore rejected by customers. But the company's track record and overall direction are quite positive: two years after becoming the first major consumer packaged-goods company to partner with the U.S. EPA's Design for the Environment (DfE) program, five SC Johnson products have earned the DfE label.

Given the company's attention to volatile chemicals and their environmental impact, it stands to reason that SC Johnson is serious about reducing its carbon footprint. It has reduced CO_2 emissions by 34% from 2000 to 2005, and looks to reduce by a total of 12% (from 2000 levels) the emissions of all manufacturing facilities worldwide by 2011. Also by 2011, the company aims to source 40% of its global electricity from green energy. Unlike many companies, SC Johnson is not buying renewable energy credits or carbon offsets, but rather is producing its own green power in some locations and buying locally generated renewable energy in others.

The company's largest manufacturing plant, Waxdale, in Racine, Wisconsin, where Windex and Scrubbing Bubbles bathroom cleaner are made, is now powered by cogeneration combustion turbines that run off both natural gas and methane from a public landfill. SC Johnson is one of a handful of companies in the United States that have developed an energy recovery system that utilizes landfill methane; SC Johnson started its in 2003. In 2007, the Center for Resource Solutions recognized SC Johnson for using Green-e certified energy at Waxdale.

In 2007, the U.S. EPA selected SC Johnson to appear in a film commemorating the 20th anniversary of the Montreal Protocol, a landmark environmental treaty to reduce ozone-depleting substances. "By embracing cooperation over confrontation, the EPA and our vital partners like SC Johnson are continuing to create a better tomorrow by protecting the earth's atmosphere today," said EPA administrator Stephen L. Johnson in lauding the company's long-term commitment to reducing volatile organic compounds. Perhaps 20 years from now, the company will be lauded again for eliminating all hazardous chemicals from its arsenal of bug and bacteria killers.

Killing Bugs, Doing Good in Africa

SC Johnson has taken a leadership role in sustainability, social progress, and entrepreneurship in the developing world, where it has found growth markets, given the high rate of malaria and incidence of bugs. The company was a major supporter of Cornell University and others in the development of the 2006 Base of the Pyramid Protocol project in Kenya, a joint project of the University of Michigan, Cornell University, the World Resources Institute, and the Johnson Foundation. The pilot business venture in Kenya, Community Cleaning Services, run by the Coalition of Youth Entrepreneurs, offers cleaning services in three poor neighborhoods in Nairobi. The idea of the project is to create partnerships between multinational companies and local entrepreneurs as a way of spreading economic development. "We believe that prosperity and responsibility can coexist," says Scott Johnson. "Our work at the base of the pyramid reinforces that we can do what's right for the business and what's right for the people around us."

Key to the Base of the Pyramid Protocol promotes collaboration and learning between the community and the employees of SC Johnson.

Vital Statistics

Main site: Racine, Wisconsin. The global company operates in more than 70 countries and sells products in more than 110 countries.

Main product: Household cleaning products and products for home storage, air care, personal care, and insect control.

Number of employees: 12,000

Green partner: EPA Design for the Environment

Success: With cogeneration, became first CPG plant in Midwest to produce nearly all its own energy through clean-burning technologies, eliminating 52,000 tons of GHGs in 2005 • Surpassed EPA Climate Leaders goals, reducing GHG emissions 17% in 2006 • Introduced hybrid cars for SCJ sales force in 2007

Challenge: Continuing to substitute effective sustainable ingredients for volatile organic compounds in its products

Awards: One of 10 Green Giants, *Fortune* magazine, 2007 • Presidential Green Chemistry Award • 2003 U.S. EPA Lifetime Atmospheric Achievement Award

In Every Deliberation

Based in the Green Mountain State, Vermont, Seventh Generation—helmed today by president and CEO Jeffrey Hollender—is one of the world's leading brands of eco-friendly home products and takes its name from the Great Law of the Iroquois: "In our every deliberation, we must consider the impact of our decisions on the next seven generations."

In 1988, former commune resident Alan Newman decided to start a mail-order green business, focusing on home care products such as detergent and cleaning sprays. When he needed additional funding and management support, he took on a partner—finance-savvy New Yorker Jeffrey Hollender.

In 1989, the *New York Times* published a flattering profile of the company that portrayed Newman as his generation's environmental prophet. However, the economic downturn of the early 1990s caused a stall in green consuming. The company faltered, and so did the partners' relationship.

Newman left the partnership to found another suc-cessful brand, Magic Hat Brewery, and to save Seventh Generation, Hollender announced he was taking the company public—on 100% recycled paper, no less. He sold the catalogue business, which at the time was responsible for 80% of the company's revenue, and started rebuilding from the ground up. He began distributing products to natural-food stores, to supermarkets, online, and to mass retailers across the United States and Canada, and expanded the product line categories, which currently include home cleaning, paper products, laundry, personal care, and baby care. By 1999, he was able to buy back the company, and came up with a new tag line and philosophical approach: "Healthier for you and the planet."

As the company grew, attracting customers desirous of environmentally friendly, toxin-free products, the competition grew, too. Hollender realized that to "bring in the green," he needed products that were not just green but of high quality and affordably priced. "People don't just buy something because it's good for the environment," Hollender says. "It has to meet other competitive requirements."

The challenge for Seventh Generation is that plant-based ingredients cost more than conventional, petroleum-based ingredients. Seventh Generation products are often comparably priced with premium conventional products, but retailers set their own prices and

OPPOSITE: A member of the latest generation using Seventh Generation's nontoxic household products

often charge larger markups on Seventh Generation products. Because of this, the company strives to use premium ingredients such as whole essential plant oils to ensure product excellence when they cannot ensure a price point. Seventh Generation products are generally the most sustainable in the natural products category.

Seventh Generation now offers an expanding array of cleaning, paper, baby, and feminine care products with the "socially responsible" stamp of the Seventh Generation R&D team, which conducts independent third-party testing on all Seventh Generation products. For years, in spite of increasing demand, Seventh Generation had to contend with a widespread belief that recycled products were inferior in quality or more expensive than alternatives, both of which were sometimes true. For example, prior to the current generation of liquid laundry detergents, Seventh Generation's version fell 80% behind Tide because it didn't contain enzymes that remove grass and blood stains and didn't have as many cleansers. In 2004, Seventh Generation's product was reformulated with enzymes and a revised surfactant system that enabled it to match Tide's performance.

"Another challenge facing businesses trying to capitalize on the green niche is that publicity about misleading environmental claims from some manufacturers has fueled a wave of consumer skepticism about green products over the past few years," explains Peter Stisser, vice president of marketing research firm Roper Starch Worldwide. The highly touted "biodegradable trash bags" of recent years are one example—trash bags are almost always sent to landfills or incinerators and are rarely exposed to the elements required for natural breakdown, rendering the environmentally friendly tag meaningless. Seventh Generation trash bags are made using recycled plastic, which eliminates the processing of petroleum into virgin plastic, reducing pollution, and requires 40% less energy in production compared to bags made from virgin plastic.

Seventh Generation believes in providing clear, comprehensive information for consumers regarding the ingredients in its products and is committed to full ingredient disclosure on its labels. All product ingredients are listed on packaging, with a Material Safety Data Sheet (MSDS) for each item posted on the company's website. Seventh Generation also sets specifications for each of its ingredients. For example, caustic sodium hydroxide must be produced by a mercury-free technology. The company also conducts annual reviews of its suppliers to ensure compliance with specifications and to monitor social and environmental policies of those companies.

Currently, the Seventh Generation line includes non-chlorine-bleached 100% recycled paper towels, bathroom and facial tissues, and paper plates; nontoxic, phosphate-free, biodegradable cleaning, dishwashing, and laundry products; plastic trash bags made from recycled plastic; chlorine-free diapers and baby wipes; and 100% organic cotton feminine hygiene products.

Seventh Generation has gained a reputation for clever and innovative marketing techniques that raise awareness of global warming. One such campaign was the creation of a virtual forest at the 2006 Natural Products Expo East trade fair. Dialing a certain number with a cell phone allowed participants to choose, plant, and grow a "seed" into a tree—and each virtual tree became an actual tree planted in Maryland the following year. Terry Galloway, arborist and director of the program Treemendous Maryland, explained, "Trees and forests are the most beneficial land use for protecting and restoring the waters of the Chesapeake Bay, Maryland's greatest natural resource and number one environmental priority." Adds Hollender, "We're saying, 'You can make a difference. You can plant a tree here.' "

Seventh Generation continued in this vein with a virtual tree-planting program in 2007 in devastated New Orleans. The One Ton Tree program was named for the amount of CO_2 an average tree removes from the atmosphere in its lifetime, and represents another attempt by the company to support urban reforestation.

Although Seventh Generation has made tremendous strides in the area of corporate responsibility while steadily increasing profits, the company faces challenges in the years ahead. Many petrochemical-based ingredients have been replaced with vegetable-sourced materials—in 2006, the synthetic mint fragrance in the toilet bowl cleaner was eliminated in favor of a natural oil—but some Seventh Generation products still contain ingredients derived from synthetic sources. Seventh Generation works constantly to maintain an effective balance on the fine line between environmentalism and profitability, such as when the company began offering more sizes of detergent bottles to meet consumer demand and battle competition, although the decision increased the amount of packaging waste.

A Mantra Embodied

One reason Seventh Generation employees like showing up for work is the company's new green headquarters in downtown Burlington. The 20,000-square-foot building is centrally located, meaning many can walk or bike to work or take energy-efficient public transportation—but if you really must drive, there are spots in the garage for plugging in electric cars. Local wood from sustainable forests, along with native stone, brick, slate, and copper, were used for construction, and furnishings, insulation, and walls were created from recycled materials. Carpets contain no formaldehyde or volatile organic compounds (VOCs) and all paint and sealants are also VOC-free. All of the lighting used is energy-efficient, although the space was designed to maximize natural light so that it is rarely necessary for artificial light to be used at all. Composting and recycling systems have also been implemented, and the building features personal and aesthetically pleasing details such as porches, cupolas, awnings, and arches, in stark contrast to so many of today's uninspired cookie-cutter office towers. Seventh Generation employees know they are working in surroundings that epitomize the products they are selling and the ethos of the company they work for.

Inside Seventh Generation headquarters in Burlington, Vermont

Vital Statistics

Main site: Burlington, Vermont
Main product: Environmentally friendly household and personal care products
Number of employees: 75
Green partners: Greenpeace • Healthy Child Healthy World
Success: Pioneered green cleaning industry twenty years ago • Annual sales growth of 40%
Challenge: Combating greenwashing by companies whose inauthentic behavior ultimately confuses the consumer
Awards: Best Bosses Award, Winning Workplaces and *Fortune* Magazine • *Advertising Age* Marketing 50 • Social Capitalist Award—*Fast Company* Magazine • Green Seal Award—Environmental Stewardship Challenge Award from the Direct Marketing Association

Can an Office-Supply Retailer Have Soul? Staples Thinks So

In 2002, when Mitt Romney was running for governor of Massachusetts, he was bird-dogged by a feisty group of student activists trying to force Staples to change its paper procurement policies. Romney was a shareholder and former board member of Staples, which was one of the companies he had helped start when he ran Bain Capital in the 1980s. The group was Green Corps, and their persistence is credited with forcing Staples to become more serious about its environmental policies.

Staples had offered recycled products since its inception in 1986, but in November 2002, the company announced formal new guidelines (its Environmental Paper Procurement Policy) that would phase out purchases of paper products from endangered forests and create an environmental affairs division to monitor progress toward achieving an average of 30% postconsumer recycled content across all paper products that Staples offers for sale. Staples, which achieved that goal in 2006, worked closely with shareholders, consultants, suppliers, and environmental groups, including ForestEthics and Dogwood Alliance, to develop the policy.

"The new policy reflects our commitment to being an environmental leader," Staples spokesperson Owen Davis said, crediting Green Corps and other student activists with catching the attention of Staples' management. "They made us take a closer look at what we were doing," Davis said.

"Staples' new policy is the beginning of the end of the practice of destroying endangered forests to make disposable paper products," said Cindy Kang, recruitment coordinator of Boston-based Green Corps, which waged a two-year campaign to change the procurement practices at Staples. "This is the result of efforts from concerned citizens across the country publicly demanding Staples stop selling our forests."

Staples, the world's largest office products company, with sales of more than $18 billion in 2006 and operations in 22 countries, quickly made good on its environmental commitment. In its 2003 Annual Environmental Report, Staples was able to claim that it had increased recycled content across all papers to more than 25%, well en route to its goal of 30%. This included paper in Staples' packaging and internal communications. Another

OPPOSITE: Solar panels have been installed at a Staples distribution center in Ontario, California.

part of its commitment was to encourage new sustainable forest development. In Indonesia in 2003, Staples worked with Japanese paper buyers, the World Wildlife Fund, and other environmental groups to secure a logging moratorium in a habitat for Sumatran elephants.

By 2005, the annual environmental report had evolved into a corporate responsibility report (Staples Soul), of which environmental awareness was just one aspect. In 2006, Staples Soul reported that using the Environmental Defense paper calculator, it estimated that by increasing its use of postconsumer recycled content in its Staples and non-Staples paper to 30%, it was saving the equivalent of 1.6 million trees, 71,800 tons of greenhouse gases, 596 million gallons of wastewater (equivalent to 900 Olympic-sized swimming pools), and 38,311 tons of waste (enough to fill 2,700 garbage trucks). Staples also sells 100% postconsumer recycled copy paper, which uses no chlorine.

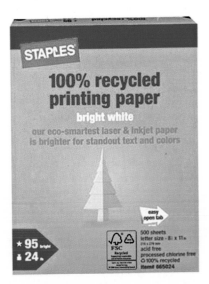

Staples offers more than 2,800 products with recycled content, ranging from 100% recycled copy paper to recycled file folders to remanufactured inkjet cartridges.

Miami mayor Manny Diaz and Staples regional vice president Royce Reed at the September 2007 groundbreaking of the Staples LEED-certified store in Miami. (David Adame/Staples)

Staples' future goals are to source more fiber from certified sustainable forests and to incorporate recycled plastics, although the company has set no public goals. Staples is working with Georgia-Pacific and the Forest Stewardship Council to explore achieving certification for forest products from small landowners in the southeastern United States, and it is also a member of the Paper Working Group, 11 major companies committed to conserving forests in sourcing paper products.

But, as Staples acknowledges, real change will come only with a change in consumer behavior and less paper use, which is why the company is seeking "environmentally preferable products beyond paper." However, beyond saying that it is "working to expand its selection," the company has no specific targets or goals in this regard.

Staples is making strides in energy conservation, now purchasing clean renewable energy for 20% of its U.S. electricity needs (up from 3% in 2003). The U.S. EPA estimates this prevents 218,000 pounds of CO_2 from entering the earth's atmosphere, the equivalent of taking 21,000 passenger cars off the road, and ranked Staples 4th in its 2007 list of Green Power retail partners (and 17th overall).

As part of its push to support renewable energy, Staples has built the largest private solar farm in New England at its distribution center in Killingly, Connecticut. The 3,184 solar roof panels provide 14% of the energy needs for the 300,000-square-foot center. Staples has also installed solar power systems in New Jersey and California and is looking to install another 15 systems over the next 3 years, as well as wind turbines in selected locations. In 2007, Staples broke ground in Miami for a green retail building registered with LEED, which will collect rainwater through rooftop gutter systems, use waterless urinals, and incorporate recycled building materials.

Despite Staples' commitment and gains, progress toward sustainability is tough to achieve. For example, the largest private solar system in New England generates enough energy to power a mere 36 homes. While the company says it is reducing "net operating expense associated with energy through an integrated approach and [improving] the net carbon impact associated with operating our business," and while net greenhouse gas emissions per square foot have dropped from 22 pounds of CO_2 per square foot in 2001 to 17 pounds in 2005, total GHG emissions are higher than they were in 2001. With offsets, Staples is reducing emissions and is ahead of its goal to reduce GHG by 7% on an absolute basis between 2001 and 2010. Staples' carbon footprint is focused in facilities and fleet operations, and to further reduce emissions it will continue to add more wind and solar power generation, introduce hybrid delivery vehicles, and sequester carbon in tropical forests.

Staples' environmental efforts have coincided with an improvement in its bottom line. For fiscal 2006, revenue rose 13%, to $18.2 billion, and net income increased 24%, to $974 million.

On the horizon, Staples envisions a move to green raw materials, including wood fiber from certified sustainable forests, agricultural waste, and lower-impact bio-based alternatives. The challenge remains to promote the manufacture and use of paper alternatives, based not on trees but on the residue from other crops such as cotton, sugarcane, and rice (so-called ag-res), which are now being produced in China, Brazil, and Thailand. After all, the U.S. Constitution was written on paper made not from trees but from hemp.

Give Us Your Cell Phones, PDAs, and Computers

Staples, which has long recycled ink and toner cartridges, also recycles used cell phones, PDAs, pagers, and batteries. Cell phones that can be refurbished are reused in developing countries; the remaining devices are recycled in a responsible manner, preventing toxics such as mercury, lead, and cadmium from entering the environment.

In 2007, Staples started accepting computers from any manufacturer or retailer for recycling, at a $10 charge. The computers are disposed of by Amandi Services, now Eco International. Staples is the first national retailer to accept computers on a daily basis (although it does not take TVs and floor-model copiers).

Vital Statistics

Main site: Framingham, Massachusetts
Main product: Reseller of office products (retail, contract, and delivery)
Number of employees: 74,000 worldwide
Green partners: EPA's Green Power Partnership and Plug-In to Recycling Program • Paper Working Group
Success: One of largest retail purchasers of green power according to EPA's Green Power Partnership list • Cut electricity consumption per square foot by approximately 15% from 2001 to 2007 • Reduced its truck fleet diesel use by 540,000 gallons in 2007
Challenge: Improving sustainable performance as a business and looking for new ways to make it easy for customers
Awards: Climate Champion Award—Clean Air–Cool Planet • Dow Jones Sustainability World Index • EPA Climate Protection Award • EPA/DOE Green Power Leadership in Green Power Purchase category

Greener Grinds

When do caffeine and conservation go hand in hand? When you're holding a Starbucks cup. The coffee company that made the Frappuccino famous is committed to environmental leadership. From the coffee beans used in its espresso machines to the paper cups with the trademark logo, the Starbucks Coffee Company is looking to reduce its environmental impact in all facets of its business.

Starbucks changed the face of coffee consumption in America beginning in the 1980s, when American coffee was typically thin and weak. Starbucks made itself into a household name by creating nationwide consumer demand for a bolder, richer, more flavorful brew. High-quality arabica beans were hand-selected and roasted for flavor, and they were purchased from small, traditional farms in middle- to high-altitude tropical forests, areas that contain some of the highest levels of biodiversity in the world.

Meanwhile, the growth of industrialized coffee plan-

tations started causing problems for growers and the environment alike. Beans grown on plantations flooded the market, causing the price of coffee to drop. Lower prices put a squeeze on small growers, and by the late 1990s many couldn't make ends meet. Industrialized, plantation-style growing techniques were also wreaking havoc on local ecosystems. To increase crop yields, many owners used chemicals and pesticides and chopped down forests, creating more sunlight for the coffee plants but destroying natural habitats for birds and other animals. Rivers were polluted with the rotting debris of the outside shell of the coffee fruit, which is discarded after removing the green bean within it.

Several years ago, it became clear to Starbucks that it could have a bigger impact on increasing the supply of high-quality coffee and improving the lives of farmers at the same time. The company created the Coffee Sourcing Guidelines in 2001 and what is now called C.A.F.E. Practices (Coffee and Farmer Equity Practices). Farmers meeting the guidelines' strict environmental, quality, economic, and social criteria became preferred suppliers for Starbucks, and Starbucks pays them a premium over the going rate for mass-produced coffee. The guidelines reward, among other things, the use of sustainable farming methods, including composting coffee pulp, rotating crops to reduce soil depletion, and eschewing the use of chemicals and fertilizers. Starbucks worked with Conser-

OPPOSITE: Starbucks' first LEED-certified store in Hillsboro, Oregon (Muriel Hastings)

vation International, a global nonprofit group, to develop 28 specific criteria for farms and farmers. In 2006, 53% of all the coffee Starbucks bought was purchased from approved C.A.F.E. Practices suppliers, more than twice the volume it purchased the year before, and in 2007, the amount will be 45% above that. Starbucks' longer-term goal is to purchase 80% of its coffee from verified C.A.F.E. Practices suppliers.

Starbucks is also purchasing more fair trade coffee. To put this in context—although Starbucks buys only about 2% of the world's coffee—the company purchased about 14% of all the Fair Trade Certified coffee in 2006. As a result, Starbucks remains the largest purchaser, roaster, and distributor of Fair Trade Certified coffee in North America.

Consumer awareness of Fair Trade Certification has increased with 27% of Americans saying in 2006 they were aware of the certification, up from 12% in 2004. As a result of growing demand, many fast-food chains and supermarket warehouses are now selling Fair Trade Certified coffee, which ensures that fair labor practices are utilized and that farmers are paid equitably.

The Starbucks corporate office, Starbucks Center in Seattle, was recently awarded LEED Gold certification, the nationally accepted benchmark for environmentally sustainable buildings. The award is doubly impressive considering the building's size (more than 2 million square feet) and its age (it was built in 1912). Starbucks launched a recycling program and began tracking water and energy consumption at Starbucks Center in 1995. More recently, the company installed energy-efficient lighting and waterless urinals in restrooms and increased its purchase of environmentally responsible supplies. Starbucks Center now buys 31% of its electricity from renewable sources and finds alternative uses for 48% of its waste, thus diverting it from landfills.

Employees working at Starbucks Center can reduce their personal environmental footprint by participating in the company's Transportation Options Program. Employees who use public transportation receive subsidies, and carpool drivers get preferred parking spaces. There are even incentives for biking to work. In 2006, 34% of Starbucks Center employees participated in the program.

Starbucks stores are becoming increasingly green as well. Among the low-impact components you will find in their stores include low-flow faucets, which reduce water usage; fluorescent lighting, which uses only half the energy of incandescent bulbs; cabinetry made from 90% postindustrial material, with no added formaldehyde, and wood products that are Forest Stewardship Council (FSC) certified; and Eco-Terr flooring, composed of 70% postconsumer recycled content and 10% postindustrial content.

Starbucks white paper cups, used for hot beverages, are made of paper fiber and the industry standard liner (low-density polyethylene plastic). The paper provides rigidity, while the plastic layer keeps the paper layer intact by protecting it from the hot beverage. In 2006, Starbucks became the first company to start using postconsumer recycled fiber in its hot cups, despite the increased cost. The company estimates that 78,000 trees were saved in the first year from using the cups, which are made from paper containing 10% postconsumer recycled fiber (PCF). Starbucks nonhot cup purchases exceed 60% PCF. The company continues to explore ways to increase PCF content in all its paper and fiber goods, and plans to implement the use of the Environmental Paper Assessment Tool (EPAT) to address the sustainability of the company's fiber purchases beyond recycled content. EPAT will enable Starbucks paper buyers to evaluate potential suppliers based on energy use, greenhouse gas emissions, water use, forest certification schemes, and a number of other important factors. However, the plastic layer also makes the hot-beverage cups unrecyclable in most paper recycling systems. Starbucks is meeting this challenge by evaluating alternatives to the current plastic coating and is currently conducting a life-cycle assessment for bio-based plastics.

There are other ways to avoid using paper cups at Starbucks. Customers who bring their own mugs get a 10-cent discount off the price of their drink. They can also use store mugs if they are planning on settling in at a seat or table. And those corrugated cardboard sleeves, made of 60% postconsumer recycled fiber, means customers don't need double cups to avoid getting burned by hot beverages.

When possible, store managers are expected to recycle their stores' waste. Still, the ability of retail stores to recycle cardboard boxes, milk jugs, and other waste products is dependent on the availability of commercial recycling services. Many local communities that offer residential recycling do not have commercial recycling, and in those locations customers are encouraged to take glass and plastic bottles with them for recycling somewhere else. In 2006, 79% of company-operated stores in the United States and Canada had recycling programs in place.

Grounds for Your Garden

The largest part of the Starbucks waste stream is, not surprisingly, coffee grounds. The good news is that not all Starbucks coffee grounds are thrown away. In 1995, a team of store managers got together and realized that collectively they had received numerous requests for the grounds, which are organic waste. Who would want used coffee grounds? Gardeners—because the organic waste is a great base for garden compost. Coffee grounds have a carbon-nitrogen ratio of 20:1, providing optimal amounts of the carbon that drives the chemical changes that turn organic matter into compost. Today, Starbucks' Grounds for Your Garden program offers complimentary bags of spent grounds to parks, schools, nurseries, and individual customers—basically to anyone who asks. It's a win-win proposition, with Starbucks reducing the amount of waste it throws away and gardeners enjoying healthier crops without using commercially produced fertilizers. If you add the grounds to your compost pile, don't worry about separating out coffee filters and tea bags—the paper breaks down rapidly during composting. Also, make sure that coffee grounds comprise no more than 25% of your compost pile's content or it will become too acidic. You can also sprinkle used grounds around plants before rain or watering for a slow-release nitrogen bath. For a faster-acting fertilizer, dilute about half a pound of grounds with five gallons of water.

Vital Statistics

Main site: Seattle, Washington	
Main product: Coffee	
Number of employees: 3,500	
Green partners: Nitze Stagen • LEED consultant Atelier Jones	
Success: Creating coffee sourcing guidelines in 2001 • Purchasing 14% of the world's fair trade coffee	
Challenge: Age of company's headquarter building made it difficult to meet some of LEED-EB's documentation requirements	
Awards: LEED-EB Gold Certification of Starbucks Center	

Capturing Carbon Dioxide Beneath the Earth's Surface

StatoilHydro is an international integrated energy company based in Norway. The company is the leading operator on the Norwegian continental shelf and has operations in 40 countries. It also leads the petroleum sector in slashing greenhouse gas emissions. StatoilHydro, 60% of which is owned by the Norwegian government, was established in October 2007 following a merger between Statoil and Hydro's oil and gas activities. The company's facilities have the lowest emission rates in the oil industry—about 88 pounds of CO_2 per unit of production. That's nearly 70% less than the global industry average of 286 pounds, according to figures from the Association of Oil and Gas Producers.

"Climate strategy forms an integrated part of our business strategy," the company states in describing its twofold approach: reduce emissions from its facilities and boost CO_2 emissions trading. Other climate-related technologies include increasing energy efficiency, maximizing carbon capture and storage, and upping its use of clean energy and renewables such as hydrogen, on- and offshore wind energy, biofuels, and tidal power.

The company pioneered the world's first facility for removal and underground storage of carbon dioxide in 1996, at its Sleipner East project in the Norwegian North Sea. In collaboration with BP and Sonatrach (the state-run Algerian oil company), StatoilHydro now operates the world's first full-scale carbon dioxide capture project at a gas field, where it injects about a million metric tons of CO_2 annually into Algeria's In Salah gas field reservoir. It operates a similar liquid-natural-gas (LNG) facility at the Snøhvit field in the Barents Sea, where it strips carbon dioxide from the gas and injects it into an empty reservoir under the seabed offshore.

"We must adopt a global perspective when developing this solution, and we must get the cost of capture and deposition so low that the technology can be applied internationally," said StatoilHydro CEO Helge Lund. "If we can cut these costs together with good partners, treatment technology developed in Norway could become a global tool."

OPPOSITE: The Sleipner East project in the Norwegian North Sea is a pioneering facility for removal and underground storage of carbon dioxide.

While environmentalists applaud the burying of carbon dioxide, they oppose the component of using carbon to force more oil out of the ground. These activists argue that, once unearthed, petroleum will inevitably be burned, creating carbon and further exacerbating climate change—and so they advocate for keeping as much petroleum as possible underground.

"[I]t would be unrealistic to imagine a development over the next 30 to 40 years where oil and gas no longer served as the dominant energy bearers," the company counters. "We do not believe that the answer lies in rapidly phasing out fossil fuels in favor of renewable energy.

"Our job thereby becomes to minimize the unfortunate consequences of our business. We've chosen to adopt an aggressive approach to the carbon dioxide challenges [and] we must constantly ask whether we're sufficiently aggressive. One way in which we are doing this is to work systematically to reduce emissions."

The Norwegian government and StatoilHydro have reached an agreement on the construction of a full-scale capture plant for carbon dioxide at a combined heat and power plant being developed at the StatoilHydro operated refinery Mongstad. A CO_2 technology development company has been established with the aim of developing and qualifying CO_2 capture technology.

A full-scale CO_2 capture and storage facility is planned to be in operation by 2014. The capture facility will strip CO_2 from both crackers and the flue gas of the combined heat and power station. In addition to supplying the refinery, this power station will provide electricity for the Troll A gas platform, the Kollsnes processing plant under contract with the Troll license, and the Gjøa field that is under construction.

Carbon storage can create profit-building credits in growing carbon trading markets, a key climate strategy for StatoilHydro. The company established an emissions trading business unit in 2004 to comply with the Kyoto Protocol and the European Union Emission Trading Scheme (EU ETS), which it considers "important tools for achieving cost-effective reductions in global emissions." According to its securities filings, StatoilHydro has invested $10 million in the World Bank's Prototype Carbon Fund and $2.5 million in its Community Development Carbon Fund (CDCF), to earn credits for emission reduction according to the Kyoto Protocol.

Goldman Sachs recently named StatoilHydro as a leader in its GS Sustain index of sustainable companies, and the company continues to make the grade on a number of other sustainable and responsible investing indexes. The Dow Jones Sustainability World Index ranked StatoilHydro the world's best oil and gas company in sustainability terms four years running, and the company remains on the FTSE4Good index, which measures the performance of companies meeting globally recognized standards of corporate responsibility by facilitating investment. Norway's Storebrand also awarded StatoilHydro its best-in-class symbol of excellence for a leading environmental and social performance.

Finally, the company scored a 72 (out of 100 potential points) in the 2006 "Corporate Governance and Climate Change: Making the Connection" report commissioned by Ceres to identify best practices in corporate climate strategy and risk management. StatoilHydro's score was more than double the industry average of 34.8 points and fell only slightly behind the top scorers, BP (90 points) and Shell (79 points).

Two wind turbines on the island of Utsira in the North Sea off Norway provide stable electricity for 10 households.

Wind into Water

StatoilHydro's insistence that renewable energy will not supplant fossil fuels as a primary energy source in the near future is not preventing the company from actively pursuing innovative clean energy solutions. In 2004, the company established a program to turn wind into water. Two wind turbines on the island of Utsira in the North Sea off Norway provide stable electricity for 10 households. They also create hydrogen for generating energy when the wind lulls. An on-site electrolyzer transforms the wind energy into hydrogen, which is then stored in tanks. The hydrogen is then fed into a fuel cell or a hydrogen-based generator, which serves as the primary energy source during low-wind periods. The plant is completely emissions-free—the only residual is water.

The project is a model for sustainable renewable energy supplies of the future—and the world's first hydrogen-driven community. "The premise is to see how well isolated communities can operate entirely energy independent of the net [electricity grids]," says project manager Torgeir Nakken. "Supply from the plant is now so consistent that we take it for granted," says power recipient Sølvy Austerheim. "In the beginning, supply was a little up and down, but it's a research project, so we kept an open mind."

One challenge is making enough hydrogen, according to Nakken. "The operational flexibility of the electrolyzer is such that we cannot utilize all surplus wind power. At the same time, the efficiency of the hydrogen engine is low, so we consume a lot of hydrogen." A subsea cable delivers electricity to the island from the mainland-based transmission network. "It's a little ironic," she says. "The land-based net went down once, blacking out the rest of the island. We still had power." The hydrogen technology remains prohibitive due to high cost and low durability. The hydrogen-fueled generator is a good near-term alternative. The hydrogen engine at Utsira is converted from a natural gas unit and has the capacity to cover the total customer load.

The ultimate goal is to make the concept commercially feasible. "It looks like we can be competitive with conventional remote-site power supply—diesel or combined wind and diesel generators—in a 5- to 10-year perspective," says Nakken. The next decision milestone is in 2008, following the completion of a feasibility study in December. "If successful, large-scale demonstrations like Utsira will pave the way for a future hydrogen marketplace. Many improvements must still be made, but we've now identified many of the corrective aspects—edging us ever closer to closing the gap."

In 2004, the Utsira project won the prestigious Platts Global Energy Award for best renewables project in New York.

Vital Statistics

Main site: Stavanger, Norway	
Main products: Oil • Gas	
Number of employees: 40,000	
Green partner: World Bank	
Success: The world's first offshore facility, Sleipner, where CO_2 is captured and stored	
Challenge: To continue to meet the energy challenge in a sustainable manner • To be part of the solution to the climate-change challenge, not the problem	
Awards: GS Leader, Goldman Sachs Index of Sustainable Companies • Dow Jones Sustainability World Index Best Oil and Gas Company in 2003, 2004, 2005, 2006, 2007.	

From Seven Cows to Seven Continents— Changing the World One Yogurt Carton at a Time

In 1983, Gary Hirshberg and his friend and fellow environmental activist Samuel Kayman founded a yogurt company with seven cows and a makeshift recipe that they devised in order to help fund Kayman's nonprofit organic farming school.

Today, Stonyfield Farm is the world's largest organic yogurt company and has managed to hold fast to its founding principles of using pure organic ingredients, supporting small farms, and fighting global warming. Hirshberg is currently the president and CEO of Stonyfield Farm, although—tellingly—he prefers to be known as its CE-Yo. Backing up his puns with solid action, Hirshberg continues to donate a full 10% of the New Hampshire company's pretax profits to environmental causes each year.

Stonyfield Farm's growth has been meteoric. Gross revenue in 2001 was $72.6 million; five years later, in 2006, it hit $263 million. Over the past 18 years, the company has grown at an annual rate of 27.4%. Such growth sparked the curiosity of French giant Groupe Danone, which acquired about 85% of the company's shares between 2001 and 2003. According to Hirshberg, Danone's ownership has not affected Stonyfield's environmental and social missions but has, in fact, allowed the company to expand into a rapidly growing organic and natural dairy business in France and across Europe.

Stonyfield has been a part of the movement to counteract global warming since its inception nearly a quarter century ago. The company's efforts to improve efficiency at its New Hampshire facility have saved enough energy to power 4,500 homes for a year and have prevented more than 14,000 metric tons of carbon dioxide from entering the atmosphere. In 2005, a 50-kilowatt solar photovoltaic array—New England's fifth largest, and a powerful source of renewable energy—was installed at the facility, and Stonyfield Farm was the first American manufacturer to offset 100% of its carbon dioxide emissions, years before Al Gore's film, *An Inconvenient Truth*.

OPPOSITE: Gary Hirshberg is chairman, president, and CE-Yo of Stonyfield Farm.

Stonyfield Farm has won national recognition for recycling, tree planting, emission offsets, energy efficiency, and efforts to reduce global warming, including the Dana and Christopher Reeve Environmental Leadership Award and the Climate Wise Partner Achievement Award from the Environmental Protection Agency.

While Stonyfield Farm strives to minimize the waste produced in the manufacturing and shipping of its product line, expanding its organic milk production is a major challenge. In 2007, Stonyfield announced that it had

Stonyfield Farm lids alert consumers to the company's sustainable practices.

succeeded in converting to organic milk for all milk used in its products. The organic milk comes from CROPP, a Wisconsin-based farmer-owned cooperative that sells certified organic products nationwide. Further afield, Stony, the company's U.K. sister brand, and Glenisk, its counterpart in Ireland, are made from milk from the Glenisk organic dairy, while Les Deux Vaches, a French sister brand, is made from milk from French organic farms. Under Groupe Danone's ownership, Stonyfield has been successful at sourcing organic milk in Europe.

With the product comes the added environmental challenge of packaging. Extensive recycling programs help minimize the waste stream. The company donates the yogurt used in product testing and other waste by-products to local hog farmers, preventing excess landfill use and the incineration of unusable yogurt. Recycline, a Massachusetts-based company, has partnered with

Stonyfield to turn containers into disposable razor handles and toothbrushes. Stonyfield Farm has also enlisted the help of the University of Michigan's Center for Sustainable Systems. One solution developed by the center entailed switching the lids on the 6-ounce containers, which required 270 tons of plastic annually, to foil. When foil was used instead, enough energy was conserved to power almost 200 households for a year. In recent years, Stonyfield's award-winning program to minimize solid waste has prevented more than 16 million pounds of material from going to landfills or incinerators, the equivalent of preventing over 8,000 metric tons of carbon dioxide emissions from entering the atmosphere.

Hirshberg wants nothing more than for Stonyfield Farm to be au courant when it comes to technology, and the company has been at the forefront of using the Internet to send out its environmental message. In 2007, the Stonyfield Shift Shout Out contest sent company representatives to college campuses to record videos showcasing students' solutions to global warming that would be posted online. "This is a generation that has no problem sharing its opinion, and using technology and the Web to do it," Hirshberg says. "Judging from their views on climate change, they also have an optimism about the challenges of global warming that reassures my generation that, yes, it's a problem we can solve, if we work together and consider all options." The company donated $5,000 to the two winners' favorite environmental groups.

Nancy Hirshberg, vice president of natural resources at Stonyfield Farm, and sister of CE-Yo, Gary.

Climate Counts

The nonprofit Climate Counts program is among Stonyfield's most significant contributions, as well as a major influence on competitors and other companies. Climate Counts originated due to Hirshberg's desire to unite consumers and corporations in the fight against global warming. The Climate Counts Company Scorecard, funded by Climate Counts, allows consumers to take into account a company's track record on climate change when making purchasing decisions. "Businesses must play a significant role in stopping global warming, and we believe the key to influencing companies lies in the hands of the consumer," explains Hirshberg. "With the Scorecard, consumers now have the power to make good climate decisions in their everyday purchases."

Companies are scored on a scale of 1 to 100, based on 22 separate criteria inspired by 4 main questions: Does the company measure its carbon footprint? What efforts has it made to reduce its own climate impact? What is its support (or lack thereof) of global warming legislation? What information does it disclose to the public about its efforts regarding climate change? Each company's scores can be seen and downloaded in pocket guide format at www.climatecounts.org.

The Climate Counts project director, Wood Turner, believes that the Scorecard effectively empowers consumers. "Most of the recent attention has been on what people and families can do to reduce their own climate footprint, such as buying compact fluorescent lightbulbs or energy-efficient appliances," Turner says. "But consumers . . . can motivate companies to take meaningful action to fight global warming. We've created this tool to help people flex their consumer muscle."

Vital Statistics

Main site: Londonderry, New Hampshire	
Main products: Organic yogurt • Organic milk	
Number of employees: 430	
Green partner: Climate Counts	
Success: World's leading organic yogurt maker • Number three yogurt brand in United States	
Challenge: Providing environmentally responsible products with the finest ingredients at a price that shoppers can afford • Being a cutting-edge low-carbon company in an economic system that externalizes the costs of carbon to society	
Awards: National Conservation Achievement Award in Corporate Leadership—National Wildlife Federation • EPA/DOE Green Power Leadership Award • EPA Business, Industry and Professional Organizations Environmental Merit Award	

Here Comes the Sun

Corporations and governments looking for ways to cut back on their fossil fuel consumption are increasingly turning to alternative energy sources, but higher costs remain an issue. SunEdison, a Maryland-based solar energy services company, has taken a giant step toward solving the problem by pioneering a business model that lets customers buy solar electric power with no up-front costs. Under the arrangement, called a solar power services agreement (SPSA), SunEdison finances, builds, operates, and maintains the solar plants and sells the solar electricity to customers at or below current utility rates. An SPSA is essentially a power purchase agreement based solely on solar power production.

SunEdison's innovative model has propelled the company into being the United States' largest solar energy services provider. Customers include the U.S. Department of Energy, Kohl's, Whole Foods, and Xcel Energy, a traditional electricity and natural gas utility company. The SPSA model is being copied by other alternative energy providers, including makers of solar thermal and geothermal heat pump systems. The Department of Energy awarded SunEdison a 2007 Green Power Leadership award for its role in advancing more widespread adoption of renewable energy.

SPSAs are a great solution for customers who want to buy clean solar energy but not the systems necessary to produce it. The modules needed to build a solar system typically represent about 40% to 50% of the total cost of a system, though manufacturing advances are causing those prices to drop by about 5% a year. In the past, the large capital outlays for equipment, coupled with a higher price per watt than regular electricity, deterred the growth of solar energy. Now, with backing from venture capital firms and banks including Goldman Sachs, SunEdison can offer prospective customers zero-emissions solar electricity with no up-front costs and no responsibilities for the system itself. Investors in SunEdison also benefit from the federal government's policy of providing incentives for green energy. They currently receive an income tax credit of up to 30% of the invest-

OPPOSITE: Xcel Energy will buy solar power generated from arid land put to use with solar power generated by SunEdison's Alamosa, Colorado, photovoltaic plant, the largest in the United States supporting substation loads.

ment (although that credit may be adjusted at the end of 2008) and a five-year accelerated depreciation schedule for the equipment.

SunEdison analyzes the technical feasibility of locating a solar power system at a site, which can be mounted on rooftops or on the ground in arid locations. It also determines the best technology to use, given engineering, space, load factors, and availability. Because the company is not a manufacturer of solar equipment, it is not wedded to any particular technology and can pick among a variety of options for the site. Then SunEdison finances, builds, maintains, and operates the facility. To make the systems more transparent and user-friendly, safety statements and detailed data about the system's production are provided to the customer.

Customers agree to long-term pricing contracts, a benefit not always possible with traditional utilities because of fluctuating fossil fuel prices. Whole Foods installed a SunEdison system in some of its stores in New Jersey in 2004. Because electricity rates in New Jersey rose significantly over the following years, SunEdison executives say Whole Foods saved 25% from what it would have spent without the solar system.

As part of its up-front feasibility study, SunEdison does an economic analysis to ensure that solar makes business sense for the prospective client. Federal and state regulations impact net prices for both system installations and ongoing solar energy costs. A patchwork of state regulations impacts how and even if solar can be deployed in a particular location. In 2007, some 26 states had set Renewables Portfolio Standards, meaning that a specific percentage of energy generated by utilities must come from renewable sources. The standards have created a market for renewable energy credits that utilities can trade to meet the goals. SunEdison executives have testified before state and federal legislators on how solar can support the increasing demand for renewable energy. Their familiarity with the issues has enabled the company to create a best practices portfolio to meet complex utility regulations. "Solar is complex. By driving standards, SunEdison is simplifying solar for customers who want green energy, and for the solar industry as a whole," said company CEO Thomas M. Rainwater.

SunEdison was founded by Jigar Shah in 2003, and Rainwater was named chief executive officer in 2007. Rainwater, who formerly held leadership positions in traditional energy companies, hopes to leverage his experience to help build SunEdison into a large, utility-scale solar energy provider. The company's biggest coup to date is Kohl's department stores, which flipped the switch

SunEdison-certified solar technicians perform routine maintenance at the 8.22 MW Alamosa solar system.

on a rooftop solar energy system in 2007 as part of the largest U.S. photovoltaic solar rollout ever. The department store chain plans to install panels on 63 of its 80 locations in California, making it a larger aggregated system than the other top five existing systems in the United States combined.

When it is completed, the installations at Kohl's will generate more than 35 million kilowatt-hours of energy annually, the equivalent of powering about 3,000 California homes. In its first year, the solar energy used by Kohl's will prevent more than 28 million pounds of carbon dioxide from being released into the atmosphere, and over the next 20 years more than 515 million pounds of emissions will be avoided. The project will help meet the goals established by the 2007 California Solar Initiative, a plan calling for the state to build solar systems that can generate 3,000 megawatts by 2017. In Colorado, Xcel Energy will buy solar power from SunEdison's new 8.2-megawatt plant there to help meet part of the state's renewable energy standard.

"Purchasing the output from the SunEdison solar plant is Xcel Energy's first foray into utility-scale solar power in Colorado; however, it continues our effort to lead utilities in renewable energy and environmental initiatives," said Tim Taylor, president and CEO, Public Service Company of Colorado, an Xcel Energy company. "It will allow us to begin building the amount of solar power generation that is needed for us to meet the solar portion of Colorado's Renewable Energy Standard of 20% renewable power generation by 2020."

Technological improvements and economies of scale should significantly reduce costs over the next few years. Manufacturing advances at silicon-panel makers are reducing the prices for solar systems, and SunEdison founder and chief strategy officer Shah would like to see a solar industry independent of government subsidies, perhaps as early as 2010.

As the rising demand for oil converges with growing global concern over the environment, the market for renewable energy is sure to grow.

Department of Energy Goes Solar

Ironically, until recently the Department of Energy's National Renewable Energy Laboratory (NREL) was powered solely by fossil fuels. That changed in 2007, when NREL announced that SunEdison would build a solar energy system near NREL's Solar Radiation Research Laboratory in Golden, Colorado. The project, expected to be completed in 2008, will provide up to 7% of the electricity that NREL uses. The project enables NREL to meet the EPA renewable-energy goal for federal facilities six years ahead of the 2013 requirement.

The 5-acre span of photovoltaic solar panels will produce approximately 750 kilowatts of power under a power purchase agreement.

Vital Statistics

Main site: Beltsville, Maryland
Main product: Solar energy services
Number of employees: 360
Green partners: Kohl's • Wal-Mart • Staples • Department of Energy National Renewable Energy Laboratory • Xcel Energy • City of San Diego • Port of Oakland
Success: First and largest solar energy services provider in North America of distributed and utility-scale solar systems
Challenge: Help consumers, utilities, and legislators understand that solar is a material resource for power
Awards: Department of Energy Green Power Award

An Open-Source Approach
to Eco-Responsibility

Sun Microsystems has pledged to reduce its U.S. carbon emissions by 20% below its 2002 baseline by 2012 and is committed to helping other companies follow suit through its driving principles: "Innovate, act, and share." By the end of 2006, the company announced that it had reduced actual greenhouse gas emissions from U.S. operations by 6.5% from 2002 levels.

Founded in 1982, Sun Microsystems developed much of the core software that fueled the information age, such as Unix and Java, and the TCP/IP sequence (the communications protocols on which the Internet runs). The company is especially renowned for its dedication to open-source software, in which information about the software is shared freely, including the software's underlying source code.

Every time you make a cell phone call, make a bid on eBay, or send an e-mail, a network connects you to a data center somewhere in the world. Electricity flows through computer chips, conveying the data to execute your task, and a corresponding poof of CO_2 goes into the atmosphere. The way Dave Douglas, vice president for eco-responsibility at Sun Microsystems, describes it, his job is to make the poofs smaller by tracking carbon usage throughout the data centers that process all this information and driving down that amount.

Worldwide, the power used by computer networks doubled between 2000 and 2005, and is expected to double again within five years, as networked services—from MySpace to a car's GPS system, online retailing, and remotely programmable thermostats—become an increasing presence in our lives. The company's challenge is to keep up with growing data demands while cutting energy use.

Sun Microsystems engineers have made Douglas's job of lowering the company's carbon emissions easier by introducing technology that is more powerful and energy-efficient than ever. The company's line of servers featuring CoolThreads technology process five times as much data per watt as servers less than half the size. The company has also developed a processor called the UltraSPARC T2, the most efficient processor on the market, using $\frac{1}{10}$ to $\frac{1}{30}$ the power of its competitors.

Because 90% of Sun Microsystems' own carbon footprint comes from electricity use, lowering the energy appetite of its data centers is a high priority. In addition to creating CO_2 emissions that cause global warming, the

OPPOSITE: Project Blackbox is a prefab virtualized data center that makes it easy for a company to deploy Sun Microsystems' energy-efficient solutions.

electricity flowing through the high-performance servers that support all of the electronic transactions generates a lot of heat—so much, in fact, that the heat threatens the performance abilities of the chips themselves.

Last year the company reengineered three of its data centers, saving space and energy while increasing computing power. In its Santa Clara, California, data center, for instance, the company reduced the number of computers needed through virtualization technology, which allows one computer to act as many servers, doing the same job with less hardware. The company also reorganized the way the servers were laid out in the building, so that hot air was deliberately concentrated in designated "hot aisles" from which it could be more efficiently vented or cooled.

Instead of blasting air-conditioning throughout the building 24/7, new air-conditioning systems were designed to respond to the needs of the system. Variable cooling systems were installed that turned on where and when needed, for instance, focusing on the hot aisles. The reengineered data centers reduced the company's overall carbon footprint by 1%.

Another innovation that saves energy is the Sun Ray, a superthin computer with no hard drive of its own. All the Sun Ray's processing is done remotely, in one of the company's newly reengineered data centers. As a result, the computer itself is highly energy-efficient. Many Sun Microsystems employees who work outside of the office use this technology. "It's more obvious each day that extreme efficiency is good for the environment and great for business," says company CEO Jonathan Schwartz.

At Sun Microsystems, the founders' green values may be more overt now than in the early days, but there was always a smooth connection between environmental ethics and the company's bottom line. Through open sourcing, Sun Microsystems encourages other companies to join in the quest for the most environmentally responsible, as well as powerful, solutions. In the absence of federal mandates to limit carbon, the company has helped build a voluntary confederation of companies working to limit their energy use.

Sun Microsystems has been a leader in making environmental responsibility easier for other companies to reduce their GHG emissions. The company launched the Eco Innovation initiative, which laid out user-friendly online tools to help other IT companies analyze and understand their environmental impact. For example, a company using the tools could reduce energy use by optimizing its own system configurations along the lines Sun Microsystems engineers have illustrated.

While a private consulting company might charge a lot to help an organization limit its carbon footprint, Sun founded OpenEco.org, the first-ever open Web community where companies can calculate, compare, and reduce their CO_2 emissions free of charge.

The company's innovations are not limited to engineering breakthroughs. For instance, it offers a take-back program that allows customers to ship products back at the end of their useful lives so that it can dispose of them responsibly. Sun Microsystems reports that it is able to recycle or reuse 95% of the materials in the returned products.

One of Silicon Valley's thorniest challenges in reducing greenhouse gas emissions is California's dependence on the automobile. A company with tens of thousands of employees generates a lot of emissions just by getting its employees to and from work each day. Without address-

The company's Open Work program allows employees to visit outpost workspaces, which cuts carbon emissions by reducing miles driven to work and the need for office space.

ing the "car" in "carbon," it is said, California will have a difficult time meeting the state's CO_2 reduction targets.

To address this challenge, Sun Microsystems created the Open Work program, which offers the option to employees to work from home or flexible offices—work spaces available for employees' use only when they need it, rather than permanent office spaces allocated to individuals. More than half of Sun's employees (17,000) participate in Open Work, which integrates leading-edge technologies and new workplace ideas so that employees work "anywhere, anytime, using any device." Using flexible offices part-time and working from home part-time allows employees to cut carbon emissions two ways—by reducing the miles driven to work and reducing the overall need for office space. Sun reports that its Open Work program reduces CO_2 emissions by 29,000 metric tons a year. The program is also allowing the company to attract and retain the best talent from around the world while reducing its office space by one-sixth. Employees who participate report that their productivity has increased by 34%, in part because they've shaved their commuting time by three hours a week. For 2006, the program accomplished the equivalent of taking 6,700 cars off the road and eliminating 18,000 tons of CO_2 emissions. Since the inception of the program in 2003, the company has saved $255 million on reduced office space costs.

Data Center to Go

Project Blackbox is a prefab virtualized data center that makes it easy for companies and other organizations to deploy Sun's energy-efficient solutions, whether for permanent facilities or for humanitarian crises such as the Indonesian tsunami or Hurricane Katrina. High-density, high-performance data centers are normally custom-built, but Sun Microsystems engineers found a way to build a standard data center that takes up one-third of the space of an average system, costs just a fraction of the price of a standard data center, and is 40% more energy-efficient than the competition. The company's modular data center was designed to fit into a standard shipping container for easy transport, so companies would not have to design custom data-center systems from the ground up. At www .sun.com/emrkt/blackbox/index.jsp the company provides open-source records and online tools to help other IT companies understand how it achieved such record-breaking energy efficiency, space savings, and performance all at once.

Vital Statistics

Main site: Santa Clara, California
Main products: Network computing infrastructure solutions • Computer systems • Software • Storage • Services • Java technology platform • Solaris operating system • StorageTek • UltraSPARC processor
Number of employees: 33,904 worldwide
Green partners: PG&E • Ceres • EPA Climate Leaders
Success: Open Work • Data center leadership • OpenEco.org: first-ever open Web community • Sun Fire T1000/T2000 server • Project Blackbox
Challenge: Reducing carbon emissions
Awards: Best in Class in approach to climate change disclosure—Carbon Disclosure Project (CDP) • First corporate Conservation Champion award

Batteries Included

TESLA MOTORS

The dream of building a practical, affordable electric car has remained elusive for over 100 years. Back in the early 1900s, Thomas Edison gave up after unsuccessfully trying to extend the life of alkaline batteries; his failure prompted him to advise Henry Ford to power the Model T with gas. Since then, attempts have been hampered by batteries that wouldn't hold a charge and by relatively cheap prices at the pump. But Martin Eberhard, an engineer and Silicon Valley entrepreneur who made his fortune in computers, wasn't deterred. Eberhard had shopped in vain for a high-performance sports car that got good mileage. Traditional sports cars were gas guzzlers, and no one was making fast electric cars that could go long distances. So in 2003, he did what any entrepreneur worth his salt would do—he created his own company, Tesla Motors, to build the car he wanted.

It was rough going during the start-up, and tension between management and creative led to Eberhard's departure from the company, in 2007. The first Tesla Roadsters rolled off the production line in 2008, sleek, speedy, and with a "tank" of battery-generated electricity capable of powering the car 220 miles before needing to be recharged. And one of the first Roadsters was earmarked for Eberhard's solar-powered garage.

For the management team at Tesla Motors, which includes chairman of the board and PayPal founder Elon Musk, reducing U.S. dependence on oil is a high priority. And since 63% of the gasoline used in America is for transportation, says Musk, cars represent a huge opportunity to do just that. Apparently others agree. The 650 cars scheduled for production the first year were sold out before the assembly line was even running, to A-list customers such as George Clooney and Matt Damon. The Roadster emits no greenhouse gases, and it even has a recyclable battery—making it the greenest production car available.

OPPOSITE: The Tesla Roadster goes from 0 to 60 in 3.9 seconds.

The Tesla Roadster's 220-mile range is a breakthrough for electric cars. Until the Roadster, electric cars had been powered first by lead-acid batteries and then nickel-metal hydride cells. Lead-acid has limited energy density, meaning that even very large batteries don't last long. They also weigh down the car, further limiting the range. The electric car that General Motors developed in the late 1990s, the EV1, had a 1,150-pound lead-acid battery that powered the car for only 90 miles in the best of conditions before needing 10 hours to recharge. Nickel-metal hydride came along a few years later, with better performance but an exorbitantly high price tag. Car manufacturers agreed that battery technology just wasn't advanced enough yet to make electric cars practical.

Fortunately, technology companies were also working to extend battery life because the success of their handheld products depended on it. They poured time and money into research and development, and as a result the lithium-ion batteries that power cell phones and laptops became both more powerful and more lightweight. One day Eberhard asked himself a question: why couldn't lithium-ion cells be used to power an electric car? Lithium-ion packs four times the energy density as lead-acid, and more power is being generated from increasingly smaller cells with each new generation of laptops. He decided to have a pack of lithium-ion batteries inserted into an electric vehicle kit car, AC Propulsion's tzero. The experiment worked. The tzero took off, reaching 60 miles per hour in 3.5 seconds and traveling 300 highway miles before the battery ran down.

The Tesla Roadster cars coming off the assembly line today have equally impressive statistics, with the added bonus of being comfortable and looking great. From the start, the Roadster was designed to be a driver's car—one that didn't compromise on style and performance the way previous electric cars had. The Tesla management team asked four automotive designers to come up with sketches, and at a company Christmas party in December 2004 employees voted on their favorites. A sketch from Lotus Design not only won the most votes but turned out to be the most practical because it was modeled on an existing Lotus chassis that was extremely lightweight—an advantage for an electric vehicle.

The car's high energy efficiency makes it inexpensive to operate. Taking into account the cost of recharging the battery, the average price to drive it is between one and two cents per mile. In a "well to wheel" analysis it performed on its own car as well as its competitors', Tesla found that the Roadster delivered twice the mileage and generated only a third the carbon dioxide as its closest rival, a hybrid. Compared to other sports cars, the Roadster is six times more efficient and produces 1/10 the emissions. The car's top speed is 120 miles per hour. It goes from 0 to 60 miles per hour in 4 seconds, putting it on par with the fastest production cars in the world, including the Ferrari Enzo and the Lamborghini Diablo.

Tesla's charge port

The Roadster is powered with a 950-pound battery pack consisting of 6,831 lithium cells, each about the size of an AA battery. The battery is recharged in about 24 hours using a conventional 110-volt cord, or in 4 hours with a specially designed charger that can be installed in a garage. Any source of energy can be used to charge the battery, including wind and solar. Tesla Motors has partnered with SolarCity, a provider of solar energy systems, to install solar panels for customers who want to charge their Roadster using a nonpolluting source of power. But using conventional coal- or natural-gas-generated electricity to charge the battery still results in substantially less pollution than internal combustion engines cause. The battery has an estimated life of about 100,000 miles, after which engineers believe there will be usable battery life, but its performance will decline.

At a cost of $98,000 each in 2008, the Roadster isn't cheap, although it's a bargain compared to the Ferrari or the Lamborghini. The Tesla team made the calculated decision to build a high-end car first and use it as an opportunity to perfect the technology. They believe that growing demand will spur innovation, as it did with laptops and cell phones. For example, better batteries will give cars increased range, which will make them more popular. The more Roadsters Tesla sells, the more cheaply it can buy batteries.

In 2009, Tesla Motors hopes to introduce a more affordable $50,000–$60,000 four-door sedan, project name Whitestar. Tesla will produce two types of Whitestars. One will run completely on batteries, and the other will contain a small gas motor that recharges the battery pack while the car is being driven. The all-electric car will have a range of about 200 miles, while the combination gas-and-battery-powered car will have an estimated range of closer to 400 miles. Later, Tesla wants to produce a $30,000 mass-market model.

Fighting Fires

In the summer of 2006, headlines announced alarming news—some Dell laptop lithium-ion batteries had burst into flames. Lithium-ion batteries have high energy density, making them efficient and economical. They also run the risk of thermal runaway, overheating that can result in an explosion, because so much energy is stored in such a small space. Thermal runaway in laptops or cell phones is usually caused by a manufacturing defect or an overcharge. The same possibilities would be true for the Roadster, but there is also the chance that thermal runaway could be caused by fire from a car crash.

Multiple safety systems are incorporated into the battery pack to safeguard against an explosion. As in laptops, the Roadster's battery pack is enclosed with aluminum instead of plastic because aluminum is structurally stronger and won't easily melt or burn. Each individual battery cell is packaged in steel cans for similar reasons. There is also a device that disconnects a battery cell if it reaches high temperatures. Cooling fluid is circulated continuously, keeping the active operating temperature of the battery pack at 25 degrees Celsius, well below the 150 degree Celsius temperature when thermal runaway occurs. Tesla has passed all the tests required by the federal motor vehicle safety standards, which involved crashing cars with batteries in them. It has also met United Nations testing standards, which imposes strict rules on transporting lithium-ion batteries.

Vital Statistics

Main site: San Carlos, California
Main product: Tesla Roadster
Number of employees: 250
Success: Manufacturing first high-performance all-electric sports car
Challenge: Price point for products
Awards: TechCrunchie for Best Clean Tech Startup—*TechCrunch* • Autopia Car of the Year—*Wired* magazine • Best Product Design, Ecodesign—*BusinessWeek*

Reducing Their Environmental Bootprint

Timberland 🌳

Timberland has always been focused on the great outdoors through its product line and today is looking outward using three primary strategies: community engagement, environmental stewardship, and global human rights. With a passionately stated effort to reduce its greenhouse gas emissions, Timberland president and CEO Jeff Swartz is tackling environmental stewardship from the boots up. "We spend every day looking for ways to reduce our environmental impact in the product development, manufacturing, and distribution processes," he explains.

The company's latest footwear products feature eco-friendly cork soles and bamboo wedge heels as Timberland takes its next steps toward sustainability.

Timberland has been particularly successful in its packaging, matching innovative design with customer education. Footwear boxes are made of 100% recycled postconsumer waste fiber and use soy-based inks for printing. Truly a different take on things, however, is the full-disclosure label on every box of shoes the company now sells. In 2006, the company launched an initiative designed to provide consumers with information about each product's social and environmental impact. Each Timberland shoe box features an Our Footprint label, modeled after the nutrition labels on food packaging. The labels disclose the average amount of kilowatt-hours needed to produce a pair of footwear; the amount of energy that was generated from renewable resources such as the sun, wind, or water; the percentage of factories that were assessed against Timberland's Code of Conduct; and the total number of hours volunteered in the community by Timberland employees.

The Our Footprint label led to the Green Index rating system, a related label that debuted on the company's Outdoor Performance line of products. The Green Index rates a product based on its average scores in three categories: climate impact (the greenhouse gas emissions created through production), chemicals used (the presence of hazardous substances), and resource consumption (the percentage of organic, renewable, and recycled materials).

OPPOSITE: Timberland recently installed a 400-kilowatt solar panel system at its California distribution center. The solar system generates nearly 60% of the energy needed to power that facility and eliminates the creation of 480,000 pounds of greenhouse gas emissions.

The Green Index offers a clear message about the transparency in environmentally responsible manufacturing Timberland espouses. Without comparable disclosure by competitors, however, it's difficult for a consumer to judge items on a like-for-like basis. Getting other manufacturers to share these details is a challenge Jeff Swartz is eager to conquer, by convincing them that detailed labeling is a plus for both producer and customer alike.

Renewable energy is another priority in Timberland's ongoing mission. Its emission reduction program includes energy reduction projects in everything from distribution centers to retail stores. Employees who purchase hybrid vehicles can pocket $3,000, and green freight standards have been developed with the help of Business for Social Responsibility.

The company provides employees a $3,000 cash incentive to purchase a hybrid vehicle, which offers higher gas mileage and lower tailpipe emissions than regular cars.

Timberland is also integrating renewable energy into its distribution centers. In 2006, Timberland's distribution center in Ontario, California, installed a large-scale solar panel. When completed, the 400 kilowatt solar power system, designed, engineered, and installed by Northern Power and manufactured by Sharp, was one of the 50 largest in the world. Timberland's European distribution center, in Enschede, Holland, is entirely powered by clean energy sources: wind, waste steam, and hydropower. And the company's manufacturing facility in the Dominican Republic uses wind and solar power to generate energy and heat water.

Timberland is extending its community education and outreach through a focused global reforestation program. In 2006, the company launched a campaign to plant one tree in England's Forest of Marston Vale for each pair of Timberland boots sold at the flagship store in London. "The response was so enthusiastic that the program will likely be expanded to the United States," says Betsy Blaisdell, Timberland's manager of environmental stewardship. In the Inner Mongolia region of northern China, Timberland is tackling desertification. By 2010, the company plans to have planted more than a million trees in the Horqin Desert.

Because Timberland believes that engaged and informed employees make for more responsible, responsive stewards of the environment, it is also effectively enlisting employees in its reforestation program. In 2007, the company hosted 170 Earth Day service events worldwide with the help of 9,000 volunteers, whose output was an estimated 53,000 service hours. The projects varied from installing portable greenhouses in New Orleans to restoring Hunt's Point Park in New York and removing invasive species from Singapore's mangrove swamps.

Timberland has also developed the Path of Service program. The program, started in 1992, offers employees 40 hours of paid time off to volunteer in their communities. A similar program, the service sabbatical, provides longer-term opportunities (three to six months) for employees to create positive, sustainable community change. Thanks to these community service programs and Timberland's nonprofit partners such as City Year, CARE, and Clean Air–Cool Planet, Timberland employees have spent more than 500,000 hours in communities around the world.

In 2006, Timberland joined the Facility Reporting Project (FRP), a multistakeholder effort launched by Ceres and the Tellus Institute to develop consistent, comparable, and credible economic, environmental, and social reporting guidance for individual facilities. Working closely with the FRP, Timberland developed its first facility-specific sustainability report for its footwear factory in the Dominican Republic. The company's goals for facility-level reporting were threefold: to build on the company's commitment to local accountability, focus on community engagement and continuous performance improvements at the local level, and provide the foundation for a dialogue between Timberland, its factory, and the factory's stakeholders.

"The facility-level CSR [corporate social responsibility] report and stakeholder dialogue have deepened our roots as a partner, employer, and community member," says Alex Hausman, CSR reporting manager at Timberland's corporate headquarters. "The continuous process of evaluation, dialogue, engagement, action, and measurement will serve as a model in communities worldwide."

Swartz does not try to pretend that a footwear company on the scale of his does not have a significant impact on the environment. The chemicals used in tanneries are harmful, and the energy required to make, transport, and sell Timberland products is significant. With assessment tools that rate leather tanneries and footwear suppliers, intense emission reduction efforts, the increase in organic cotton, and the switch to water-based adhesives, Timberland is working on the premise that knowledge is power—green power.

Bagging the Boots

Timberland wants to sell you a pair of shoes, and it knows you'll need something to carry them home in, but the company prefers it be reusable.

One of the company's recent retail campaigns offered Timberland customers the opportunity to purchase a reusable, recyclable shopping bag, and as a reward for their responsible choice, every time customers used the bag they received 10% off their purchase price. Don't have $5.50 for the earth? Timberland had a Plan B for less eco-conscious consumers as well. For every customer who chose to forgo the reusable bags, the company made a 10-cent donation to the Conservation Fund.

Vital Statistics

Main site: Stratham, New Hampshire
Main products: Premium-quality footwear • Apparel • Accessories
Number of employees: 6,000
Green partners: Clean Air–Cool Planet • The Climate Group • Organic Exchange • Ceres
Success: Industry-first ingredients label on footwear • Development of a rating system to measure and report on the environmental impact of products
Challenge: Reducing impact on the environment
Awards: 100 Best Corporate Citizens—*CRO* magazine

Running the Numbers

TOSHIBA
Leading Innovation >>>

Toshiba Corporation manufactures a dizzying array of products, ranging from DVD players, notebook PCs, home appliances, and mobile phones to elevators, medical equipment, and semiconductors. But despite the company's diversification, it has adopted a uniform and comprehensive approach to sustainability that spans nearly all of its product lines. That approach earned it the number five spot in *Newsweek*'s 2007 worldwide ranking of the most sustainable companies. How can executives managing vastly different businesses, which each face unique environmental challenges, all use the same framework? It all boils down to numbers.

Toshiba has developed quantitative techniques for measuring its environmental progress against its goals.

One such technique is the innovative Factor T, a mathematical formula that enables the company to find the right balance between environmental friendliness and quality. This methodology recognizes that technical advancements aren't always compatible with environmental goals. But rather than making product decisions based on an either/or basis, Toshiba executives have a tool to help them balance that trade-off. Factor T (the *T* stands for *Toshiba*) is a computation calculated by multiplying the degree in improvement of product value by the degree of the reduction of environmental impact. The T Factor is calculated compared to an earlier version of the same product, so that the company can measure whether the newest model is an improvement over the old.

For example, in the case of a notebook PC, value can be assigned according to specifications, including the PC's thin and light design, long battery life, and how well it resists water and screen distortion. The environmental factor could be derived by taking into account how much energy it uses while operating and how many of its parts can be reused or recycled at the end of its life cycle. If this number is greater than the number of last year's notebook PC, then success has been achieved; the higher the T Factor, the greater the accomplishment.

The T Factor number associated with each product is based on the product's eco-efficiency (the value of the product divided by the environmental impact of a

OPPOSITE: By using steam instead of air for cooling the high-temperature unit of a gas turbine, the gas turbine inlet temperature is maintained at 2700°F instead of the conventional 2,300°F. As a result, heat efficiency has been enhanced greatly, which translates into a reduction of 1 million tons in CO_2 emissions per power plant each year compared with a conventional oil-fired thermal power plant.

product), which can be aggregated to produce a single number indicating Toshiba's overall track record in improving its sustainability. In 2006, Toshiba calculated that its overall business processes and products were 59% more environmentally friendly than in 2000.

The goal for 2010 is to improve by 100% over 2000. To accomplish this goal, Toshiba has a three-pronged strategy. The company wants to reduce carbon dioxide and greenhouse gas emissions that result from product use and also during the production process itself. It is also looking at ways to reduce the use of chemicals in products and to reduce chemical emissions during manufacturing. The company's third strategy is to reduce waste and increase recycling. All of these strategies are backed up by numerical targets for improvement, with published data available to the general public for tracking results on an annual basis. For example, in 2006, the company succeeded in its goal of producing a higher number of ecologically sound products; in fact, Toshiba exceeded its target. It was not successful in reducing emissions from the use of chemicals, and the report indicates specific steps to improve performance.

One such cutting-edge product is Toshiba's notebook PC, which rates among the highest in the industry for being green. Of the eleven notebook PCs rated highest by the Green Electronics Council, eight are manufactured by Toshiba (as of January 2008). The highest-rated, the

Portégé R500, uses 50% less energy than it did when it was introduced in 2000, and has 47% fewer life-cycle carbon dioxide emissions. Its screen uses light-emitting diode (LED) backlighting for its liquid crystal display instead of the more common compact fluorescent backlighting, which contains harmful mercury.

More than 90% of the parts in the Portégé R500 are reusable and recyclable, and Toshiba sponsors a free take-back program so that consumers can easily recycle their computers. For a small fee, Toshiba also recycles computers made by other manufacturers. In 2007, the company co-sponsored major electronic waste efforts in New York City and in California that contributed to diverting a corporate-wide U.S. total of 1.5 million pounds of unwanted computers, TVs, VCRs, DVD players, and cell phones. That electronic waste otherwise probably would have ended up in landfills. Globally, Toshiba recycled 67,351 tons of product in 2006.

Toshiba partners with outside agencies to recycle as well. It has partnered with eBay on the ReThink Initiative, which offers information, tools, and solutions that make it easy to sell, donate, or recycle used computers and electronics. The company also teamed up with the Rechargeable Battery Recycling Corporation (RBRC) to help customers avoid throwing portable rechargeable batteries and old cell phones in the trash. Toshiba products with an RBRC label will have an 800 number on

---

Toshiba Group's T Factor is the value factor of a new product multiplied by its Environmental Impact Reduction Factor. As the value factor and the environmental impact reduction factor rise, the product's overall value rises proportionately.

$$\boxed{\textbf{T Factor}} = \boxed{\begin{array}{c}\textbf{Value Factor}\\ \text{(degree of improvement of product value)}\end{array}} \times \boxed{\begin{array}{c}\textbf{Environmental Impact}\\\textbf{Reduction Factor}\\ \text{(degree of reduction of environmental impacts)}\end{array}}$$

As the value of the product rises and the degree of its environmental impact lessens, the T Factor rises.

Overall value, including convenience and comfort, is based on customer input. The higher the value of the new product compared with the benchmark product, the greater the value factor.

Environmental impact is calculated by using the lifecycle assessment method. The lower the environmental impact of the new product compared with the benchmark product, the greater the environmental impact factor.

For example: in the case of a notebook PC

- Light and thin
- Long battery life
- Robust design
- Water-resistant structure
- Distortion protection screen
- High-speed processing and large-capacity data storage

- Low energy consumption
- Mercury free
- Adoption of substrates free from halogen/antimony compounds
- Fewer materials

Factor T is a mathematical formula that enables the company to find the right balance between environmental friendliness and quality.

them directing individuals to the proper donation spot.

Efforts to become more environmentally aware are targeted internally as well as externally. Toshiba America Medical Systems, which sells diagnostic and medical imaging systems, will replace its fleet of 180 company cars for sales and service employees with hybrid vehicles by 2010. At the corporate level, after analyzing the rental car data provided by Hertz, Toshiba executives determined that more than 74% of employee rental cars were full-size cars. Since midsize cars get on average 20% better mileage, employees could significantly reduce emissions simply by renting smaller cars. Toshiba partnered with Hertz so that Toshiba's online reservation system was automatically set at the midsize car level, and immediately saw the balance of rentals reverse to the more fuel-efficient models.

In 2000, Toshiba launched its green procurement policy, and it currently uses 5,000 suppliers that meet its criteria. Again relying on a quantitative assessment tool, Toshiba utilizes a 22-point environmental performance survey to rank suppliers; priority is given to those ranking highest. Toshiba also gives feedback to suppliers, advising them on how to raise their environmental scores.

Joining Forces

Our growing dependence on electronics—phones, computers, DVD players—means parallel growth in the problem of what to do with old, oftentimes toxic equipment. Ten states have enacted legislation requiring electronic waste recycling, and others are likely to follow suit. In response, Toshiba announced in late 2007 a joint venture with two other major manufacturers to create a company that manages the collection and recycling of electronic equipment.

Toshiba America Consumer Products partnered with Panasonic Corporation of North America and Sharp Electronics Corporation to create the new company. Called the Electronic Manufacturers Recycling Management Company (MRM), it provides cost-effective services to manufacturers complying with the recently enacted electronics recycling requirements in Minnesota. In its first few months of operation, MRM has already worked with 10 electronics manufacturers and has managed the recycling of over 2 million pounds of electronic waste. By developing and managing collective electronic recycling programs, MRM hopes to reduce the burdens placed on individual manufacturers as they comply with state laws. In addition to planning for recycling programs in several states, MRM is also positioned to offer recycling services as needed in other states or on a national scale. At the same time, the company aims to help electronics manufacturers, state and local governments, and consumers increase their awareness of what to do with old equipment, reflecting its continuing commitment to environmental responsibility.

Vital Statistics
Main sites: Tokyo, Japan, and New York, New York
Main products: Digital products • Electronic devices • Social infrastructure
Number of employees: 191,000
Green partners: ReThink Initiative • Rechargeable Battery Recycling Corporation (RBRC) • Green Electronics Council (EPEAT) • Energy Star • Plug-In to eCycling • U.S. EPA's Performance Track • Hertz Rental Car • Best Buy
Success: Integrating environmental vision and strategy throughout varied businesses
Challenge: Communicating environmental accomplishments to the public
Awards: Dow Jones Sustainability World Index • Plug-In to eCycling recognition • EPEAT product design recognition

With Pedal to the Medal, Toyota Accelerates into Hybrids

TOYOTA

Toyota has been known as a conservative follower of fashion, a maker of solid but stolid cars. No longer. With the bestselling Prius as its flagship, Toyota is introducing hybrids across its brand lineup and has sold more than 1 million to date. The company's strategy is in direct response to global environmental threats such as climate change, which is being triggered by rising CO_2 emissions from automobiles and other sources. "If automakers don't reduce smog-forming emissions, greenhouse gases, and the need for petroleum, we won't be in business," said former Toyota president Fujio Cho. Toyota showed a record $14 billion profit in its fiscal year ending March 2007.

The company is responsible for the world's best-selling car, the Corolla. More than 11 million Corollas have been sold over the past 40 years. Toyota also manufactures the bestselling sedan in the United States, the Camry, and is neck and neck with General Motors as the world's largest automaker. But it's the Prius, what *Fortune* magazine calls "the first vehicle to provide a serious alternative to the internal combustion engine since the Stanley Steamer ran out of steam in 1924," that has really captured the public imagination. It is, says *Fortune,* "a car designed for a world of scarce oil and surplus greenhouse gases."

Toyota, which has long been known for its efficient and process-oriented manufacturing, its solid yet uninspiring cars, and its tendency to follow rather than lead, hit a home run with the innovative Prius. With a 1993 mandate from then-president Eiji Toyoda to develop an alternative to the gas-fueled engine, the Prius was introduced in 1997, the first commercially produced hybrid. It exhibited some of the character of early Japanese imports from the 1970s: slow, small, quirky. In 2000, when it was first introduced in the United States, it took 13 seconds to accelerate from 0 to 60 miles per hour, 3 seconds more than the little Corolla. *Car and Driver* magazine reported, "The Prius alternatively lurches and bucks down the road, its engine noise swelling and subsiding for no apparent reason."

But with its relentless push to innovate and improve, the Prius quickly evolved for the U.S. market. And by

OPPOSITE: With an unwavering commitment to environmental protection, Toyota strives to create clean and efficient products and to conserve resources before their vehicles even hit the road.

2003 and 2004, when the second generation was introduced (Toyota provided five chauffeur-driven Priuses for the 2003 Academy Awards), high gas prices made Toyota's quixotic quest seem prescient. U.S. sales, 60% of global sales, hit 53,000 units in 2004, 108,000 in 2005, and more than 500,000 in 2006. *Consumer Reports* named the Prius, which gets 40 to 50 miles per gallon, the "most satisfying vehicle" each year from 2004 to 2007. "It's the hottest car we've ever had," said Jim Press, former president of Toyota Motor Sales. In 2004, General Motors vice chairman Bob Lutz had dismissed hybrids as "an interesting curiosity." By 2005, his tune had changed: "The manifest success of the Prius caused a rethink on everybody's part."

Today, Toyota has added hybrid versions of the Highlander SUV, three of the four vehicles in its luxury Lexus line, and the Camry, and is projecting total hybrid sales of 1 million by 2010. The combination of new hybrids with Toyota's typical fuel-efficient gas engines—the gas-engine Camry saves an estimated 220 gallons per year versus the average midsize car—has pushed Toyota's overall fleet fuel efficiency well above the industry corporate average fuel efficiency (CAFE).

Toyota's Environmental Action Plan covers a life cycle ranging from engineering, development, and design to manufacturing to sales and logistics. Their efforts have made them an industry leader in reducing energy and water usage, landfill waste, and emissions of volatile organic compounds.

Since driving cars and trucks accounts for more than 85% of the GHG emissions from a vehicle's life cycle (compared to manufacturing and shipping),* the fuel efficiencies are having their impact on CO_2 emissions. According to a report by Environmental Defense, Toyota's CO_2 emissions rate dropped by 3% from 2004 to 2005, while America's Big Three (General Motors, Ford, and DaimlerChrysler) saw a worsening of their fleet-average CO_2 emissions. However, Toyota's "carbon burden" grew more than any other Big Six manufacturer (125%), due solely to increased sales. Carbon burden, a term coined by Environmental Defense, factors in both the efficiency of vehicles and the carbon intensity of the fuel they run on, as well as new vehicle sales. "The ability of Toyota...to gain market share while cutting emissions is a clear example of innovative design paying off for the bottom line and the environment," said John DeCicco, senior fellow at Environmental Defense.

In manufacturing efficiency, Toyota is well ahead of its own benchmark goals for its first five-year environmental plan for 2002 to 2006. For Toyota, CO_2 per vehicle produced in 2005 was 0.94 metric tons, 22% less than 2000. (Ford, by contrast, emitted 1.3 metric tons per vehicle produced in 2006; GM does not divulge such figures.) Today, 85% of each Toyota car manufactured is recyclable. Energy consumed per vehicle produced was down 30% since 2000. Toyota also derives savings from efficient lighting and heat recovery systems. In 2006, Toyota won the Energy Star Award for Sustained Excellence, as energy consumed dropped 7% per vehicle (with a 4% increase in production).

In its second North American Environmental Plan, Toyota's goal is to "achieve best-in-class fuel efficiency performance" and reduce total energy usage in manufacturing by 27% over 2002's usage. Toyota looks to achieve a 10% reduction in CO_2 emissions per vehicle by 2012, again with 2002 as a base, and to maintain "zero landfill" at its manufacturing facilities, which means that Toyota gives away or sells every waste product it creates to companies that recycle the waste.

*Yvan Ardenti and Stefano Gilardi, "The Carbon Intensity of Car Manufacturers," March 2007. Centre Info. Study released at TBLI Conference, Paris.

Toyota's green image has come under fire from some environmentalists, such as the Natural Resources Defense Council and the Union of Concerned Scientists, for its marketing of the Tundra truck, one of the largest vehicles on the market. At the same time, Toyota joined forces with American manufacturers to lobby against raising the CAFE standard to 35 miles per gallon. Meanwhile, the new LS 600 Lexus is a V-8 "luxury" hybrid that sells for more than $100,000 and gets only 20–22 miles per gallon, which advances neither Toyota's green image nor the cause of carbon reduction.

In its main and more sedate hybrid line, Toyota is working feverishly to produce a lithium battery replacement for the conventional nickel-metal hydride battery, which is expected to increase fuel efficiency to 60–70 miles per gallon. It now appears the third-generation Prius will launch in 2009 with conventional nickel-metal hydride batteries. Meanwhile, the competition in the hybrid market is picking up. GM's first lithium-ion hybrid, the Saturn VUE Green Line plug-in, is expected by late 2009, and Honda is looking to introduce next-generation diesels.

"We need to improve the production engineering and develop better technology in batteries, motors, and inverters," says Toyota CEO Katsuaki Watanabe. "My quest is to produce a third-generation Prius quickly and cheaply."

Hybrids Join Corporate Fleets

As every car sales operation knows, the cornerstone of a solid long-term business is inclusion in corporate fleets, such as rental cars, cab companies, and sales forces. To date, hybrids have typically been excluded from fleets, perhaps because of legacy relationships with other manufacturers or concerns about durability and image. But, of course, it's now much easier being green.

The Yellow Cab Company in Dallas, Texas, for one, is introducing hybrids into its fleet, with 10 to 15 expected by the end of 2007. By 2011, the company hopes that every cab will be a hybrid. The current choice: the 2007 Toyota Camry.

Most hybrids aren't big or sturdy enough to meet taxi requirements, says Jack Bewley, president of Dallas's Yellow Cab Company. But the Camry is about the same size as the Ford Taurus, which the company currently uses—and the Camry gets 34 miles per gallon, 14 more than the Taurus.

In a much bigger deal, the City of Chicago signed an $8.7 million contract in 2007 to buy as many as 300 Toyota hybrids, part of a long-term plan to replace gas guzzlers in the city's 5,400-car fleet. Over the next three years the city will purchase 100 Prius sedans, 100 Camrys, and 100 Highlander SUVs. In 2008, the Chicago police department expects to buy 300 alternative-fuel police sedans that run on E85, a blend of 85% ethanol and 15% gasoline.

"Government and corporate fleets represent the real growth area for hybrids," says Art Spinella, president of CNW Marketing Research. "Better than a quarter of all hybrids being sold are either for commercial or government use."

Vital Statistics

Main site: Toyota City, Japan	
Main product: Automobiles	
Number of employees: 36,866 (United States)	
Success: Launched the first mass-produced gasoline-electric hybrid vehicle, the Prius, in 1997 • Offers six hybrid models in the United States • Sold more than 1.3 million hybrids worldwide	
Challenge: Achieving harmony with society and environment	

Reengineering a Cell Phone Network to Reduce CO$_2$

Vodafone is the world's largest mobile phone service provider, handling more than 250 million subscribers worldwide (including Verizon Wireless customers in the United States). Admittedly, mobile phones and the networks that service them have unavoidable impacts on the environment. But Vodafone has adopted an environmental ethic to help limit its carbon footprint: by reducing its energy consumption and that of its partners worldwide to reduce not only its environmental impact but also costs. In recent years, Vodafone has employed innovative tactics to increase its energy efficiency at its base stations and utilized renewable energy to help drive down CO$_2$ emissions.

Vodafone's environmental challenge is a formidable one, considering few industries are growing as fast as mobile phone companies. In the developing world alone, the number of active cell phones is doubling each year. So even as Vodafone becomes more energy-efficient, its overall carbon emissions are increasing as traffic on its networks continues to rise and it expands into emerging markets such as India.

Even though Vodafone saw a 25% increase in data traffic on its networks between 2006 and 2007, it was still able to reduce its overall CO$_2$ emissions from its data networks by 12% over the previous year and CO$_2$ emissions per unit of data by 29%. Vodafone's target is to reduce network CO$_2$ emissions per unit of data by 40% by the year 2011. In the same time period, overall CO$_2$ emissions are projected to increase by 15%–20% as its network traffic grows.

Energy usage for Vodafone networks accounts for more than 80% of the company's CO$_2$ emissions. So utilizing innovative energy solutions, such as renewable

OPPOSITE: Vodafone concept store

energy, is one of the ways Vodafone is reducing its environmental impact. In 2006 and 2007, renewable energy made up 17% of total network energy use. To increase its use of renewable energy and reduce overall CO_2 output, Vodafone implemented a renewable energy pilot program at some of its base stations, which transmit data as users make and receive phone calls. Starting with a base station in Greece, the company replaced a diesel generator with solar panels and a wind turbine, along with a backup fuel cell. A three-month test demonstrated that in remote locations with low power loads, solar and wind energy can generate sufficient power while reducing maintenance costs. Vodafone now has 123 solar base stations in Greece and 70 in Egypt. The company expects to bring even more solar and wind base stations online in the future—especially in regions with temperate climates.

All of these base stations use cooling systems to prevent equipment from overheating. The energy used to cool these stations accounts for approximately 25% of overall network energy usage. Traditionally, air-conditioning systems have been used to cool equipment and prevent possible network failures. But Vodafone's newer base stations use fresh air to cool network equipment. This system, known as free cooling, reduces the need for air-conditioning, which uses coolants composed of CFCs and HFCs—both harmful greenhouse gases that contribute to global warming. Vodafone has installed free-cooling systems at base stations in Germany, Greece, Ireland, and Spain. In Germany alone, free cooling is used at 1,555 base stations and has reduced energy usage by 80% compared to base stations with standard cooling systems. In warmer climates, where free cooling isn't as effective during the day, Vodafone has installed alternative equipment to enable free cooling at night.

Vodafone has taken other steps to dramatically increase its energy efficiency—by 33% since 2005. Other energy-saving initiatives include shutting down base stations in high-density areas when demand is low and identifying stations that don't require battery backup.

Since Vodafone doesn't manufacture telephones or other consumer electronics, it doesn't have direct control over the environmental impacts of those products. But it has made progress recycling its own waste. In 2006 and 2007, 97% of Vodafone's 9,959 tons of waste network equipment was reused or recycled, and all Vodafone subsidiaries have systems in place for efficient recycling of network equipment.

Vodafone estimates that consumers in high-income countries typically replace their mobile phones every eighteen months.

While Vodafone can control the safe and responsible disposal and recycling of its own equipment, it has no control over what happens to mobile phones used by its subscribers when they upgrade to newer models. Vodafone estimates that consumers in high-income countries typically replace their mobile phones every 18 months, regardless of the condition of the phone. "Currently, 90 million handsets are being sent to landfills every year—a crying shame when you think that 65%–85% can be either recycled or reused," says Tim Yates, chief marketing officer, Vodafone UK. To encourage customers to keep their phones longer, Vodafone offers customers special discounts and free airtime credit. In the United Kingdom alone, 20% of Vodafone customers chose to keep their old phones when renewing their contract in 2006.

Vodafone has started mobile phone recycling programs in Albania, Romania, and Egypt and is working with the Forum for the Future, a U.K.-based think tank, to introduce recycling in other developing countries, where most of the mobile phone growth is occurring. In 2006, Vodafone collected 1.4 million phones—30% of which were resold for use in developing countries. And for Vodafone, it doesn't stop at recycling. In many of the markets, all funds raised from the resale of the recycled phones are donated to charities, such as Global Cool, an environmental campaign committed to helping people reduce their personal CO_2 emissions.

Through direct and indirect tactics, Vodafone is employing innovative solutions to reduce its energy usage and overall CO_2 emissions in an effort not only to shrink its own carbon footprint but also to encourage its subsidiaries, affiliates, and customers to reduce theirs as well.

How to Recycle a Mobile Phone Base Station

Vodafone, like other mobile phone companies, often replaces network equipment. Outdated equipment is resold or recycled through partners such as Shields Environment, world leaders in maximizing network assets in the telecommunications industry. Equipment that cannot be resold is broken down and its hazardous materials are removed. Materials from lead-acid batteries are separated to produce bullion (which is refined into lead alloys), gypsum, and a co-polymer that can be sold. The remaining materials—acids—are neutralized, and the hazardous material that cannot be recycled is stored while scientists seek ways to recycle it. The remaining nonhazardous materials, such as cardboard, aluminum, and steel, are returned to productive use, and all plastics are incinerated to produce energy. Lastly, the circuit boards are sent to a specialist refiner to recover precious metals, including palladium, copper, gold, and silver. To top it off, Vodafone gets a cut of the return on the metals.

Vital Statistics

Main site: Newbury, England
Main product: Mobile phone networks
Number of employees: 63,000
Green partners: Forum for the Future • Global Cool
Success: Network carbon dioxide emissions per unit of data transmitted decreased by 29%
Challenge: To reduce network carbon dioxide emissions per unit of data transmitted by 40% by 2011 (from 2005)

Greener National Parks

A Xanterra Parks & Resorts escape offers experiences and activities as varied as the environments in which they operate, from the wetlands of the Everglades to the harsh desert conditions of California's Death Valley. As the largest national and state park concessioner in the United States, Xanterra is serious about preserving and protecting the fragile ecosystems that host its many hotels, lodges, restaurants, and campsites.

With more than 18 million people annually visiting state and national parks where Xanterra operates, the company has sizeable challenges in accommodating visitors and, at the same time, being respectful of its host—Mother Nature. The company's current environmental goals stem from a 2004 retreat attended by Xanterra's company-wide environmental management team and renowned environmental scientist Hunter Lovins. With the belief that businesses need to be economically as well as ecologically stable, the company developed Ecologix, Xanterra's company-wide, intranet-based environmental management system (EMS). It represents a "logical integration of ecology and business" that puts in place institutional programs to protect the ecosystems that envelop the company's hotels, restaurants, shops, and operational facilities. Ecologix, certified to the ISO 14001 international EMS standard, sets forth ambitious but achievable goals that act as the main objectives toward a truly sustainable business by 2015. The goals encompass fossil fuels, renewable energy, emissions and transportation, solid and hazardous waste, water usage, and sustainable cuisine.

Xanterra has implemented a multifaceted strategy to reduce fossil fuel use by 30% by 2015. They are doing it by building a 1-megawatt solar photovoltaic energy system (see sidebar); by using renewable, clean-burning biodiesel in many boilers and vehicles; by powering a portion of electricity demands at seven national park locations with wind power; and by retrofitting more than 50,000 light fixtures at all locations. Strategic conservation programs that designate areas for targeted shutdowns, installing energy control systems in rooms and facilities, and upgrading to Energy Star–rated equipment also contribute to the reductions. Xanterra was the first organization to build several U.S. Green Building Council LEED-certified buildings in national parks and has also pioneered Ecologix Environmental Suites, ultragreen

OPPOSITE: Xanterra Parks & Resorts' solar photovoltaic system at Zion Lodge in Zion National Park

rooms at Zion Lodge in Zion National Park. This multipronged strategy has resulted in a 17% reduction in overall CO_2 emissions during the past seven years.

Solid waste is an inevitable by-product of the hospitality industry, and it is augmented by the guests the company serves. In 2006, the company recycled 5.94 million pounds of solid waste; everything from packaging to food refuse to scrap metal was either recycled, composted, or diverted from landfills. This almost triples the 1.87 million pounds recycled in 2000. And every pound counts: at the Painted Desert Oasis at Petrified Forest National Park, more than 1,400 pounds of food waste was collected by employees to be used by local Navajo ranchers for their animals.

Xanterra has been greening its hazardous waste practices by isolating each waste stream and recycling it according to its composition, or, in the case of solvents, completely phasing them out in favor of green cleaners that pass the triple test of cost-effectiveness, cleaning effectiveness, and environmental performance. In 2003, Xanterra banned the sale of fishing lures, weights, lines, and other fishing equipment made of lead to keep the known neurological toxin out of its national park marinas—most of which are certified to the Clean Marina Standards.

With facilities located near some of the nation's cleanest lakes, fragile ecosystems such as the Everglades, and a resort in Death Valley, the country's driest location, there was a clear imperative to reduce the volume of water usage company-wide. Installing ultra-low-flow faucets and toilets and waterless urinals saves hundreds of thousands of gallons of water per year. At Zion, reducing irrigation of landscaped areas by 40% resulted in water savings of more than 9 million gallons in one season.

In 2001, Xanterra developed a Sustainable Cuisine program that initially began as a seafood policy to ensure that Xanterra avoided serving endangered fish in its 64 restaurants. Today, Sustainable Cuisine has grown into an aggressive company-wide program that includes seafood, poultry, meat, wine, coffee, produce, and soy milk. Employees throughout the country are aware of local opportunities to use food that is harvested using practices that are good for the environment. Chris Lane, Xanterra's vice president of environmental affairs, emphasizes the company's commitment to Sustainable Cuisine. "From the beginning, our goal has been to educate our guests and employees around the country about the importance of making environmentally responsible cuisine decisions. Xanterra has greatly benefited from the steamroller effect of increased awareness and the resulting ideas for additional initiatives."

In the late 1800s, architect Mary Jane Colter was hired by the Fred Harvey Company (which Xanterra acquired in 1968) to design buildings that reflected their natural settings, like Lookout Studio at the Grand Canyon.

One of the largest industries on earth, the tourism industry has a tremendous impact on the world's environment. It is also notoriously slow to track and report its environmental impact. Xanterra aims at being an industry innovator when it comes to setting an environmental example by establishing the standards by which other tourist-related organizations can measure themselves. Xanterra is the first hospitality company to publish a periodic sustainability report publicly disclosing its entire environmental performance. That performance is based on the company's unique Ecometrix tracking system—targeted environmental performance metrics that measure resource usage. This also means holding suppliers and vendors accountable for their impacts as well. To that end Xanterra has developed an Environmentally Preferable Procurement (EPP) program that provides quantifiable goals and targets as well as guidelines for staff members when making purchases. Xanterra sends a letter to all vendors and prints a policy on all packaging that explains environmental goals and vendor responsibilities. It also asks for participation in certain initiatives, such as minimizing waste generation, using environmentally preferable products and supplies, reducing consumption of natural resources (water, energy, materials), and evidencing proper waste disposal.

An additional challenge is not only minimizing the company's own impact but that of its guests. Xanterra educates guests about its environmental programs and how they can be involved through recycling, the use of efficient transportation systems, and purchasing environmentally preferable products it sells to guests. It also provides signage in guest rooms suggesting ways in which a guest can conserve resources, provides displays explaining renewable energy systems at particular locations, explains Sustainable Cuisine items, provides each guest room with a sustainability report and property-specific environmental information, and offers an environmental survey to some guests.

Xanterra has set out to accomplish an enormous task, and through its environmental policies and goals it has achieved enough to show that environmental performance within the tourism industry is not only tangible and quantifiable but economically advantageous as well. It continues to prove that being a good environmental steward is a necessary and attainable goal.

Desert Sun

In an effort to significantly reduce greenhouse gas emissions and dependence on fossil fuels, Xanterra is installing one of the largest renewable energy systems in the country. The 1-megawatt solar photovoltaic (PV) energy system at its Death Valley operations will harness the sun's energy to generate more than one-third of the annual electricity needs for Xanterra's operations there. This system, larger than five football fields, will include more than 5,700 solar panels and generate, on-site, more than 2.2 million kilowatt-hours (kWh) per year. Over the next 30 years, Xanterra's PV system will eliminate the emission of more than 284,000 tons of carbon dioxide, nitrogen oxide, and sulfur dioxide—primary contributors to global warming, acid rain, and smog.

Vital Statistics

Main site: Denver, Colorado
Main products: Tourism • Concessions • Resorts in national and state parks and private resorts
Number of employees: 8,500
Green partners: National Park Service • World Wildlife Fund
Success: Largest renewable energy system in tourism industry • Two LEED-certified buildings • Sustainability reporting • Ecologix Green Suites • Sustainable Cuisine • Clean Marina certifications • ISO 14001 certifications • Greenhouse gas emission reduction of 17% in eight years • 51% solid waste diversion rate
Challenge: Protecting the environment without sacrificing guest service
Awards: EPA Performance Track Corporate Leader • U.S. Department of the Interior Environmental Achievement Award • Geotourism Award for Sustaining the Environment of a Place • National Park Service Environmental Achievement Award—Travel Industry Association • Good Earthkeeping Award—American Hotel and Lodging Association • Innovation in Design Award—*Environmental Design and Construction* magazine • Environmental Achievement Award—American Society of Travel Agents

A Green Book Made by a Green House

RANDOM HOUSE

BERTELSMANN

Though the old adage says "Never judge a book by its cover," today Random House believes that its books should be a reflection of the company's commitment to green initiatives, and is thinking hard about how to produce book covers, jackets, and pages more responsibly.

When you compare a book to a cell phone or a garbage bag, for instance, it looks comparatively harmless: a book is nontoxic, biodegradable, never becomes obsolete, and it can be recycled, reused, and requires no additional energy to use (except brain power).

But a book's paper is made from trees, which are harvested from forests the world round, and the decimation of those forests is a major factor in climate change.

Random House alone purchases more than 120,000 tons of paper for book production each year—88% of the company's overall annual emissions. So in 2006 the publishing house took action by announcing an environmental paper strategy, committing to an increase in the use of recycled uncoated paper from 3% to 30% by 2010.

Producing *Green Biz* in an environmentally responsible manner was integral to the subject matter. As with the companies profiled in *Green Biz*, Random House had to balance multiple objectives: the book had to be beautiful, economically feasible, and it had to be green. A simple initial decision was to refrain from jacketing the book to save on the amount of paper used in the package. Choosing the paper and printing location was more complicated. Until recently, printing in color on recycled paper was problematic because the paper was porous and dingy. However, rising public awareness has encouraged paper mills to develop a brighter, smoother sheet from postconsumer waste (PCW) recycled paper. Random House's production department sourced a 100% PCW-recycled 100-pound OGP paper that takes color ink as well as any traditional art paper, and found an FSC-certified printer in China to print the book.

At first glance it would seem that Random House could have greatly reduced the book's carbon footprint by printing in the United States: Shipping the books by boat from China to Long Beach, California, and then by rail to the Random House warehouse in Maryland generates twice the CO_2 emissions of printing domestically (1.6 metric tons opposed to .8 metric tons). However, upon closer inspection it became clear that the saving of 5.5 tons of emissions by printing on 100% PCW would result in total fewer emissions. The following graph shows the difference between printing in the United States on 30% postconsumer recycled paper and printing on 100% postconsumer recycled paper in China.

Assumptions	
Book weight	3.5 lbs
Paper weight	3 lbs
Print run size	5,000 lbs
Paper waste	1,320 lbs
Total paper used	16,320 lbs

Domestic Printing	
Paper	
PCW recycled content	30%
CO_2 emissions [1]	41,271 lbs
CO_2 emissions	18.7 metric tons
Transport	Madison, WI, to Westminster, MD (truck)
Distance traveled [2]	831 miles
	7,271 short ton miles
CO_2 emissions	0.8 metric tons
Fulfillment [3]	0.3
Corporate overhead [4]	0.1
Total	
CO_2 emissions	**19.9** metric tons

International Printing		
Paper		
PCW recycled content	100%	
CO_2 emissions [1]	29,230 lbs	
CO_2 emissions	13.3 metric tons	
Transport	Hong Kong to Long Beach, CA (sea freight)	Long Beach, CA, to Westminster, MD (rail)
Distance traveled [2]	7,255 miles	2,660 miles
	63,481 short ton miles	23,275 short ton miles
CO_2 emissions	0.9 metric tons	0.7 metric tons
Fulfillment [3]	0.3	
Corporate overhead [4]	0.1	
Total		
CO_2 emissions	**15.3** metric tons	

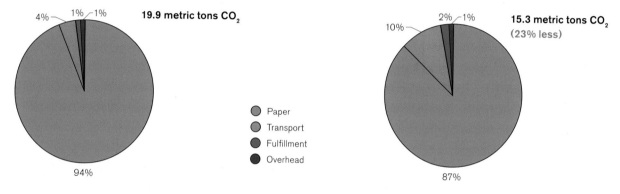

19.9 metric tons CO_2

4% 1% 1%
94%

15.3 metric tons CO_2
(23% less)

10% 2% 1%
87%

- Paper
- Transport
- Fulfillment
- Overhead

(1) Estimates based on information obtained from www.papercalculator.org; assumes 16,320 lbs of paper and 30% or 100% PCW content
(2) From Google Maps
(3) Prorated from total RH fulfillment emissions based on print run
(4) Prorated from total RH corporate overhead emissions based on print run

The Greening of Random House

While sustainable paper sourcing is by far the most crucial and immediate issue for the book publishing industry, educating and involving employees is also important for a business whose mission is to inform as well as entertain.

In early 2008, Random House received LEED certification for its headquarters in New York City, only the second existing building (as opposed to new construction) in the city to receive the designation. It was a fitting testament to the effective and thorough scrutiny made by the in-house green committee of every aspect of the building's operations, from paper recycling, energy sourcing, and water conservation to choice of lighting, cleaning products, and coffee cups.

Fifteen percent of the building's energy comes from wind energy provided from Sterling Planet. The lighting system has sensors that automatically shut off perimeter office lighting when there is no movement. Floor and lobby lighting are dimmed or shut down at off-peak hours. Four thousand lightbulbs in the building were recently replaced with energy-efficient and power-reducing bulbs.

Company Contacts

Alcoa Inc.
Alcoa Corporate Center
201 Isabella Street
Pittsburgh, PA 15212-5858
www.alcoa.com

Advanced Micro Devices, Inc. (AMD)
One AMD Place
Sunnyvale, CA 94088-3453
www.amd.com

Aspen Skiing Company
117 Aspen Business Center
Snowmass Village, CO 81615
www.aspensnowmass.com

Aveda Corporation
4000 Pheasant Ridge Drive NE
Blaine, MN 55449-7106
www.aveda.com

Bank of America Corporation
100 North Tryon Street
Charlotte, NC 28255
www.bankofamerica.com

Baxter International Inc.
One Baxter Parkway
Deerfield, IL 60015-4625
www.baxter.com

Ben and Jerry's Homemade, Inc.
30 Community Drive
South Burlington, VT 05403-6828
www.benjerry.com

The Body Shop International plc
New City Court
20 St. Thomas Street
London SE1 9RG
United Kingdom
www.thebodyshopinternational.com

BP plc
1 St. James Square
London, SW1Y 4PD
United Kingdom
www.bp.com

Bristol-Myers Squibb Company
345 Park Avenue
New York, NY 10154-0037
www.bms.com

British Telecommunications plc (BT)
81 Newgate Street
London, EC1A 7AJ
United Kingdom
www.bt.com

Citi
399 Park Avenue
New York, NY 10043
www.citi.com

Clif Bar & Company
1610 Fifth Street
Berkeley, CA 94710-1715
www.clifbar.com

The Coca-Cola Company
1 Coca-Cola Plaza
Atlanta, GA 30313-2499
www.coca-cola.com

FPL Group, Inc.
700 Universe Boulevard
Juno Beach, FL 33408
www.fplgroup.com

General Electric Company
3135 Easton Turnpike
Fairfield, CT 06432
www.ge.com

Goldman Sachs
85 Broad St.
New York, NY 10004
www.goldmansachs.com

Google Inc.
1600 Amphitheatre Parkway
Mountain View, CA 94043
www.google.com

Green Mountain Coffee Roasters, Inc.
33 Coffee Lane
Waterbury, VT 05676
www.greenmountaincoffee.com

Herman Miller, Inc.
855 East Main Avenue
Zeeland, MI 49464-0302
www.hermanmiller.com

Hewlett-Packard Company
3000 Hanover Street
Palo Alto, CA 94304-1185
www.hp.com

American Honda Motor Co., Inc.
1919 Torrance Boulevard
Torrance, CA 90501-2746
www.honda.com

HSBC Holdings plc
8 Canada Square
London E14 5HQ
United Kingdom
www.hsbc.com

IBM Corporation
1 New Orchard Road
Armonk, NY 10504-1722
www.ibm.com

IKEA Group
1700 East Bayshore Road
Palo Alto, CA 94303-2559
www.ikea.com

Intel Corporation
2200 Mission College Boulevard
Santa Clara, CA 95054-1549
www.intel.com

Interface Corporation
2859 Paces Ferry Road
Suite 2000
Atlanta, GA 30339
www.interfaceinc.com

Levi Strauss & Co.
1155 Battery Street
San Francisco, CA 94111
www.levistrauss.com

McDonald's Corporation
2111 McDonald's Drive
Oak Brook, IL 60523
www.mcdonalds.com

Mohawk Fine Papers Inc.
465 Saratoga Street
Suite 1
Cohoes, NY 12047-4626
www.mohawkpaper.com

National Grid
25 Research Drive
Westborough, MA 01582
www.nationalgridus.com

Nike, Inc.
1 SW Bowerman Drive
Beaverton, OR 97005-6453
www.nike.com

Novo Nordisk A/S
Novo Allé
2880 Bagsværd
Denmark
www.novonordisk.com

Patagonia, Inc.
259 West Santa Clara Street
Ventura, CA 93001
www.patagonia.com

Pacific Gas and Electric Company
(PG&E)
245 Market Street, #438
San Francisco, CA
www.pge.com

Rio Tinto plc
5 Aldermanbury Square
London EC2V 7HR
United Kingdom
and
120 Collins Street
Melbourne, Australia 3000
www.riotinto.com

SC Johnson & Son, Inc.
1525 Howe Street
Racine, WI 53403-5011
www.scjohnson.com

Seventh Generation, Inc.
60 Lake Street
Burlington, VT 05401-5218
www.sevengeneration.com

Staples, Inc.
500 Staples Drive
Framingham, MA 01702
www.staples.com

Starbucks Corporation
2401 Utah Avenue South
Seattle, WA 98134
www.starbucks.com

StatoilHydro
Forusbeen 50
N-4035 Stavanger
Norway
www.statoil.com

Stonyfield Farm
10 Burton Drive
Londonderry, NH 03053
www.stonyfield.com

SunEdison
12500 Baltimore Avenue
Beltsville, MD 20705
www.sunedison.com

Sun Microsystems, Inc.
4150 Network Circle
Santa Clara, CA 95054
www.sun.com

Tesla Motors
1050 Bing Street
San Carlos, CA 94070
www.teslamotors.com

The Timberland Company
200 Domain Drive
Stratham, NH 03885
www.timberland.com

Toshiba America, Inc.
1251 Avenue of the Americas
Suite 4110
New York, NY 10020
www.toshiba.com

Toyota Motor Sales, U.S.A., Inc.
19001 South Western Avenue, A404
Torrance, CA 90501
www.toyota.com

Vodafone Group plc
Vodafone House
The Connection
Newbury, Berkshire RG14 2FN
United Kingdom
www.vodafone.com

Xanterra Parks & Resorts
6312 South Fiddlers Green Circle
Suite 600N
Greenwood Village, CO 80111-4943
www.xanterra.com

Green Partners

1% for the Planet
www.onepercentfortheplanet.org
A global group of 757 companies that donate 1% of their sales to more than 1,500 environmental organizations worldwide.

American Forests
www.americanforests.org
Provides action opportunities to targeted audiences to enable them to improve their environment with trees.

Austin Energy (Green Choice)
www.austinenergy.com
The nation's 10th largest community-owned electric utility. Green Choice is its successful green power program.

Businesses for Social Responsibility
www.bsr.org
Provides socially responsible business solutions to many of the world's leading corporations.

CarbonFund.org
www.carbonfund.org
Supports renewable energy, energy efficiency, and reforestation projects globally that reduce carbon dioxide emissions through the purchase of carbon offsets.

CARE
www.care.org
Fights global poverty, placing a special focus on assisting poor women.

Center for Sustainable Innovation
www.sustainableinnovation.org
Conducts research, development, training, and consulting for and with companies around the world interested in achieving sustainability in the conduct of human affairs.

Ceres
www.ceres.org
A national network of investors, environmental organizations, and other public interest groups working with companies and investors to address sustainability challenges such as global climate change.

Chicago Climate Exchange
www.chicagoclimatex.com
Launched in 2003, the world's first voluntary, legally binding integrated trading system to reduce emissions of all six major greenhouse gases (GHGs) with offset projects worldwide.

City Year
www.cityyear.org
Program giving the opportunity to young people to perform extensive community service.

Clean Air–Cool Planet
www.cleanair-coolplanet.org
Partners with companies to develop economically efficient and innovative climate policies and mobilizes civic engagement to implement practical climate solutions.

Climate Counts
www.climatecounts.org
Nonprofit organization funded by Stonyfield Farm and launched in collaboration with Clean Air–Cool Planet.

The Climate Group
www.theclimategroup.org
Devised by a group of companies, governments, and other supporters to create new momentum in the international effort to stop climate change.

Climate Savers Computing Initiative
www.climatesaverscomputing.org
A nonprofit group of eco-conscious consumers, businesses, and conservation organizations started by Google and Intel in 2007.

Clinton Climate Initiative
www.clintonfoundation.org
President William J. Clinton's foundation dedicated to a business-oriented fight against climate change in practical, measurable ways.

Colorado Office of Energy
www.colorado.gov/energy
The governor of Colorado's Energy Office.

Community Office for Resource Effeciency
www.aspencore.org
Nonprofit organization promoting renewable energy, energy efficiency, and green building in western Colorado and beyond.

The Conservation Fund
www.conservationfund.org
An environmental nonprofit dedicated to protecting America's most important landscapes and waterways.

Conservation International
www.conservation.org
Nonprofit applying innovations in science, economics, policy, and community participation to protect the earth's biodiversity around the world.

Constellation New Energy
www.newenergy.com
An electricity supplier to business, commercial, and industrial accounts nationwide.

Dogwood Alliance
www.dogwoodalliance.org
A network of more than 70 groups around the Southern United States working to engender broad-based support to end unsustainable forestry.

Earthwatch
www.earthwatch.org
An international nonprofit organization that brings science to life for people concerned about the earth's future.

Eco International
www.enviroinc.com
E-waste recycling infrastructure incorporating the companies of Amandi, Envirocycle, and Nxtcycle, among others.

EI Solutions
www.eispv.com
Installs large-scale solar power systems.

Environmental Defense
www.environmentaldefense.org
A nonprofit that links science, economics, and law to create innovative, equitable, and cost-effective solutions to environmental problems.

Environmental Protection Agency
www.epa.gov
The branch of the U.S. government protecting human health and the environment.

EPA Climate Leaders
www.epa.gov/stateply
An industry-government partnership that works with companies to develop comprehensive climate change strategies.

EPA Design for the Environment
www.epa.gov/dfe
Works to replace traditional harmful chemicals, materials, and technologies with more environmentally conscious methods and technologies.

EPA Energy Star Computer Program
www.energystar.gov
With the U.S. Department of Energy, aims to protect the environment through energy-efficient products and practices.

EPA Green Power Partnership
www.epa.gov/grnpower
Lists partners who are buying green power.

EPA Performance Track
www.epa.gov/perftrac
Recognizes and drives environmental excellence by encouraging facilities with strong environmental records to set public, measurable goals to improve the quality of the nation's air, water, and land.

EPA SmartWay Transport Partnership
epa.gov/smartway
A collaboration with the freight industry to increase energy efficiency while reducing greenhouse gases and air pollution.

Environmental Resources Trust
www.ert.net
An environmental nonprofit dedicated to harnessing the power of markets to meet environmental aspirations.

Equator Principles
www.equator-principles.com
A benchmark developed by the banking industry for managing social and environmental issues in project financing.

Forest Ethics
www.forestethics.org
Aims to protect endangered forests by transforming the paper and wood industries in North America.

Forest Stewardship Council
www.fscus.org
A nonprofit organization devoted to encouraging the responsible management of the world's forests.

FuturGen Industrial Alliance
www.futuregenalliance.org
A $1 billion public-private partnership to design, build, and operate the world's first coal-fueled, zero-emissions power plant.

Global Cool
www.globalcool.org
U.K.-based group dedicated to instructing individuals on how to reduce their carbon footprints.

Global Forest Watch
www.globalforestwatch.org
The forest-related arm of the World Resources Institute.

Global Roundtable on Climate Change
www.earth.columbia.edu/grocc
Brings together high-level stakeholders to discuss and explore core scientific, technological, and economic issues to shape sound public policies on climate change.

Global Water Challenge
www.globalwaterchallenge.org
Works to provide clean water and sanitation to those in need.

Green Electronics Council
www.greenelectronicscouncil.org
Supports the effective design, manufacture, use, and recovery of electronic products.

Green Grid Consortium
www.thegreengrid.org
A global consortium dedicated to advancing energy efficiency in data centers and business computing ecosystems.

Green Power Market Development Group

www.thegreenpowergroup.org

A collaboration of the World Resources Institute and 12 leading corporations dedicated to building corporate markets for green power.

Green Seal

www.greenseal.org

Promotes the manufacture, purchase, and use of environmentally responsible products and services.

Green Suppliers Network

www.greensuppliers.gov

With the U.S. Department of Commerce, assists companies to practice lean manufacturing techniques coupled with sound environmental strategies.

Green-e

www.green-e.org

Independent certification and verification program for renewable energy and greenhouse gas emission reductions in the retail market.

Greening Australia

www.greeningaustralia.org.au

Organization dedicated to solving Australia's environmental problems through practical experience, community engagement, and science.

Greenpeace International

www.greenpeace.org

Commited activists fighting global warming, the destruction of ancient forests, and the deterioration of our oceans.

Healthy Child Healthy World

www.healthychild.org

Dedicated to creating a healthy environment for children.

Global Greengrants Fund

www.greengrants.org

Bringing together those who can offer financial support with grassroots groups in developing countries to make a change.

International Finance Corporation

www.ifc.org

Fosters sustainable economic growth in developing countries by financing private sector investment, mobilizing capital in the international financial markets, and providing advisory services to businesses and governments.

Jane Goodall Institute

www.janegoodall.org

A global nonprofit founded by renowned primatologist Jane Goodall that empowers people to make a difference for all living beings.

Kew Gardens

www.kew.org

The Royal Botanic Gardens, just southwest of London. Mission is to build and share knowledge about plants and fungi to show the vital role plants play on the planet.

Leave No Trace

www.lnt.org

Nonprofit organization dedicated to the responsible enjoyment and active stewardship of the outdoors by all people.

Metafore's Paper Working Group

www.metafore.org

Nonprofit organization that specializes in working with businesses to implement innovations relating to evaluating, selecting, and manufacturing environmentally preferable wood and paper products.

National Center for Atmospheric Research

www.ncar.ucar.edu

Plans, organizes, and conducts atmospheric and related research programs in collaboration with universities.

National Park Service

www.nps.gov

Cares for almost 400 natural, cultural, and recreational sites across the nation to preserve, protect, and share the legacies of the United States.

National Renewable Energy Laboratory (Department of Energy)

www.nrel.gov

The website of the National Renewable Energy Laboratory, a facility of the U.S. Department of Energy (DOE) for renewable energy, energy efficiency research, development and deployment.

National Resources Defense Council

www.nrdc.org

Uses law, science, and the support of 1.2 million members and online activists to protect the planet's wildlife and wild places, and defend endangered natural places.

NativeEnergy

www.nativeenergy.com

Offers carbon offsets that help build Native American, farmer-owned, community-based renewable energy projects.

The Nature Conservancy

www.nature.org

Conservation organization to protect ecologically important lands and waters.

Organic Exchange

www.organicexchange.org

A charitable organization committed to expanding organic agriculture, with a specific focus on increasing the production and use of organically grown fibers.

Organic Farming Research Foundation

www.ofrf.org

Fosters the improvement and widespread adoption of organic farming practices.

Pew Center on Global Climate Change

www.pewclimate.org

Brings together business leaders, policy makers, scientists, and other experts to spread information about climate change.

Pyramid Protocol Project

www.bop-protocol.org

Engages in and develops partnerships with low-income communities and works to develop business solutions that are beneficial to corporations and communities.

Rainforest Alliance

www.rainforest-alliance.org

Works to conserve biodiversity and ensure sustainable livelihoods by transforming land-use practices, business practices, and consumer behavior.

Rechargeable Battery Recycling Corporation
www.rbrc.org
Sponsors a national program, Call2Recycle, that helps people recycle their used portable rechargeable batteries and old cell phones.

Regional Greenhouse Gas Initiative
www.rggi.org
A cooperative effort of nine Northeast and Mid-Atlantic states to design a regional cap-and-trade program initially covering carbon dioxide emissions from power plants in the region.

Resources for the Future
www.rff.org
Conducts independent research, rooted primarily in economics and other social sciences, on environmental, energy, and natural resource issues.

Rethink Initiative
www.rethink.ebay.com
Addresses the problem of e-waste with information for its online community.

Roundtable on Sustainable Palm Oil
www.rspo.org
Researches and develops criteria for the sustainable production and use of palm oil.

Solar America Initiative (U.S. Department of Energy)
www.eere.energy.gov/solar
Part of an initiative to accelerate the development of advanced photovoltaic materials with the goal of making solar energy cost-competitive with other forms of renewable electricity by 2015.

Sterling Planet
www.sterlingplanet.com
Innovative supplier of renewable energy, energy efficiency, and low-carbon solutions.

United Nations Environment Programme
www.unep.org
Provides leadership and encourages partnership in caring for the environment by inspiring, informing, and enabling nations and peoples to improve their quality of life without compromising that of future generations.

UNEP Finance Initiative
www.unepfi.org
A global partnership between UNEP and the financial sector.

U.S. Climate Action Partnership
www.us-cap.org
A group of businesses and organizations encouraging the federal government to enact legislation for significant reduction in greenhouse gas emissions.

The U.S. Climate Partnership
www.usclimatepartnership.org
Dedicated exclusively to developing and implementing cost-effective greenhouse gas practices, strategies, and performance targets for all companies addressing the problem.

U.S. Green Building Council
www.usgbc.org
Nonprofit organization dedicated to sustainable building design and construction.

University of Michigan Center for Sustainable Systems
http://css.snre.umich.edu
Develops sustainable concepts for the design, evaluation, and improvement of complex systems through research and education.

University of Vermont Center for Sustainable Agriculture
www.uvm.edu/~susagctr
Integrates university and community expertise to promote sustainable farming systems throughout Vermont and the region.

Wildlife Conservation Society
www.wcs.org
Manages national and international conservation projects, research, and education programs.

Woods Hole Research Center
www.whrc.org
Conducts research, identifies policies, and supports educational activities that advance the well-being of humans and of the environment.

World Business Council for Sustainable Development
www.wbcsd.org
A CEO-led, global association of some 200 companies dealing exclusively with business and sustainable development.

World Resources Institute
www.wri.org
An environmental think tank focused on finding practical ways to protect the earth and improve people's lives.

World Wildlife Fund
www.worldwildlife.org
The leader in wildlife conservation and preservation of animal habitats around the world. A global environmental organization dedicated to conserving biological diversity, protecting natural resources, and reducing pollution.

Green Terms and Abbreviations

A complex and descriptive vocabulary has developed in response to the awareness of climate change and the work being done on overall environmental impact. These definitions have been reprinted courtesy of the EPA (www.epa.gov), The U.S. Green Building Council (www.usgbc.org), the National Learning Center for Private Forest and Range Landowners (www.forestandrange.org), and the World Bank Carbon Finance Unit (www.carbonfinance.org).

Air pollution: The presence of contaminants or pollutant substances in the air that interfere with human health or welfare, or produce other harmful environmental effects.

Alternative fuels: Substitutes for traditional liquid oil-derived motor vehicle fuels such as gasoline and diesel. Includes mixtures of alcohol-based fuels with gasoline, methanol, ethanol, compressed natural gas, and others.

Backwashing: Reversing the flow of water back through the filter medium to remove entrapped solids.

Biodegradable: Capable of decomposing under natural conditions.

Biodiversity: Diversity of species, genes, ecosystem function, and habitats.

Biofuels: Fuels made from biomass resources, or their processing and conversion derivatives. Biofuels include ethanol, biodiesel, and methanol.

Brownfields: Abandoned, idled, or underused industrial and commercial facilities/sites where expansion or redevelopment is complicated by real or perceived environmental contamination. They can be in urban, suburban, or rural areas. EPA's Brownfields Initiative helps communities mitigate potential health risks and restore the economic viability of such areas or properties.

Building envelope: The exterior surface of a building's construction—the walls, windows, floors, roof, and floor. Also called building shell.

Building integrated photovoltaics (BIPV): Photovoltaics that are integrated into building structures, so the solar modules also serve a structural role in the building.

By-product: Material, other than the principal product, generated as a consequence of an industrial process or as a breakdown product in a living system.

Carbon dioxide (CO_2): A colorless, odorless, nonpoisonous gas that is a normal part of the earth's atmosphere. Carbon dioxide is a product of fossil fuel combustion as well as other processes. It is considered a greenhouse gas, as it traps heat (infrared energy) radiated by the earth into the atmosphere and thereby contributes to the potential for global warming. The global warming potential of other greenhouse gases is measured in relation to that of carbon dioxide, which by international scientific convention is assigned a value of 1. Also see **Global warming potential (GWP)** and **Greenhouse gas.**

Carbon dioxide equivalent (CO_2e): The universal unit of measurement used to indicate the global warming potential of each of the six greenhouse gases. Carbon dioxide—a naturally occurring gas that is a by-product of burning fossil fuels and biomass, land-use changes, and other industrial processes— is the reference gas against which the other greenhouse gases are measured.

Carbon displacement: Offsetting of CO_2 emissions from fossil fuel combustion by substituting fossil fuels with bioenergy.

Certified emission reduction (CER): A unit of greenhouse gas emission reduction issued pursuant to the Clean Development Mechanism of the Kyoto Protocol, and measured in metric tons of carbon dioxide equivalent. Also see **VER (verified emissions reduction).**

Certified wood: Wood products bearing the FSC (Forest Stewardship Council) logo, which guarantees that the wood is from a certified well-managed forest.

Chain of custody (COC) certification: Chain of custody certification provides a guarantee about the production of FSC-certified products. Chain of custody is the path taken by raw materials from the forest to the consumer, including all successive stages of processing, transformation, manufacturing, and distribution.

Chlorinated hydrocarbons: (1) Chemicals containing only chlorine, carbon, and hydrogen. These include a class of persistent, broad-spectrum insecticides that linger in the environment and accumulate in the food chain. Among them are DDT, aldrin, dieldrin, heptachlor, chlordane, lindane, endrin, mirex, hexachloride, and toxaphene. Other examples include TCE, used as an industrial solvent. (2) Any chlorinated organic compounds including chlorinated solvents, such as dichloromethane, trichloromethylene, and chloroform.

Chlorofluorocarbon (CFC): Any of a family of inert, nontoxic, and easily liquefied chemicals used in refrigeration, air-conditioning, packaging, insulation, or as solvents and aerosol propellants. Because CFCs are not destroyed in the lower atmosphere, they drift into the upper atmosphere, where their chlorine components destroy ozone. Also see **Fluorocarbon, Hydrochlorofluorocarbon.**

Clean coal technology: Any technology not in widespread use prior to the Clean Air Act Amendments of 1990. This act will achieve significant reductions in pollutants associated with the burning of coal.

Clean fuels: Blends or substitutes for gasoline fuels, including compressed natural gas, methanol, ethanol, and liquified petroleum gas.

Climate change (also **global climate change**): The term is sometimes used to refer to all forms of climatic inconsistency, but because the earth's climate is never static, the term is more properly used to imply a significant change from one climatic condition to another. In some cases, "climate change" has been used synonymously with the term "global warming"; scientists, however, tend to use the term in the wider sense to also include natural changes in climate. Also see **Global warming.**

Closed-loop recycling: Reclaiming or reusing wastewater for nonpotable purposes in an enclosed process.

Combined heat and power (CHP) plant: A plant designed to produce both heat and electricity from a single heat source.

Compost: A humus- or soil-like material created from aerobic, microbial decomposition of organic materials such as food scraps, yard trimmings, and manure.

Compressed natural gas (CNG): An alternative fuel for motor vehicles; considered one of the cleanest because of low hydrocarbon emissions and relatively non-ozone-producing vapors. However, vehicles fueled with CNG do emit a significant quantity of nitrogen oxide.

Construction and demolition waste: Waste building materials, dredging materials, tree stumps, and rubble resulting from construction, remodeling, repair, and demolition of homes, commercial buildings, and other structures and pavements. May contain lead, asbestos, or other hazardous substances.

Cooling pond: A natural or man-made body of water that is used for dissipating waste heat from power plants.

Cooling tower: Structure that dissipates the heat from water-cooled systems by spraying the water through streams of rapidly moving air.

Cost/benefit analysis: A quantitative evaluation of the costs that would be incurred by implementing an environmental regulation versus the overall benefits to society of the proposed action.

Cost-effective alternative: An alternative control or corrective method identified after analysis as being the best available in terms of reliability, performance, and cost. Although costs are one important consideration, regulatory and compliance analysis does not require EPA to choose the least expensive alternative. For example, when selecting or approving a method for cleaning up a Superfund site, the agency balances costs with the long-term effectiveness of the methods proposed and the potential danger posed by the site.

Cost recovery: A legal process by which potentially responsible parties who contributed to contamination at a Superfund site can be required to reimburse the trust fund for money spent during any cleanup actions by the federal government.

Cost sharing: A publicly financed program through which society, as a beneficiary of environmental protection, shares part of the cost of pollution control with those who must actually install the controls.

Cradle-to-grave or manifest system: A procedure in which hazardous materials are identified and followed as they are produced, treated, transported, and disposed of by a series of permanent, linkable, descriptive documents (manifests).

Dioxin: Any of a family of compounds known chemically as dibenzo-p-dioxins. Concern about them arises from their potential toxicity as contaminants in commercial products. Tests on laboratory animals indicate that it is one of the more toxic man-made compounds.

Ecological risk assessment: The application of a formal framework, analytical process, or model to estimate the effects of human action(s) on a natural resource and to interpret the significance of those effects in light of the uncertainties identified in each component of the assessment process. Such analysis includes initial hazard identification, exposure and dose-response assessments, and risk characterization.

Electric hybrid vehicle: An electric vehicle that either (1) operates solely on electricity, but contains an internal combustion motor that generates additional electricity (series hybrid) or (2) contains an electric system and an internal combustion system and is capable of operating on either system (parallel hybrid).

Electric power grid: A system of synchronized power providers and consumers connected by transmission and distribution lines and operated by one or more control centers. In the continental United States, the electric power grid consists of three systems: the Eastern Interconnect, the Western Interconnect, and the Texas Interconnect. In Alaska and Hawaii, several systems encompass areas smaller than the state (e.g., the interconnect serving Anchorage, Fairbanks, and the Kenai Peninsula; individual islands).

EMAP data: Environmental monitoring data collected under the auspices of the Environmental Monitoring and Assessment Program. All EMAP data share the common attribute of being of known quality, having been collected in the context of explicit data quality objectives and a consistent quality assurance.

Emission cap: A limit designed to prevent growth in emissions and future stationary sources from eroding any mandated reductions. Generally, such provisions require that any emission growth from facilities under the restrictions be offset by equivalent reductions at other facilities under the same cap. Also see **Emissions trading.**

Emission factor: The relationship between the amount of pollution produced and the amount of raw material processed. For example, an emission factor for a blast furnace making iron would be the number of pounds of particulates per ton of raw materials.

Emission inventory: A listing, by source, of the amount of air pollutants discharged into the atmosphere of a community; used to establish emission standards.

Emission standard: The maximum amount of air-polluting discharge legally allowed from a single source, mobile or stationary.

Emissions trading: The creation of surplus emission reductions at certain stacks, vents, or similar emissions sources and the use of this surplus to meet or redefine pollution requirements applicable to other emissions sources. This allows one source to increase emissions when another source reduces them, maintaining an overall constant emission level. Facilities that reduce emissions substantially may "bank" their credits or sell them to other facilities or industries.

Energy efficiency, electricity: Refers to programs that are aimed at reducing the energy used by specific end-use devices and systems, typically without affecting the services provided. These programs reduce overall electricity consumption (reported in megawatt-hours), often without explicit consideration for the timing of program-induced savings. Such savings are generally achieved by substituting technologically more advanced equipment to produce the same level of end-use services (e.g., lighting, heating, motor drive) with less electricity. Examples include high-efficiency appliances; efficient lighting programs; high-efficiency heating, ventilating, and air-conditioning (HVAC) systems or control modifications; efficient building design; advanced electric motor drives; and heat recovery systems.

Energy-efficient motors (also **high-efficiency motors** and **premium motors**): Virtually interchangeable with standard motors, but differences in construction make them more energy-efficient.

Energy exchange: Any transaction in which quantities of energy are received or given in return for similar energy products.

Energy management system: A control system capable of monitoring environmental and system loads and adjusting HVAC operations accordingly in order to conserve energy while maintaining comfort.

Energy recovery: Obtaining energy from waste through a variety of processes (e.g., combustion).

Energy Star: In 1992, the U.S. Environmental Protection Agency (EPA) introduced Energy Star as a voluntary labeling program designed to identify and promote energy-efficient products to reduce greenhouse gas emissions. Computers and monitors were the first labeled products. The Energy Star label is now on over 50 product categories including major appliances, office equipment, lighting, and home electronics. The EPA has also extended the label to cover new homes and commercial and industrial buildings.

Environmental Paper Assessment Tool (EPAT): A project of the Paper Working Group that establishes consistent language and metrics to measure environmentally preferable paper. The Paper Working Group is a collaboration between 11 leading companies and Metafore with the shared goal of making environmentally preferable paper products more widely available and affordable.

Environmental sustainability: Long-term maintenance of ecosystem components and functions for future generations.

Feedstock: Raw material used for the generation of bioenergy and the creation of other bioproducts.

Fluorocarbon (FC): Any of a number of organic compounds analogous to hydrocarbons in which one or more hydrogen atoms are replaced by fluorine. Once used in the United States as a propellant for domestic aerosols, they are now found mainly in coolants and some industrial processes. FCs containing chlorine are called chlorofluorocarbons (CFCs). They are believed to be modifying the ozone layer in the stratosphere, thereby allowing more harmful solar radiation to reach earth. Also see **CFC.**

Fossil fuel: Fuel derived from ancient organic remains (e.g., peat, coal, crude oil, and natural gas).

Fuel economy standard: The Corporate Average Fuel Economy (CAFE) standard, effective in 1978. It enhanced the national fuel conservation effort, imposing a miles-per-gallon floor for motor vehicles.

Fuel efficiency: The proportion of energy released by fuel combustion that is converted into useful energy.

Geothermal/ground source heat pump: These heat pumps are underground coils to transfer heat from the ground to the inside of a building.

Gigawatt: A measure of electrical power equal to 1 billion watts or 1 million kilowatts. A large coal or nuclear power station typically has a capacity of about 1 gigawatt.

Global Effluent Guidelines (GEG): Wastewater guidelines established by Levi Strauss that suppliers must meet to do business with the company.

Global warming: An increase in the near-surface temperature of the earth. Global warming has occurred in the distant past as the result of natural influences, but the term is most often used to refer to the warming predicted to occur as a result of increased emissions of greenhouse gases. Scientists generally agree that the earth's surface has warmed by about 1 degree Fahrenheit in the past 140 years. The Intergovernmental Panel on Climate Change (IPCC) recently concluded that increased concentrations of greenhouse gases are causing an increase in the earth's surface temperature and that increased concentrations of sulfate aerosols have led to relative cooling in some regions, generally over and downwind of heavily industrialized areas. Also see **Climate change.**

Global warming potential (GWP): The ratio of the warming caused by a substance to the warming caused by a similar mass of carbon dioxide. CFC-12, for example, has a GWP of 8,500, while water has a GWP of zero.

Greenhouse effect: The warming of the earth's atmosphere attributed to a buildup of carbon dioxide or other gases. Some scientists think that this buildup allows the sun's rays to heat the earth while making the atmosphere opaque to infrared radiation, thereby preventing a counterbalancing loss of heat.

Greenhouse gas: A gas, such as carbon dioxide or methane, that contributes to potential climate change.

Halogen: A type of incandescent lamp with higher energy efficiency than standard.

Hazardous waste: By-products of society that can pose a substantial or potential hazard to human health or the environment when improperly managed. Possesses at least one of four characteristics (ignitability, corrosivity, reactivity, or toxicity), or appears on special EPA lists.

Hydrocarbon (HC): Chemical compound that consists entirely of carbon and hydrogen.

Hydrochlorofluorocarbon (HCFC): A compound consisting of hydrogen, chlorine, fluorine, and carbon. The HCFCs are one class of chemicals being used to replace the CFCs. They contain chlorine and thus deplete stratospheric ozone, but to a much lesser extent than CFCs. Also see **CFC.**

Joule: Metric unit of energy, equivalent to the work done by a force of 1 newton applied over a distance of 1 meter; 1 joule = 0.239 calories.

Kilowatt: A measure of electrical power equal to 1,000 watts; 1 kW = 3,412 BTU/hr.

Kilowatt-hour (kWh): A measure of energy equivalent to the expenditure of 1 kilowatt for 1 hour. For example, 1 kWh will light a 100-watt lightbulb for 10 hours.

LEED: The Leadership in Energy and Environmental Design (LEED) Green Building Rating System encourages and accelerates global adoption of sustainable green building and development practices through the creation and implementation of universally understood and accepted tools and performance criteria.

Life cycle of a product: All stages of a product's development, from extraction of fuel for power to production, marketing, use, and disposal.

Material Safety Data Sheet (MSDS): A compilation of information required under the OSHA Communication Standard on the identity of hazardous chemicals, health, and physical hazards, exposure limits, and precautions. Section 311 of SARA (Superfund Amendments and Reauthorization Act) requires facilities to submit MSDSs under certain circumstances.

Methane: A colorless, nonpoisonous, flammable gas created by anaerobic decomposition of organic compounds. A major component of natural gas used in the home.

Methanol: An alcohol that can be used as an alternative fuel or as a gasoline additive. It is less volatile than gasoline; when blended with gasoline it lowers the carbon monoxide emissions but increases hydrocarbon emissions. Used as pure fuel, its emissions are less ozone-forming than those from gasoline. Poisonous to humans and animals if ingested.

Metric ton: Common international measurement for the quantity of greenhouse gas emissions. A metric ton is equal to 2,205 pounds.

Natural gas: Underground deposits of gases consisting of 50% to 90% methane (CH_4) and small amounts of heavier gaseous hydrocarbon compounds such as propane (C_3H_8) and butane (C_4H_{10}).

Nitrate: A compound containing nitrogen that can exist in the atmosphere or as a dissolved gas in water and can have harmful effects on humans and animals. Nitrates in water can cause severe illness in infants and domestic animals. A plant nutrient and inorganic fertilizer, nitrate is found in septic systems, animal feedlots, agricultural fertilizers, manure, industrial wastewaters, sanitary landfills, and garbage dumps.

Nitric oxide (NO): A gas formed by combustion under high temperature and high pressure in an internal combustion engine; it is converted by sunlight and photochemical processes in ambient air to nitrogen oxide. NO is a precursor of ground-level ozone pollution, or smog.

Nonrenewable fuels: Fuels that cannot be easily made or "renewed," such as oil, natural gas, and coal.

Off-site facility: A hazardous waste treatment, storage, or disposal area that is located away from the generating site.

Offsets: A concept whereby emissions from proposed new or modified stationary sources are balanced by reductions from existing sources to stabilize total emissions.

On-site facility: A hazardous waste treatment, storage, or disposal area that is located on the generating site.

Ozone (O_3): Found in two layers of the atmosphere, the stratosphere and the troposphere. In the stratosphere (the atmospheric layer 7 to 10 miles or more above the earth's surface), ozone is a natural form of oxygen that provides a protective layer shielding the earth from ultraviolet radiation. In the troposphere (the layer extending up 7 to 10 miles from the earth's surface), ozone is a chemical oxidant and major component of photochemical smog. It can seriously impair the respiratory system and is one of the most widespread of all the pollutants for which the Clean Air Act required EPA to set standards. Ozone in the troposphere is produced through complex chemical reactions of nitrogen oxides, which are among the primary pollutants emitted by combustion sources; hydrocarbons, released into the atmosphere through the combustion, handling, and processing of petroleum products; and sunlight.

Ozone depletion: Destruction of the stratospheric ozone layer that shields the earth from ultraviolet radiation harmful to life. This destruction of ozone is caused by the breakdown of certain chlorine- and/or bromine-containing compounds (chlorofluorocarbons or halons), which break down when they reach the stratosphere and then catalytically destroy ozone molecules.

Ozone layer: Defined by the EPA as the protective layer of atmosphere in the stratosphere, 7 to 10 miles or more above the ground, that absorbs some of the sun's ultraviolet rays, reducing the amount of potentially harmful radiation reaching the earth's surface. Ozone depletion is caused by the breakdown of certain chlorine- and/or bromine-containing compounds such as CFCs or halons.

PET, PETE (polyethylene terephthalate): Thermoplastic material used in plastic soft drink and rigid containers.

Petroleum: Crude oil or any fraction thereof that is liquid under normal conditions of temperature and pressure. The term includes petroleum-based substances comprising a complex blend of hydrocarbons derived from crude oil through the process of separation, conversion, upgrading, and finishing, such as motor fuel, jet oil, lubricants, petroleum solvents, and used oil.

Petroleum derivatives: Chemicals formed when gasoline breaks down in contact with groundwater.

Photovoltaic and solar thermal energy (as used at electric utilities): Energy radiated by the sun as electromagnetic waves (electromagnetic radiation) that is converted at electric utilities into electricity by means of solar (photovoltaic) cells or by concentrating (focusing) collectors.

Photovoltaic cell: An electronic device consisting of layers of semiconductor materials fabricated to form a junction (adjacent layers of materials with different electronic characteristics) and electrical contacts and being capable of converting incident light directly into electricity (direct current).

Pollution prevention: Reducing the amount of energy, materials, packaging, or water in the design, manufacturing, or purchasing of products or materials in an effort to increase efficient use of resources, reduce toxicity, and eliminate waste.

Postconsumer: Status of a material or finished product that served its intended use as a consumer item. It may be recycled and incorporated into other materials (which are then identified as containing postconsumer recycled content or recovered material).

Postindustrial (also **preconsumer**): This refers to waste produced during the manufacturing process of virgin material and rerouted from one step in the process to the next. This does not refer to recycled material.

Power Purchase Agreement (PPA): The contract to buy the electricity generated by a power plant.

Rapidly renewable: Materials that are not depleted when used, but are typically harvested from fast-growing sources and do not require unnecessary chemical support. Examples include bamboo, flax, wheat, wool, and certain types of wood.

Recycle/reuse: Minimizing waste generation by recovering and reprocessing usable products that might otherwise become waste (i.e., recycling of aluminum cans, paper, and bottles).

Renewable energy resources: Energy resources that are naturally replenishing but flow-limited. They are virtually inexhaustible in duration but limited in the amount of energy that is available per unit of time. Renewable energy resources include biomass, hydro, geothermal, solar, wind, ocean thermal, wave action, and tidal action.

Site inspection: The collection of information from a Superfund site to determine the extent and severity of hazards posed by the site. It follows and is more extensive than a preliminary assessment. The purpose is to gather information necessary to score the site, using the Hazard Ranking System, and to determine if it presents an immediate threat requiring prompt removal.

Smelter: A facility that melts or fuses ore, often with an accompanying chemical change, to separate its metal content.

Emissions cause pollution. Smelting is the process involved.

Sulfur dioxide (SO_2): A pungent, colorless gas formed primarily by the combustion of fossil fuels; becomes a pollutant when present in large amounts.

Surfactant: A detergent compound that promotes lathering.

Sustainable forest management: Forest management that ensures that forest resources will be managed to supply goods and services to meet the current demands of society while conserving and renewing the availability and quality of the resource for future generations.

Treatment plant: A structure built to treat wastewater before discharging it into the environment.

Used oil: Spent motor oil from passenger cars and trucks collected at specified locations for recycling (not included in the category of municipal solid waste).

Verified emission reduction (VER): A unit of greenhouse gas emission reduction that has been verified by an independent auditor but which has not yet undergone the procedures and may not yet have met the requirements for verification, certification, and issuance of CERs under the Kyoto Protocol. Buyers of VERs assume all carbon-specific policy and regulatory risks. Buyers therefore tend to pay a discounted price for VERs, which takes the inherent regulatory risks into account.

Volatile organic compound (VOC): A variety of chemicals emitted as gases from certain solids or liquids.

Waste: (1) Unwanted materials left over from a manufacturing process. (2) Refuse from places of human or animal habitation.

Waste characterization: Identification of chemical and microbiological constituents of a waste material.

Waste exchange: Arrangement in which companies exchange their wastes for the benefit of both parties.

Waste feed: The continuous or intermittent flow of wastes into an incinerator.

Waste generation: The weight or volume of materials and products that enter the waste stream before recycling, composting, landfilling, or combustion takes place. Also can represent the amount of waste generated by a given source or category of sources.

Waste heat recovery: Recovering heat discharged as a by-product of one process to provide heat needed by a second process.

Waste minimization: Measures or techniques that reduce the amount of wastes generated during industrial production processes. The term is also applied to recycling and other efforts to reduce the amount of waste going into the waste stream.

Waste piles: Noncontainerized, lined or unlined accumulations of solid, nonflowing waste.

Waste reduction: Using source reduction, recycling, or composting to prevent or reduce waste generation.

Waste stream: The total flow of solid waste from homes, businesses, institutions, and manufacturing plants that is recycled, burned, or disposed of in landfills; segments thereof, such as the residential waste stream or the recyclable waste stream.

Waste-to-energy facility (also municipal-waste combustor): Facility where recovered municipal solid waste is converted into a usable form of energy, usually via combustion.

Waste treatment lagoon: Impoundment made by excavation or earth fill for biological treatment of wastewater.

Waste treatment plant: A facility containing a series of tanks, screens, filters, and other processes by which pollutants are removed from water.

Waste treatment stream: The continuous movement of waste from generator to treater and disposer.

Wastewater: The spent or used water from a home, community, farm, or industry that contains dissolved or suspended matter.

Wastewater operations and maintenance: Actions taken after construction to ensure that facilities constructed to treat wastewater will be operated, maintained, and managed to reach prescribed effluent levels in an optimum manner.

Wastewater treatment plant: A facility containing a series of tanks, screens, filters, and other processes by which pollutants are removed from water. Most treatments include chlorination to attain safe drinking water standards.

Water pollution: The presence in water of enough harmful or objectionable material to damage the water's quality.

Watt: A unit of power, or work done per unit time, equal to 1 joule per second. It is used as a measure of electrical and mechanical power. One watt is the amount of power that is delivered to a component of an electric circuit when a current of 1 ampere flows through the component and a voltage of 1 volt exists across it.

Index

A

acid rock drainage (ARD), 157
"additionality" concept, 1
Alcoa, 14–17
alternative energy
  Baxter International, 36
  BP, 46–49
  Clif Bar & Company, 64
  description of strategy, 1
  FPL Group, 70–73
  Google, 82–84
  Hewlett-Packard, 96–97
  HSBC, 105
  IBM, 108
  Intel, 117
  Interface, 121
  Mohawk, 130–32
  National Grid, 136, 137
  Novo Nordisk, 144–45
  Pacific Gas and Electric Company,
    152
  Staples, 168
  StatoilHydro, 174–77
  SunEdison, 182–85
  Timberland, 196
  Vodafone, 208
  Xanterra Parks & Resorts, 212–13
alternative transportation
  Bank of America, 33
  Clif Bar & Company, 65

  description of strategy, 2
  Google, 82, 85
  Green Mountain Coffee Roasters, 88
  Honda, 98–101
  McDonald's, 129
  Mohawk, 132
  Pacific Gas and Electric Company,
    153
  SC Johnson & Son, 161
  Seventh Generation, 165
  Starbucks, 172
  Tesla Motors, 190–93
  Timberland, 196
  Toshiba, 201
  Toyota, 202–5
Amazon National Park, 17
AMD (Advanced Micro Devices),
  18–21
Aspen Skiing Company, 22–25
Aveda, 26–29

B

Bank of America, 30–33
Base of the Pyramid Protocol project,
  161
batteries, lithium-ion, 193
Baxter International, 34–37
beeswax candles, 93
Ben & Jerry's, 38–41
biodiesel, 12

biodiversity and land conservation
  Alcoa, 17
  BP, 48
  Bristol-Myers Squibb, 52–52
  description of strategy, 2
  Goldman Sachs, 81
  Green Mountain Coffee Roasters, 89
  Pacific Gas and Electric Company,
    153
  Rio Tinto, 154–57
  Timberland, 196
biofuels, 49
block caving, 154
The Body Shop, 42–45
BP (British Petroleum), 46–49
Braungart, Michael, 8
Bristol-Myers Squibb, 50–53
"brownwashing," 4
BT, 54–57
bunker fuel, 12

C

carbon dioxide capture project,
  174–76
Carbon Disclosure Project (CDP), 4
carbon trading, 5
certification
  Aveda, 28
  Ben & Jerry's, 40
  The Body Shop, 42–45

certification *(cont.)*

Clif Bar & Company, 64

description of strategy, 2–3

Green Mountain Coffee Roasters, 86–89

IKEA, 110–12

McDonald's, 126, 128–29

Mohawk, 130, 132

Patagonia, 148–49

Staples, 168

Starbucks, 170–72

Stonyfield Farm, 180

Timberland, 194–97

Chicago Climate Exchange (CCX), 33

Citi, 58–61

Clif Bar & Company, 62–65

climate change

Alcoa, 14

Aspen Skiing Company, 22–24

Bank of America, 30

Citi, 58–60

description of strategy, 3

Google, 84–85

HSBC, 102–5

Pacific Gas and Electric Company, 150–52

Rio Tinto, 154–57

Stonyfield Farm, 178, 180–81

Coca-Cola, 66–69

Coffee and Farmer Equity Practices (C.A.F.E.), 170

coffee grounds, 173

composting, 173

consumer messaging and labeling

Ben & Jerry's, 38

Clif Bar & Company, 64

description of strategy, 4

General Electric, 74–76

Levi Strauss & Co., 122, 124

National Grid, 134–37

Pacific Gas and Electric Company, 153

Seventh Generation, 162–64

Stonyfield Farm, 180–81

Timberland, 194–96

cooking-oil fuel, 129

Cool Commute program, 65

cradle-to-cradle production, 8, 92

D

Dairy Stewardship Alliance, 41

Department of Energy, 185

E

Eco Innovation initiative, 188

emissions measurement, reduction, and trading

Alcoa, 14–17

AMD, 20–21

Bank of America, 33

Baxter International, 36

BP, 48

Bristol-Myers Squibb, 52

Citi, 60

description of strategy, 4–5

Hewlett-Packard, 96–97

Honda, 98, 100

HSBC, 104–5

IBM, 106–8

Intel, 120

Levi Strauss & Co., 124–25

Mohawk, 130

National Grid, 136

Novo Nordisk, 144–45

SC Johnson & Son, 160

Sun Microsystems, 186–88

employee engagement

Bank of America, 33

BT, 54–56, 57

description of strategy, 5

Google, 82, 84–85

Herman Miller, Inc., 90–92

Hewlett-Packard, 97

IBM, 108

Interface, 121

Timberland, 196

energy, alternative. *See* alternative energy

energy efficiency

AMD, 18–20

Baxter International, 36

description of strategy, 6

Hewlett-Packard, 94–96

Intel, 114–17

McDonald's, 128

National Grid, 134–37

Pacific Gas and Electric Company, 150–53

Seventh Generation, 164

Sun Microsystems, 186–88

Vodafone, 206–9

Evolution locomotives, 77

F

fair trade, 3, 44, 86, 88, 172

Fijian marine organisms, 53

flexible work hours, 54

Forest Stewardship Council (FSC), 3, 28, 110, 130, 132

FPL Group, 70–73

G

General Electric, 74–77

Global Climate Confidence Index, 105

Global Reporting Initiative (GRI) guidelines, 11

Goldman Sachs, 78–81

Gombe National Park, 89

Goodall, Jane, 89

Google, 82–85

green building

Aspen Skiing Company, 25

Bank of America, 30–32

Citi, 60

description of strategy, 6

Goldman Sachs, 80

Herman Miller, Inc., 90, 92–93

Honda, 101

HSBC, 105

IBM, 109

McDonald's, 128

Random House, 215

Seventh Generation, 165

Staples, 168–69

Starbucks, 172

Xanterra Parks & Resorts, 210–13

Green-e, 1

Green Grid, 21

greenhouse gas (GHG) emissions, 5

Greenhouse Gas Protocol, 5

Greenlist management system, 158–60

green manufacturing

Alcoa, 14–16

Coca-Cola, 68–69

description of strategy, 7
Herman Miller, Inc., 92
Honda, 101
IKEA, 113
Interface, 120
Novo Nordisk, 144
Patagonia, 148–49
Random House, 214–15
SC Johnson & Son, 160
Toyota, 202–5
Green Mountain Coffee Roasters,
    86–89
"greenmuting," 4
green product design
    AMD, 20
    The Body Shop, 44–45
    description of strategy, 7
    General Electric, 77
    Herman Miller, Inc., 92
    Hewlett-Packard, 94
    Interface, 120–21
    Levi Strauss & Co., 122–24
    Nike, 138–40
    Patagonia, 148–49
    Seventh Generation, 162–65
    Tesla Motors, 190–93
    Toshiba, 198–200
"greenwashing," 4, 164, 205

H
Herman Miller, Inc., 90–93
Hewlett-Packard, 94–97
Honda, 98–101
honeybees, 93
HSBC, 102–5
hybrid locomotive, 77
hybrid trucks, 12, 153
hydrogen research, 49, 101

I
IBM, 106–9
ICT carbon emissions, 57
IKEA, 110–13
information communications technology
    (ICT), 57
Intel, 114–17
Interface, 118–21
iron-making, 154

L
land conservation. *See* biodiversity and
    land conservation
LEED certification, 6, 32, 60, 80,
    92–93, 116, 128, 169, 172,
    210, 215
Levi Strauss & Co., 122–25
lithium-ion batteries, 193

M
Manufacturers Recycling Management
    Company (MRM), 201
Marine Stewardship Council
    (MSC), 3
McDonald's, 126–29
McDonough, William, 8, 92
Mohawk, 130–33

N
National Grid, 134–37
NativeEnergy, 64
Nature Conservancy, 52
Nike, 138–41
Novo Nordisk, 142–45
nuclear power, 72

O
OpenEco.org, 188
Open Work program, 188–89
organic materials and products, 2,
    86–89, 140, 148–49, 180

P
Pacific Gas and Electric Company,
    150–53
palm oil, 45, 113
Patagonia, 146–49
product stewardship
    description of strategy, 8
    Herman Miller, Inc., 92
    Hewlett-Packard, 94
    Interface, 120–21
    Nike, 138
    Novo Nordisk, 144
    StatoilHydro, 174–77
    Toshiba, 198–201
Project Big Green, 109
Project Blackbox, 189

public policy leadership
    Alcoa, 17
    Aspen Skiing Company, 22–24
    Baxter International, 36
    description of strategy, 8
    General Electric, 74, 77
    Pacific Gas and Electric Company,
        150–52
    Sun Microsystems, 188

R
Random House, 214–15
recycling and resource conservation
    AMD, 20
    Ben & Jerry's, 38
    Coca-Cola, 68
    description of strategy, 9
    Herman Miller, Inc., 92
    Hewlett-Packard, 94–96
    Intel, 116, 117
    Interface, 120–21
    Mohawk, 132–33
    Nike, 138–41
    Patagonia, 148–49
    Staples, 169
    Starbucks, 172–73
    Stonyfield Farm, 180
    Sun Microsystems, 188
    Toshiba, 200–201
    Vodafone, 206–9
    Xanterra Parks & Resorts, 210–13
renewable energy credits (RECs), 1, 36,
    72, 73, 117
renewable fuels, 12
Rio Tinto, 154–57

S
San Jose Unified School District, 33
SC Johnson & Son, 158–61
Seventh Generation, 162–65
smelting technologies, 16
solar energy, 33, 48–49, 72, 82, 96–97,
    152, 168, 182–85, 196, 208, 213
Staples, 166–69
Starbucks, 170–73
StatoilHydro, 174–77
Stonyfield Farm, 178–81
SunEdison, 182–85

Sun Microsystems, 186–89
Sun Ray computers, 188
supply chain accountability/ethical
    sourcing
    Aveda, 28
    The Body Shop, 42–44, 45
    BT, 56
    description of strategy, 10
    Green Mountain Coffee Roasters,
        86–89
    Hewlett-Packard, 97
    IKEA, 110–12
    Levi Strauss & Co., 122, 124
    McDonald's, 126, 128–29
    Mohawk, 130, 132
    Nike, 140
    Seventh Generation, 164
    Staples, 166–68
    Starbucks, 170–72
    Stonyfield Farm, 180
    Toshiba, 201
    Xanterra Parks & Resorts, 212–13
sustainability reporting
    Aspen Skiing Company, 22
    Aveda, 26, 28
    Bank of America, 30
    Baxter International, 34–36
    Ben & Jerry's, 38
    BP, 48
    Bristol-Myers Squibb, 50, 52
    BT, 56
    Citi, 60
    Coca-Cola, 66–68
    description of strategy, 10–11
    Goldman Sachs, 78–80
    Green Mountain Coffee Roasters,
        88–89
    Herman Miller, Inc., 93
    HSBC, 102
    Intel, 114, 118
    Nike, 138
    Novo Nordisk, 142
    Seventh Generation, 164
    Starbucks, 170

Sun Microsystems, 186
Timberland, 194, 196–97
Sustainable Cuisine, 212
sustainable/green investing
    Bank of America, 30, 32–33
    Citi, 60–61
    description of strategy, 11
    Goldman Sachs, 78–80
    HSBC, 102–4
sustainable packaging and shipping/
    logistics
    Aveda, 26–28
    The Body Shop, 44–45
    Clif Bar & Company, 64
    Coca-Cola, 68, 69
    description of strategy, 12
    Green Mountain Coffee Roasters, 88
    IBM, 108
    IKEA, 112
    Intel, 117
    McDonald's, 128
    Patagonia, 149
    SC Johnson & Son, 158
    Timberland, 194, 197

T

Tanzanian Gombe Reserve Coffee, 89
telecommuting, 5, 54–56
Tesla Motors, 190–93
T Factor, 198–200
Tierra de Fuego, 81
Timberland, 194–97
Toshiba, 198–201
toxic materials alternatives
    Baxter International, 36–37
    description of strategy, 9–10
    Intel, 116
    Mohawk, 132
    Nike, 138, 140
    SC Johnson & Son, 158–60
Toyota, 202–5
transportation. See alternative
    transportation
trigeneration, 20

U
Utsira project, 177

V
Vodafone, 206–9

W
waste management
    Baxter International, 36
    Ben & Jerry's, 38–40
    description of strategy, 12
    Honda, 101
    Interface, 121
water management
    Baxter International, 36
    Bristol-Myers Squibb, 52–53
    Coca-Cola, 66–68
    description of strategy, 13
    Intel, 116
    Levi Strauss & Co., 124, 125
    McDonald's, 129
    Rio Tinto, 156–57
Wildlife Conservation Society
    (WCS), 81
Wildlife Habitat Council, 52
wind power, 49, 70–72, 130
work-at-home programs, 108,
    189
workplace transformation
    Ben & Jerry's, 40–41
    BT, 54–56
    description of strategy, 13
    Google, 82, 84
    IBM, 108
    Seventh Generation, 165
    Sun Microsystems, 188–89
World Wildlife Fund (WWF), 66, 68, 112,
    144

X
Xanterra Parks & Resorts, 210–13

Y
Yawanawa-Aveda partnership, 29